Your Spanish Exchange

This comprehensive vocabulary and phrase book is one of a new series of books written specifically to help students of all ages on foreign exchanges.

Helen & Nigel Harrison

YOUR SPANISH EXCHANGE

Yarker Publishing

First published in Great Britain in 1997 by
Yarker Publishing
Gordon House
276 Banbury Road
Summertown
Oxford
OX2 7ED

Printed in Great Britain by
Redwood Books

British Library Cataloguing-in-Publication Data
A catalogue record for this book is available from
the British Library

ISBN 1-901609-02-2

ACKNOWLEDGEMENTS

Grateful thanks to
Luis Buitrago who translated the text
and to
Soraya Sanchez-Tirador & Rosemary Watts
for their assistance in checking the text.

Acknowledgement also to
Waddingtons Games Limited &
McDonald's Restaurants Limited

CONTENTS

THE EXCHANGE 13-26

Arriving & unpacking 13-15
Daily routine & night-time 15-19
Planning the next day 19-20
Speaking & understanding problems 21-22
General problems 23-26
Homesickness 23
Wanting to be alone 23
Tiredness 24
Foreign food 24
Leaving 25

THE HOME 27-72

The living room 29-33
The dining room 34-36
The study 36-37
The kitchen 37-46
The utility room 47-54
The bedroom 54-57
The bathroom 57-63
Gardens 63-70
Pets 71-72

GAMES 73-130

Playing board games 73-78
Monopoly 79-88
Cluedo 89-95
Card games 96-113
Chess, draughts & dominoes 122-130
Jigsaws 119-121
Shorter games & outdoor games 122-130

COMPUTERS 131-138
Hardware & software 131-133
The keyboard 133-135
Word processing 135-137
The Internet 137-138

COMPUTER GAMES 139-144
Loading 139
Controls 140
Scoring 141-144

TELEVISION, VIDEO & RADIO 145-151
Controls 146-147
Recording 148
Programmes, news & weather 148-150
Hiring videos 151

MUSIC 153-158
Listening to music 153-156
Lessons & practice 157-158

READING 159-166
Books 159-161
Newspapers 161-162
Magazines 162
The library 163
Horoscopes 165-166

FOOD 167-187
Meals & diets 167-169
Typical British & Spanish food 170-172
Cooking terms & ingredients 173-183
Barbecues 184-185
McDonald's 186-187

CINEMA & THEATRE.......... 189-200
Cinema.......... 189-190
Theatre.......... 191-197
Ballet.......... 197-198
Opera.......... 198-200

PARTIES & CLUBS.......... 201-203

FAIRS, CIRCUS & ZOO.......... 205-213
Fair.......... 205-211
Circus.......... 211-212
Zoo.......... 213

SIGHTSEEING.......... 215-233
Stately homes & castles.......... 215-223
Churches.......... 224-226
Art galleries & exhibitions.......... 227-231
Vineyards.......... 231-233

WALKS.......... 234-246
Walking the dog.......... 234
Picnics.......... 235-236
Route.......... 236
Problems.......... 237
View.......... 239-242
Paddling.......... 240
Walking & weather conditions.......... 241-242
Trees & wild life.......... 243-245
Fruit picking.......... 245-246

PHOTOGRAPHY.......... 247-253
Cameras.......... 247-250
Video cameras.......... 251-253

SPORT.. 255-300
Tennis.......................... 255-261
Riding.......................... 262-267
Skiing.......................... 268-275
Football & rugby.................. 276-281
Ice skating....................... 282-283
Table tennis...................... 284-286
Golf............................ 287-289
Motor racing...................... 290-291
Athletics......................... 292-296
Cricket.......................... 297-300

SWIMMING.............................. 301-308
Swimming pools.................... 301-305
Tubes........................... 306
Strokes.......................... 306
Underwater swimming & diving....... 307-308

THE BEACH............................ 309-317
Equipment........................ 309
Snorkelling....................... 310
Sandcastles....................... 310
Shell collecting & shrimping.......... 311
Beach games...................... 311-312
Water skiing...................... 313
Problems......................... 314
Cruises.......................... 314-315
Sunbathing....................... 316-317

FAMILY & FRIENDS 319-330
Immediate family 319-320
Relatives by marriage 321
Separation & divorce 321-322
Liking / not liking people 322-324
Babies 325-326
Engagements & weddings 327-329
Funerals 330

CONTACTING PEOPLE 331-339
By post 331-335
By telephone 335-339

SCHOOL & COLLEGE 341-357
Schools 341-346
Staff & pupils 346-347
School day & timetable 348-349
Studying & exams 350-353
Higher education 354-357

STATIONERY 359-362

CURRENT EVENTS 363-369
Elections & economy 363-364
Emergencies & war 365
Law & order 366-367
Monarchy 368
National lottery 369

TRAVEL 371-402
- Signs 371-373
- Trains 373-379
- Underground trains 380-381
- Buses 382-383
- Planes 383-389
- Ferries 390-391
- Cars 392-398
- Driving lessons & driving test 397-398
- Bikes 399-402

EMERGENCIES 403-434
- Accidents 403-405
- Illness & parts of the body 406-417
- Doctors 417-422
- Hospitals 422-425
- Dental treatment 426
- Opticians 427-428
- Preventive medicine 428-432
- Crime 433-434

PROBLEMS 435-438
- Loss & damage 435-436
- Filling in forms 437-438
- Equipment not working properly 438

THE EXCHANGE
EL INTERCAMBIO

ARRIVING — *LA LLEGADA*

MEETING THE FAMILY — *CONOCIENDO A LA FAMILIA*

MEETING THE FAMILY	*CONOCIENDO A LA FAMILIA*
Hello!	*¡Hola!*
I'm…	*Me llamo / soy…*
Are you Madame / Monsieur..?	*¿Eres Señor o Señora..?*
Thank you for coming to meet me.	*Gracias por venir a recogerme.*
I recognized you from the photos you sent me.	*Te reconocí por la foto que me enviaste.*
I'm very pleased to meet you.	*Encantado de conocerte.*
This is a present for you from my family.	*Este regalo es para tí de parte de mi familia.*
It's really good to see you again.	*Me alegro de verte de nuevo.*

THEY MAY SAY TO YOU — *PUEDEN PREGUNTAR / PREGUNTARTE*

THEY MAY SAY TO YOU	*PUEDEN PREGUNTAR / PREGUNTARTE*
Did you have a good journey?	*¿Has tenido un buen viaje?*
What was the flight like?	*¿Cómo fue el vuelo?*
What was the crossing like?	*¿Cómo fue la travesía?*
Would you like to go to the toilet?	*¿Quieres / quiere ir a los servicios?*
Would you like something to eat or drink?	*¿Te / le gustaría comer o beber algo?*
Are you hungry / thirsty?	*¿Tienes / tiene hambre / sed?*
Are you tired?	*¿Estás / está cansado(a)?*

ARRIVING cont. — *LA LLEGADA cont.*

THEY MAY SAY TO YOU cont. — *PUEDEN PREGUNTAR / PREGUNTARTE cont.*

I'll show you round the house.	*Te voy a enseñar la casa.*
I'll show you your room.	*Te voy a mostrar tu habitación.*
Do you want to unpack now or later?	*¿Quieres / quiere deshacer las maletas ahora o más tarde?*
Would you like to ring your family to say you have arrived safely?	*¿Te gustaría llamar a tu familia para decir que has llegado bien?*
Shall I dial the number for you?	*¿Quieres que marque el número por tí?*

YOU MIGHT WANT TO SAY — *SI QUIERES DECIR*

Yes, the journey was fine, thank you.	*El viaje fue bien, gracias.*
No, it was a dreadful journey.	*No, fue un viaje horrible.*
We got held up.	*Nos retrasamos.*
The flight was very late leaving.	*El vuelo salió con retraso.*
The flight was bumpy.	*El vuelo estuvo movido.*
The crossing was rough.	*La travesía estuvo movida.*
I was seasick.	*Me dieron naúseas.*

ARRIVING cont. / *LA LLEGADA cont.*

YOU MIGHT WANT TO SAY cont. / *SI QUIERES DECIR cont.*

Could I ring my parents, please?	*¿Podría llamar a mis padres, por favor?*
I like your house / your room.	*Me gusta tu casa / habitación.*
Where is the loo / the toilet?	*¿Dónde están los servicios?*
Could I have a wash, please?	*¿Podría lavarme, por favor?*
Could I have a drink of water, please?	*¿Podría beber un vaso de agua, por favor?*

UNPACKING / *DESHACIENDO EL EQUIPAJE*

Shall I unpack my case now?	*¿Deshago las maletas ahora?*
Where shall I put my clothes?	*¿Dónde puedo poner mi ropa?*
You can use this half of the wardrobe.	*Puedes utilizar la mitad del armario.*
These drawers are for you.	*Estos cajones son tuyos.*

SLEEPING ARRANGEMENTS / *PREPARANDOSE PARA DORMIR*

I hope you don't mind sharing a room with me?	*Espero que no te importe compartir la habitación conmigo?*
Do you prefer to have a room on your own or be with me?	*¿Prefieres una habitación para tí solo o conmigo?*

ARRIVING cont. / *LA LLEGADA cont.*

SLEEPING ARRANGEMENTS cont. / *PREPARANDOSE PARA DORMIR cont.*

This is your bed.	*Ésta es tu cama.*
Do you prefer a duvet or blankets?	*¿Prefieres un cobertor o unas mantas?*
Would you like another pillow?	*¿Quieres otra almohada?*
Would you like the window open?	*¿Quieres que deje la ventana abierta?*
Do you prefer the window shut?	*¿Quieres que deje la ventana cerrada?*

NEEDING SOMETHING / *NECESITANDO ALGO*

Do you need anything?	*¿Necesitas algo?*
Do you want something?	*¿Quieres algo?*
Have you got..?	*¿Tienes / tiene…?*
• any more hangers?	*más perchas?*
• a towel?	*una toalla?*
I forgot to bring …	*Me olvidé traer…*
• an alarm clock.	*un despertador*
• a hairdryer	*un secador de pelo*
• a comb	*un peine*
• my toothbrush	*mi cepillo de dientes*
Could I borrow..?	*¿Podría prestarme…?*

ARRIVING - DAILY ROUTINE cont. — *LA LLEGADA - LA RUTINA DIARIA cont.*

What time do you usually get up?	*¿A qué hora te levantas normalmente?*
Will you wake me when you get up?	*¿Me puedes / puede despertar cuando te/se levantes / levante?*
What time shall I set my alarm for?	*¿A qué hora pongo el despertador?*
Would you like to lie in tomorrow?	*¿Quieres quedarte en la cama hasta tarde mañana?*
I'm really tired. Could I sleep until late tomorrow?	*Estoy muy cansado(a). ¿Podría dormir hasta tarde mañana?*
We have to get up early tomorrow because we are going out.	*Tenemos que levantarnos temprano mañana porque vamos a salir.*
What time do you have breakfast?	*¿A qué hora desayunas?*
What do you like for breakfast?	*¿Qué tomas para desayunar?*
I usually have toast and cereal.	*Normalmente tomo tostadas y cereales.*
What time do you have dinner?	*¿A qué hora cenas?*

NIGHT-TIME — *POR LA NOCHE*

What time do you usually go to bed?	*¿A qué hora te vas a la cama?*
You look tired.	*Pareces cansado(a).*
Would you like to go to bed?	*¿Te gustaría ir a la cama?*
I am really tired.	*Estoy muy cansado(a).*
I would like to go to bed now.	*Me gustaría ir a la cama ahora.*
Can I stay up a little longer, please?	*¿Puedo quedarme levantada un poco más, por favor?*
Can I read in bed for a bit, please?	*Puedo leer en la cama un poco, por favor?*

DAILY ROUTINE cont. / *LA RUTINA DIARIA cont.*

LIGHTS ON OR OFF? / *¿LAS LUCES ENCENDIDAS O APAGADAS?*

Could you leave the light on, please?	*¿Podría dejar las luces encendidas, por favor?*
Do you like a light on at night?	*¿Quieres dejar un luz encendida por la noche?*
I prefer to sleep in the dark.	*Prefiero dormir con la luz apagada.*
I get nervous without a light.	*Me pongo nervioso con la luz apagada.*
I am frightened of the dark.	*Me da miedo la oscuridad.*
Would you like this nightlight left on all night?	*¿Quieres que deje esta luz encendida toda la noche?*

TOO HOT OR TOO COLD? / *¿DEMASIADO CALOR O FRIO?*

Are you warm enough?	*¿Estás caliente?*
Would you like an extra blanket?	*¿Quieres una manta extra?*
Yes please / No thank you.	*Sí, por favor / No, gracias.*
Are you too hot?	*¿Tienes demasiado calor?*
Would you like a thinner duvet?	*¿Quieres un cobertor más delgado?*
Would you like a hot water bottle?	*¿Quieres una bolsa de agua caliente?*
Could I have a hot water bottle, please?	*¿Quisiera una bolsa de agua caliente, por favor?*
Would you like me to put the electric blanket on before you go to bed?	*¿Quieres que conecte / enchufe la manta eléctrica antes de que te vayas a la cama?*
Don't forget to turn the electric blanket off before you get into bed.	*No olvides desconectar / desenchufar la manta eléctrica antes de irte a dormir.*

DAILY ROUTINE cont. / *LA RUTINA DIARIA cont.*

PROBLEMS AT NIGHT / *PROBLEMAS POR LA NOCHE*

Call me if you want anything in the night.	*Llámame si quieres algo por la noche.*
I had a nightmare.	*Tuve una pesadilla.*
I had a dream.	*Tuve un sueño.*
I can't get to sleep.	*No puedo dormirme.*
I was scared.	*Estaba asustado(a).*
I heard a noise.	*Oí un ruido.*
I don't want to be on my own.	*No quiero quedarme solo(a).*
I am missing home.	*Echo de menos mi casa.*
Could I have a drink of water, please?	*¿Podría beber agua, por favor?*

DECIDING WHERE TO GO FOR A DAY OUT / *DECIDIENDO DONDE PASAR UN DIA FUERA DE CASA*

What would you like to do today?	*¿Qué te gustaría hacer hoy?*
We thought we would go out somewhere.	*Pensamos que podríamos ir a alguna parte / algun lugar*
Would you like to do some sightseeing?	*¿Te gustaría hacer turismo?*
Would you like to go to…?	*¿Te gustaría ir a...?*
Have you ever been there before?	*¿Has estado/ido allí antes?*
Would you like to visit…?	*¿Te gustaría visitar..?*
It will be a long day.	*Va a ser un día muy largo / completo.*

DAILY ROUTINE cont. / *LA RUTINA DIARIA*

DECIDING WHERE TO GO FOR A DAY OUT cont. / *DECIDIENDO DONDE PASAR UN DIA FUERA DE CASA cont.*

How long will it take?	*¿Cuánto se tarda?*
What time would we have to get up ?	*¿A qué hora nos tendríamos que levantar?*
What time will we need to leave?	*¿A qué hora tendríamos que salir?*
What time would we get back?	*¿A qué hora estaremos de vuelta?*
Do you feel up to doing that?	*¿Te apetece hacer eso?*
We thought we would go out for a meal.	*Pensamos que ibamos a salir a comer.*
Would you like to go shopping?	*¿Te gustaría ir de compras?*
Is there anything you need to buy?	*¿Necesitas comprar algo?*

WHAT TO TAKE WITH YOU. / *QUE LLEVAR CONTIGO*

Bring your camera, if you have one.	*Trae tu cámara, si tienes una.*
What should I wear?	*¿Qué debo ponerme?*
Wear old clothes / smart clothes.	*Lleva ropa vieja / ropa de vestir.*
Wear walking shoes.	*Lleva zapatos para andar.*
Wear comfortable shoes.	*Lleva zapatos cómodos.*
Wear boots.	*Lleva botas.*
Bring a mack or a coat.	*Trae un impermeable o un abrigo.*
Bring your money.	*Coge dinero.*

SPEAKING PROBLEMS — *PROBLEMAS DE COMUNICACION*

CAN YOU SPEAK SLOWER, PLEASE? — *¿PUEDES HABLAR MÁS DESPACIO, POR FAVOR?*

I don't understand what you said.	*No entiendo lo que dices.*
Can you repeat that, please?	*¿Puedes repetirlo, por favor?*
Pardon?	*¿Cómo?*
Can you talk really slowly, please?	*¿Puedes hablar mucho más despacio, por favor?*

HOW DO YOU SPELL THAT? — *¿CÓMO SE DELETREA?*

Can you write that down for me, please?	*¿Puedes escribirlo, por favor?*
How do you pronounce this word?	*¿Cómo se pronuncia esta palabra?*

LACK OF VOCABULARY — *FALTA DE VOCABULARIO*

I do not know the word in Spanish.	*No sé la palabra en español.*
I've forgotten the Spanish word.	*He olvidado la palabra en español.*
What's that called in Spanish?	*¿Cómo se llama eso en español?*
Have you a dictionary?	*¿Tienes un diccionario?*
I need to look a word up in the dictionary.	*Necesito buscar una palabra en el diccionario.*
What does that mean?	*¿Qué significa?*
I can only say a few words.	*Sólo puedo hablar un poquito.*
You are really fluent.	*Hablas perfectamente.*
I am beginning to understand more.	*Empiezo a entender más.*
I am nervous of speaking.	*Me pongo nervioso cuando hablo.*

SPEAKING PROBLEMS cont. — *PROBLEMAS DE COMUNICACION cont.*

ASKING TO BE CORRECTED — *PARA QUE TE CORRIJAN LOS ERRORES*

Will you correct my mistakes, please?	*¿Puedes corregir mis errores, por favor?*
Was that right?	*¿Es correcto? ¿Está bien?*
What was wrong?	*¿Es incorrecto? ¿Está mal dicho?*
Was my pronunciation wrong?	*¿Estuvo mal mi pronunciación?*

NOT GETTING ENOUGH PRACTICE AT SPEAKING SPANISH — *SI NO PRACTICAS ESPANOL SUFICIENTEMENTE*

Can we speak in English for an hour and then Spanish for an hour?	*¿Podemos hablar en inglés por una hora y otra hora en español?*
Shall we play this game in Spanish?	*¿Jugamos en español?*
We could play it in English next time.	*¿Podemos jugar a esto en inglés la próxima vez?*
Can you teach me how to play a Spanish card game in Spanish?	*¿Puedes enseñarme un juego de cartas en español?*
I know I am rather slow but I would like to practise my Spanish a bit more.	*Sé que aprendo lentamente, pero me gustaría practicar me español un poco más.*
I know it's annoying for you when I try to speak Spanish but I won't get any better unless I try.	*Sé que es aburrido para tí cuando intento hablar en español pero no voy a mejorar sino lo intento.*

GENERAL PROBLEMS / *PROBLEMAS GENERALES*

HOMESICKNESS / *ECHAR DE MENOS EL HOGAR*

You are very kind but I am feeling homesick.	*Eres muy amable pero echo de menos mi casa.*
I am missing home.	*Echo de menos me casa.*
I am missing my parents - could I possibly ring them up?	*Echo de menos a mis padres. ¿Podría llamarles?*
If I ring them, they will ring me straight back.	*Si les llamo, ellos me llamarán aquí inmediatamente.*
I am happy really. I'm sorry. It's just a bit of a strain speaking Spanish.	*Perdone, estoy feliz, solo un poco agobiado hablando en español.*
I will be O.K. in a minute.	*Estaré bien en un momento.*

WANTING TO BE ALONE / *CUANDO QUIERES ESTAR SOLO(A)*

Do you mind if I go to my room to write some letters?	*¿Te importa si voy a mi habitación a escribir unas cartas?*
I would really like to write to my family to tell them what I have been doing.	*Me gustaría escribir a mi familia para decirles lo que he estado haciendo.*
I am in the middle of a good book at the moment and would like to read for a bit, if that's O.K.?	*Estoy en el medio de un libro muy bueno ahora y me gustaría leer por un rato, si no te importa.*
Could I go to sleep for half an hour? I am feeling tired.	*¿Podría ir a dormir por media hora? Estoy cansado(a).*

GENERAL PROBLEMS | *PROBLEMAS GENERALES*

TIREDNESS | *CANSANCIO*

I feel rather tired and would prefer to have a quiet day, if you don't mind.	*Me siento cansado(a) y preferiría pasar un dia tranquilo, si no te importa.*
Could we just stay at home and watch a video or something?	*¿Qué te parece si nos quedamos en casa y vemos un video o algo?*

FINDING THE FOOD STRANGE | *SI LA COMIDA ES EXTRANA*

Could I try just a tiny bit, please?	*¿Puedo probar un poquito, por favor?*
I am not very hungry at the moment.	*No tengo mucha hambre de momento.*
I don't usually eat very much.	*Normalmente, no como mucho.*
Could I possibly have my meat cooked a bit longer, please?	*¿Podría hacer más la carne, por favor?*
Do you have any… that I could eat? (See "Food" - pages 167-187)	*¿Tiene algo de... que pueda comer?*

LEAVING — *LA DESPEDIDA*

SAYING YOUR THANKS — *DANDO GRACIAS*

Thank you.	***¡Gracias!***
Thank you for having me to stay.	*Gracias por haber cuidado de mí.*
I've had a lovely time.	*Lo he pasado fenomenal.*
You have been very kind.	*Han sido muy amables.*
Thank you for taking me to see so much.	*Gracias por llevarme a ver tantas cosas.*
I particularly enjoyed going to..	*Particularmente me encanto ir a...*
You really helped me to improve my Spanish.	*Me habeis ayudado muchísimo a mejorar mi español.*

FUTURE PLANS — *PLANES PARA EL FUTURO*

I will phone you when I get home.	***Te llamaré cuando llegue a casa.***
Write to me.	*Escríbeme.*
I hope I'll see you next year.	*Espero verte el próximo año.*
Would you like to come to stay in England?	*¿Te gustaría ir y quedarte en Inglaterra?*

THE HOME
LA CASA

HOUSES AND FLATS — *CASA Y PISOS (APARTAMENTOS)*

TYPES OF HOUSES — *TIPOS DE CASAS*

TYPES OF HOUSES	*TIPOS DE CASAS*
a flat	*piso*
a terraced house	*casas adosadas*
a semi-detached house	*casa adosada (duplex)*
a detached house	*casa*
a cottage	*casa de campo*
old	*viejo(a)*
eighteenth / nineteenth century	*del siglo dieciocho / diecinueve*
modern	*moderna*
ultra-modern	*ultramoderna*
homely	*casero(a)*
smart	*elegante*
stylish	*con estilo*
charming	*encantador(a)*

THE OUTSIDE OF THE HOUSE — *EL EXTERIOR DE LA CASA*

THE OUTSIDE OF THE HOUSE	*EL EXTERIOR DE LA CASA*
the gate	*la verja*
the entrance	*la entrada*
the drive	*el camino / la entrada*
the path	*el camino*
the front / back door	*la puerta principal / la puerta de atrás*
the front / back garden	*La parte de delante / de atrás del jardín*
the chimney	*la chimenea*
the roof	*el tejado*
the windows	*las ventanas*

INSIDE THE HOUSE — *EL INTERIOR DE LA CASA*

the basement	***el sótano***
a cellar	*una bodega*

the ground floor	***el piso de abajo***
the porch	*el porche*
the lobby	*el recibidor*
the hall	*el hall*
the living room	*el cuarto de estar*
the dining room	*el comedor*
the study	*el estudio*
the kitchen	*la cocina*
the utility room	*el trastero*
the downstairs loo	*el cuarto de baño de abajo*
the cloakroom	*el vestíbulo*

the stairs	***las escaleras***
the staircase	*la escalera*
downstairs	*abajo*
upstairs	*arriba*
to go downstairs / upstairs	*bajar / y subir las escaleras*

the lift	***el ascensor***
to press the button	*pulsar el botón*
Which floor do you want?	*¿Qué piso quiere?*
The first / second/ third / fourth floor, please.	*El primero / segundo / tercero / cuarto / por favor.*
The fifth / sixth / seventh / eighth floor, please.	*El quinto / sexto / séptimo / octavo piso, por favor.*

INSIDE THE HOUSE — *EL INTERIOR DE LA CASA*

the first floor	***el primer piso***
the main bedroom	*la habitación principal / el dormitorio principal*
the spare bedroom	*la habitación de invitados*
my parents' room	*la habitación de mis padres*
my room	*mi dormitorio / mi habitación*
your room	*tu dormitorio / tu habitación*
the toilet	*el servicio*
the bathroom / the shower	*el baño / la ducha*

the attic	***el ático***
the playroom	*la habitación de los juguetes*
the junk room	*el trastero*
the games room	*la habitación para jugar*

INDIVIDUAL ROOMS — *LAS HABITACIONES*

THE LIVING ROOM — *EL CUARTO DE ESTAR*

For comprehensive details on using the equipment see Sections on "T.V., Video & Radio" (145-151), "Music" (153-158), "Contacting people by phone" (335-339) & "Reading" (159-166).

FURNITURE	*MUEBLES*
an armchair	***sillón (m)***
to sit in	*sentarse*
to relax	*relajarse*
to get up from	*levantarse de*
to plump up the cushion	*almohadillar el cojín*
a sofa	***un sofá***
to put your feet up	*poner los pies encima*

THE LIVING ROOM cont. — *EL CUARTO DE ESTAR*

a rocking chair	***la mecedora***
to rock	*mecer*
a book case	***la librería***
a shelf	*la estantería*
to read (See "Reading" 159-166)	*leer*
a table	***una mesa***
an occasional table	*una mesa pegable*
a vase of flowers	*un florero*
a card table	***una mesa de juego***
to play cards	*jugar a las cartas*
(See "Games - Cards" 96-113)	

CLOCKS — *RELOJES*

a grandfather clock	*un reloj de caja*
to wind up	*dar cuerda*
to strike the hour	*marcar las horas*
a cuckoo clock	*un reloj de cuco*
a digital clock	*un reloj digital*
What time is it?	*¿Qué hora es?*
Is the clock fast / slow?	*¿Esta el reloj adelantado / retrasado?*
It's ten minutes fast / slow.	*Está diez minutos adelantado / retrasado.*

LIGHTING — *ILUMINACION/ LAS LUCES*

lamps	***lámparas (f)***
to turn on / off	*encender / apagar*
a standard lamp / a lampshade	*lámpara / tulipa (f)*
a central light	*la luz central*
wall lights	*la luz de la pared / los apliques*
a dimmer switch	*el regulador de intensidad*
to dim the lights	*regular la intensidad de la luz*

THE LIVING ROOM cont. — *EL CUARTO DE ESTAR*

LIGHTING — *ILUMINACION / LAS LUCES*

a candlestick	***los candelabros***
a candle	*la vela*
to light	*encender*
a match	*una cerilla*
by candlelight	*a la luz de las velas*
to blow out	*apagar / soplar*

EQUIPMENT — *APARATOS*

(See "T.V., Video & Radio" 145-151)

the radio	***la radio***
to turn on / off	*encender / apagar*
to listen to	*escuchar / oír (la radio)*
the television	***la television***
to turn on / off	*encender / apagar*
to watch	*ver*
the video player	***el video (la máquina de video)***
to record a programme	*grabar un programa*
to hire a video	*alquilar un video*
to watch a video	*ver un video*
the hi-fi (See "Music" 153-158)	***el equipo de alta frecuencia***
the record player	*el tocadiscos*
a record	*el disco*
the cassette player	*el casset / el grabador*
a cassette	*el casset / una cinta de musica*
the C.D. player	*el equipo de compact disc*
a C.D.	*el disco compacto / CD*
to listen to	*escuchar*
to turn up / to turn down	*subir / bajar el volumen*

THE LIVING ROOM cont. — *EL CUARTO DE ESTAR*

EQUIPMENT cont. — *APARATOS cont.*

(For detailed expressions to do with telephones - see 335-339)

THE TELEPHONE	*EL TELEFONO*
to ring	*llamar*
to answer	*contestar*
to pick up	*coger*
to use	*usar*
an extension	*una extension*
an answer phone	*el contestador automático*
a message	*un mensaje*
to listen	*escuchar*
to play back	*volver a escuchar / rebobinar*

FURNISHING AND DECORATION — *AMUEBLANDO Y DECORANDO*

a rug	*alfombrilla / carpeta (f)*
a carpet	*moqueta / carpeta (f)*
the wallpaper	*papel para la pared*
the colour of the paint	*el color de la pintura*
the curtains	*las cortinas*
the blinds	*las persianas*

THE LIVING ROOM cont. — *EL CUARTO DE ESTAR*

THE HEATING — *LA CALEFACCION*

Central heating	***La calefacción central / centralizada***
to turn the heating on / off	*poner / quitar la calefacción*
to turn the thermostat up / down	*subir / bajar el termostato*
Is the heating on?	*¿Está la calefacción puesta / encendida?*
to feel the radiator	*tocar el radiador*
Do you mind if we turn the heating on / off / up / down.	*¿Te importa si enciendo, apago, subo, bajo la calefacción?*
a fireplace	***la chimenea (el hogar)***
to light the fire	*encender el fuego*
a match / to strike	*una cerilla / golpear*
a real fire	*fuego real (m)*
to get it going well	*hacer que prenda bien*
kindling / firelighters	*leña menuda / astillas (f)*
old newspapers	*periódicos viejos (usados) (m)*
logs / coal	*leños (m) / carbón (m)*
a pair of tongs	*un par de tenazas*
a poker	*atizador (m)*
to sit by the fire	*sentarse cerca del fuego*
to toast crumpets	*bollos o hojuelas para tostar*
a toasting fork	*un pincho*
to burn	*quemar, prendar*
an electric fire	***un fuego eléctrico / la calefacción electrica***
a gas fire	***un fuego de gas / la callefación de gas***
to turn on / off	*encender / apagar*

THE DINING ROOM — *EL COMEDOR*

THE DINING TABLE — *LA MESA DE COMER*

the chairs	*las sillas*

LAYING THE TABLE — *PONIENDO LA MESA*

Would you like me to lay the table for you?	***¿Quieres/quiere que ponga la mesa?***
How many people shall I lay for?	*¿Para cuánta gente tengo que ponerla?*
Where do you keep..?	***¿Donde tienes/tiene...?***
• the table mats	• *los salvaplatos / salvamanteles (m)*
• a tablecloth	• *el mantel*
• napkins	• *las servilletas*
What cutlery do we need?	***¿Qué cubiertos necesitamos?***
• knives	• *cuchillos (m)*
• forks	• *tenedores (m)*
• soup spoons	• *cucharas soperas (f)*
• fish knives and forks	• *cuchillos para pescado y tenedores (m)*
• dessert spoons and forks	• *cucharillas (f) y tenedores (m)*
• teaspoons	• *cucharillas (f)*
• serving spoons	• *cazos (m) / cucharones (m)*
What crockery shall I put out?	***¿Qué platos pongo?***
• dinner plates	• *la porcelana*
• side plates	• *platos pequeños (m)*
• dishes	• *platillos (m)*
• serving plates	• *bandejas (f)*

THE DINING ROOM — *EL COMEDOR*

LAYING THE TABLE cont. — *PONIENDO LA MESA cont.*

What glasses do we need?	***¿Qué vasos necesitamos?***
• water glasses	• *vasos de agua (m)*
• a jug of water	• *una jarra para el agua*
• red wine glasses	• *copas (f) para el vino tinto*
• white wine glasses	• *copas para el vino blanco*
• champagne glasses	• *copas de champán*

Do you want..?	***¿Quieres/quiere...?***
salt and pepper	*sal (f) y pimienta (f)*
mustard	*mostaza (f)*
butter	*mantequilla (f)*
preserves	*conservas (f)*
marmalade	*mermelada (f)*
cereals	*cereales (m)*
fruit juice	*zumo (m) de fruta*
sugar	*azúcar(f)*
milk	*leche (f)*
cream	*crema (f)*

Do you want candles?	***¿Quiere/quiere velas?***
a candelabra	*un candelabro*
a candle	*una candela / una vela*
to light	*encender la luz*
a match	*una cerilla*
to blow out	*soplar / apagar*

CLEARING THE TABLE.	***RECOGIENDO / LIMPIANDO LA MESA***
Would you like me to clear the table?	*¿Quieres / quiere que recoja la mesa?*
Where shall I put..?	*¿Dónde pongo...?*
Where do you keep..?	*¿Dónde guardas...?*

THE DINING TABLE cont. — *LA MESA DE COMER cont.*

SEATING ARRANGEMENTS	***DONDE SENTAR***
Would you like to sit there?	*¿Te gustaría sentarte aquí?*
Sit next to me.	*Siéntate junto a mí.*
Sit opposite me.	*Siéntate en frente de mí.*
Sit anywhere.	*Siéntate en cualquier sitio.*

THE STUDY — *EL ESTUDIO*

For comprehensive details on using the equipment see "Computers" 131-138, "Computer Games" 139-144 and "Contacting people by phone" 335-339.

a desk	***una mesa del estudio / un escritorio***
a drawer	*un cajón*
the desk top	*la sobremesa, el tapete*
a desk lamp	*lámpara de oficina (f)*
an anglepoise lamp	*lámpara de estudio*
a calculator	*calculadora (f)*
a diary	*diario (m)*
an address book	*una agenda, libreta de direcciones*
a blotter	*secante (m)*
a pen holder	*un porta plumas*
a paperweight	*un pisapapeles*
a telephone (See 335-339)	*un teléfono*
a chair	***una silla***
to sit down	*sentarse*
to get up	*levantarse*

THE STUDY cont. ***EL ESTUDIO***

a bookcase	***una librería***
a bookshelf	*una estantería*
a book	*un libro*
to read (See 159-166)	*leer*
a typewriter (See 133-137)	*una máquina de escribir*
a computer (See 131-138)	*una computadora / un ordenador*

THE KITCHEN — *LA COCINA*

THE COOKER — *LA COCINA*

gas	***gas (m)***
to turn on / off	*encender / apagar*
to turn up / down	*subir / bajar*
to light	*encender*
a match	*una cerilla*
automatic	*automático/a*
electricity	***electricidad (f)***
halogen	*halógeno*
a ceramic hob	*virocerámica*
an Aga	*una Aga / una cocina Aga*
a Rayburn	*un Rayburn*
a microwave	***el microondas***
to microwave	*pasar por el microondas*
to heat up	*calentar*
to defrost	*descongelar*
to set the timer for five minutes	*ajustar el reloj para cinco minutos*
	programar

THE KITCHEN cont.	*LA COCINA cont.*
THE COOKER cont	*LA COCINA cont.*

THE OVEN	***EL HORNO***
the oven door	*la puerta del horno*
to open	*abrir*
to shut	*cerrar*
temperature	***la temperatura***
to adjust	*ajustar*
high / medium / low	*alta / media / baja*
degrees	*grados (m)*
Fahrenheit	*Fahrenheit*
Centigrade	*centígrados*
Gas Mark Four	*Indicador de gas al cuatro*
a shelf	***una estantería***
top / middle / bottom	*de arriba / del medio / de abajo*
a glass door	*una puerta de cristal*
an oven light	*una luz del horno*
cooking time	***tiempo (m) de cocion/ preparación***
an auto-timer	*marcador de tiempo automático(m)*
a minute timer	*marcador de minutos (m)*
to set	*ajustar / programar*

THE HOB	***LA VITROCERAMICA***
a ring	*un hornillo*
front / back	*delantero / trasero*
left / right	*izquierdo / derecho*

THE KITCHEN cont — *LA COCINA cont.*

OVEN UTENSILS	*UTENSILIOS PARA EL HORNO (m)*
a casserole	*la cacerola*
a roasting dish	*la bandeja para asados*
an oven tin	*el molde para hornos*
a round tin	*el molde redondo para hornos*
an oblong tin	*el molde oblongo*
a cake tin	*el molde para pasteles*
a bun tray	*la bandeja de buñuelos*
a loaf tin	*el molde para pan*
a deep tin	*la lata*
an oven glove	*el guante de horno*

COOKING VERBS abc)	*VERBOS PARA COCINAR*
to bake	*cocer al horno*
to be nearly ready	*estar casi a punto*
to boil	*hervir*
to casserole	*hacer a la cacerola*
to check	*comprobar*
to cook	*cocinar*
to cover	*cubrir*
to heat gently / quickly	*calentar a fuego lento / a mucha temperatura*
to put on	*poner*
to roast	*tostar / asar*
to see if it's done	*ver si está hecho*
to simmer	*hacer que hierva un poco*
to take off	*apartar*

EQUIPMENT	*UTENSILIOS (m)*
a saucepan / a lid	***cazo con tapa (m)***
large / medium / small	*grande / mediano / pequeño*
to cover partially	*cubrir parcialmente*
to cover / to uncover	*cubrir / descubrir*

THE KITCHEN - EQUIPMENT cont.	*LA COCINA - UTENSILIOS (m) cont.*
a frying pan	*una sartén*
a fish slice	*una rodaja de pescado*
a wooden spoon	*una cuchara de madera*
to stir	*mover, agitar*
a wok	*una sartén*
to stir fry	*freír moviendo / sofreír*

THE SINK	*EL FREGADERO*
the bowl	*el cuenco / el escurridor de cubiertos*
the draining board	*el escurreplatos*
the taps	***los grifos***
hot / cold	*caliente / frío*
a mixer tap	*el grifo de agua templada*
to turn on / off	*encender / apagar*
too hot	*demasiado caliente*
not hot enough	*no es demasiado caliente*
to fill the sink with water	*llenar el fregadero*
washing up liquid	***el detergente para platos / el fairy***
to squirt	*mojar / poner en remojo*
bubbles	*burbujas (f)*
grease / greasy	*grasa / grasoso(a)*
clean / dirty	*limpio(a) / sucio(a)*
to rinse off	*secar / aclarar*
sink equipment	***los utensilios para el fregadero(m)***
a brush / a sponge	*un cepillo / una esponja*
a wire wool pad	*estropajo de aluminio (m)*
a dishcloth	*estropajo (m)/ trapo para platos*
to brush / to rub	*cepillar / raspar*
to scour	*fregar / restregar*
to wash	*lavar*

THE KITCHEN cont — *LA COCINA cont.*

DRYING DISHES — *SECAR LOS PLATOS*

to drain	*escurrir*
a rack	*un escurreplatos*
a cutlery basket	*un escurrecubiertos*
to leave to dry	*dejar que se sequen*
to dry	*secar*
a tea towel	*un trapo para secar*
to put away	*recoger / poner en su sitio*
to stack	*amontonar*

THE FRIDGE — *FRIGORIFICO*

to refrigerate	*poner en el frigorífico*
the fridge door	*la puerta del frigorífico*
a bottle rack	*un estante para botellas*
an egg rack	*la huevera*
a salad drawer	*un cajón para la fruta*
an ice compartment	*un compartimiento para hielo*
an ice cube tray	*una bandeja de cubitos de hielo / cubitera (f)*
ice cubes	*cubito de hielo (m)*
a shelf	*estantería (f)*

THE FREEZER — *CONGELADOR (m)*

to freeze	*congelar*
to defrost	*descongelar*
to thaw out	*descongelar / deshelar*
to melt	*derretir*
the fast freeze button	*el botón para congelar rápidamente*
maximum / minimum	*máximo / mínimo*

THE KITCHEN cont — *LA COCINA cont.*

THE DISHWASHER — *FREGAPLATOS / LAVAVAJILLAS (m)*

to load / unload	*cargar / vaciar*
to stack	*amontonar / apilar*
to turn on / off	*encender / apagar*
a drawer	*un cajón*
a cutlery basket	*una cesta para cubiertos*
to need	*necesitar*
dishwasher powder / salt / rinse aid	*detergente para lavavajillas (m) / sal (f) / enjuage de lavavajillas* (m)

DISHWASHER PROGRAMMES — *PROGRAMAS DE LAVADO*

a normal wash	*un lavado normal*
a quick wash	*un lavado rápido*
a delicates programme	*un programa para cosas delicados*
a long wash	*un lavado de larga duración*
rinse and hold	*escurrir y secar*

KITCHEN WASTE — *LA BASURA EN LA COCINA*

the waste bin	*cubo de basura (m)*
to empty	*vaciar*
to be full	*estar lleno*
a dustbin	*cubo de basura (m) / recogedor (m)*
a waste disposal unit	*unidad trituradora de desperdicios (f)*

THE KITCHEN cont / *LA COCINA cont.*

KITCHEN CUPBOARDS / *LOS ARMARIOS DE LA COCINA*

a wall unit	*un armario*
a base unit	*una unidad de cocina*
a carousel	*un carrusel*
the work surfaces	***la encimera***
kitchen paper	*papel de cocina (m)*
a knife rack	*un cuchillero*
a herb rack	*una estanteria para especias*
a china cupboard	***el armario de la vajilla***
a dinner plate	*un plato grande llano*
a side plate	*un plato pequeño llano*
a cup	*una taza*
a saucer	*un platillo para taza*
a soup bowl	*un cuenco*
a dish	*un plato*
an egg cup	*una huevera*
a serving dish	*una bandeja*
a milk jug	*una jarra de leche*
a sugar bowl	*un cuenco para el azúcar*
a butter dish	*un plato para la mantequilla*
a glass cupboard	***una vitrina***
a tumbler	*un vaso de whisky*
a wine glass	*una copa*
a glass jug	*una jarra de cristal*

KITCHEN CUPBOARDS cont. — *LOS ARMARIOS DE LA COCINA cont.*

a cutlery drawer	***un cajón de los cubiertos***
a knife / a fork	*un cuchillo / un tenedor*
a spoon	*una cuchara*
a teaspoon	*una cucharilla*
a dessertspoon	*una cucharilla de postres*
a tablespoon	*una cuchara para servir*
a serving spoon	*un cucharón*
a soup ladle	*un cazo*
a measuring spoon	*una cuchara de medidas*

a kitchen tool drawer	***el cajón de herramientas para la cocina***
a can / bottle opener	*un abrelatas / un sacacorchos*
a potato peeler	*un pelador*
a sharp knife	*un cuchillo afilado*
a bread knife	*un cuchillo para el pan*
a potato masher	*un amasador de patatas*
a lemon zester	*un pelador de limones*
a fish slice	*una rodaja de pescado*
kitchen tongs	*tenacillas de cocina (f)*
a whisk	*un batidor / batidora (una)*
a balloon whisk	*un levantanatas*
a spatula	*una espátula*
a garlic press	*un triturador de ajo / almidez*
a skewer	*un pincho/ una broqueta/ una brocheta*

OTHER KITCHEN EQUIPMENT — *LOS UTENSILIOS DE COCINA*

The kettle	***Olla para hervir agua / hervidor***
an electric kettle	*una olla para hervir agua (f) / hervidor eléctrico (m)*
to turn on / off	*apagar / encender*
to boil / to pour	*hervir / echar*

OTHER KITCHEN EQUIPMENT — *LOS UTENSILIOS DE COCINA*

The bread bin	***Lata (f) para el pan / panera (f)***
the bread board	*la tabla de cortar el pan*
the bread knife	*el cuchillo de cortar el pan*
to cut	*cortar*
to butter	*poner mantequilla (f)*
to soften	*emblandecer*
too hard	*demasiado duro(a)*
a butter dish	*un plato para la mantequilla*
a butter knife	*un cuchillo para la mantequilla*
to melt	*derretir*
a loaf of bread	*una barra de pan (m)*
a slice of bread	*un trozo / un pedazo de pan (m)*
crumbs	*migajas (f)*

The toaster	***La tostadora***
to make toast	*hacer una tostada*
to set the toaster	*poner la tostadora*

A pastry board	***Una tabla de amasar***
a rolling pin	*el amasador / el rollo de amasar*
cutters	*cortadores (f)*

A coffee grinder	***Molinillo de café (m)***
coffee beans	*el(los) grano(s) de cafe*
to grind	*moler*
a coffee maker	*la cafetera*
filter paper	*el filtro de papel*
a plunger	*un desatascador*

OTHER KITCHEN EQUIPMENT cont. — *LOS UTENSILIOS DE COCINA cont.*

Scales	***Báscula (f)***
to weigh	*pesar*
to measure	*medir*
to balance	*equilibrar*
weights	*pesas (f)*

A food processor	***Procesador de comida (m)***
a goblet	*una copa*
a lid	*una tapa / una tapadera*
to liquidize	*pasar por la licuadora*
fast / slow	*rápido / lento*
to purée	*hacer puré (f)*
to chop	*cortar en rodajas (f)*
to mix	*mezclar*
to blend	*combinar / mezclar*

Smaller equipment	***Utensilios más pequeños (m)***
an electric hand whisk	*una batidora eléctrica*
a salt mill	*un salero*
a pepper mill	*un molinillo de pimienta*
a lemon squeezer	*un esprimidor de limones*
a sieve	*un tamiz*
a colander	*un colador*
a steamer	*un vaporizador*
a salad spinner	*un escurridor de lechuga*
a measuring jug	*una jarra de medir*
a pestle and mortar	*una maja y un mortero*

THE UTILITY ROOM — *EL TRASTERO*

WASHING, DRYING & IRONING CLOTHES — *LAVADO / SECADO/ PLANCHADO DE LA ROPA*

Dirty clothes	***La ropa sucia***
soiled	*manchado / sucio*
a stain	*una mancha*
stain remover	*quita manchas (f)*
to treat quickly	*limpiar rápidamente*
to pre-soak	*poner remojo*
to bleach	*blanquear*
to scrub	*restregar*
clean clothes	*limpiar ropa (f)*

The washing machine	***La lavadora***
to open the door	*abrir la puerta*
to put the clothes in	*poner la ropa dentro*
to put the powder in	*poner el detergente*
biological powder	*detergente verde / ecológico (m)*
non-biological powder	*detergente no ecológico (m)*
washing liquid	*detergente (m)*
pre-wash spray	*spray (m) /riego de pre-lavado (m)*
to add conditioner	*añadir acondicionador (m) / suavizante (m)*

To choose a cycle	***Elegir un programa***
to press a button	*pulsar un botón*
to turn a dial	*dar la vuelta al botón*
Type of wash (abc)	***Tipo de lavado (m)***
boil	*hervir*
coloured	*color*
cool / hot	*temperatura ambiente / caliente(f)*
rinse	*aclarar*
white	*ropa blanca*
cottons / woollens	*algodón (m) / géneros (m) de lana*

WASHING, DRYING & IRONING CLOTHES cont. / *LAVADO / SECADO/ PLANCHADO DE LA ROPA*

Type of spin	***tipo de secado (m)***
short	*en corto*
long	*de larga duración*

DRYING CLOTHES / *SECANDO LA ROPA*

Outside	***Fuera***
a washing line	*tendedero (m)*
a prop	*un tendedero*
to peg	*pinzar / colgar / poner pinzas / tender*
a peg	*una pinza*
a peg bag	*una bolsa para las pinzas*
a linen basket	*un cesto para el lino*
to dry	*secar*
to put out / to take in	*sacar / meter*
It's raining.	*está lloviendo*

Inside	***Dentro***
an airer	*un colgador de ropa*
a clothes horse	*un tendedero con patas*
by the fire	*cerca del fuego*
on a radiator	*sobre el radiador*

In the tumble drier	***En la secadora***
to put the clothes in	*poner la ropa dentro*
to take them out	*sacar la ropa*
to set them timer	*programar el tiempo*
hot / cool	*caliente / templado*
a conditioning sheet	*un suavizante*
to prevent static	*prevenir la fuerza estática*
to clean the grill	*limpiar el filtro*
to remove the fluff	*remover la pelusa*

IRONING CLOTHES — *PLANCHAR LA ROPA*

The ironing board	***La tabla de planchar***
to put up	*montar*
to take down	*desarmar*
the iron	*la plancha*
to iron	*planchar*
to do the ironing	*hacer la plancha*

A steam iron	***Una plancha de vapor***
to fill with water	*echar agua (f)*
to run out of water	*acabarse el agua*
to squirt	*remojar*
to steam	*echar vapor (m)*

The temperature of the iron	***La temperatura de la plancha***
a cool / warm / hot iron	*una plancha templada /caliente*
too cold / too hot	*demasiado frio(a) / demasiado caliente*
to scorch	*hervir de calor*
a burn	*una quemadura*

The ironing	***La plancha***
creased	*impecable*
crumpled	*arrugado(a)*
to fold	*doblar*
to smooth out	*suavizar*
to turn the clothes the right way	*poner la ropa del derecho*
inside out	*del revés*
to air	*sacudir*

DOING THE CLEANING — *HACER LA LIMPIEZA*

Vacuuming	***Pasar el aspirador***
a vacuum cleaner	*una aspiradora*
to undo the flex	*desenrollar el cable*
to plug in	*enchufar*
a power point	*un enchufe*
to switch on	*enchufar*
a carpet	*una alfombra*
a solid floor	*un suelo sólido*
an upright cleaner	*una aspiradora vertical*
a cylinder cleaner	*una aspiradora con ruedas (de tambor)*
to empty the dustbag	*vaciar las bolsas*

Cleaning tools for the vacuum	***Herramientas para limpiar de una aspiradora***
a thin nozzle	*una boquilla fina*
a soft / hard brush	*un cepillo blando (de cerdas blanda) / duro (de cerdas duras)*
a wide brush	*un cepillo ancho*
the hose	*el tubo / el fuelle*
to suck up	*aspirar / succionar*
poor / good suction	*mala / buena succión*

Brushing	***Cepillado***
a broom	*un cepillo*
a soft brush	*un cepillo de cerdas blandas*
a hard brush	*un cepillo de cerdas duras*
a dustpan	*un recogedor*
to sweep up	*barrer*
a pile	*un montón*
to collect	*recoger*
to throw away	*tirar*
dust / dirt	*polvo (m) / suciedad (f)*

DOING THE CLEANING *HACER LA LIMPIEZA*

Washing surfaces	***Lavar / fregar suelos***
a bucket	*un cubo*
water	*agua (f)*
cleaning agent	*detergente (m)*
disinfectant	*desinfectante (m)*
to disinfect	*desinfectar*
a spray	*un spray / un pulverizador*
to spray	*pulverizar*
a sponge	*una esponja*
to soak	*mojar / empapar*
to squeeze	*estrujar*
to wring out	*escurrir / retorcer*
to wipe	*pasar un paño*
to rub	*restregar*
a mop	*una mopa / una fregona*
a scrubbing brush	*un cepillo de restregar*
to scrub	*restregar / raspar*

Polishing	***Abrillantar***
a duster	*plumero (m)*
to dust	*pasar el paño / quitar el polvo*
the dust	*el polvo*
a cobweb	*telaraña (f)*
to polish	*abrillantar*
polish	*abrillantador (m)*
spray polish	*abrillantador en sprai*
a tin of polish	*lata (f) de abrillantador*
furniture polish	*abrillantador para muebles (m)*
floor polish	*abrillantador para el suelo*
beeswax	*cera de abeja (f)*
to apply lightly	*aplicar ligeramente*
to make something shine	*sacar brillo a algo*
to buff up	*restregar*
to clean the silver / the brass	*limpiar la plata / el bronce*

DOING THE CLEANING cont. *HACER LA LIMPIEZA cont.*

CLEANING THE BATHROOM	*LIMPIANDO EL BANO*
Cleaning the loo	***Limpiando la taza del baño***
a lavatory brush	*el cepillo*
lavatory cleaner	*el detergente para la taza*
to squirt	*remojar*
to wipe	*restregar*
to flush the toilet	*tirar de la cadena*
to put out more loo rolls	*poner rollos de papel higiénico*
Cleaning…	***Limpiando...***
the basin	*el lavabo*
the bath	*el baño*
the mirrors	*los espejos*
the shelves	*las estanterías*

REMOVING RUBBISH	*SACAR LA BASURA*
To empty …	***Vaciar...***
the ashtrays	*los ceniceros*
the waste bins	*el cubo de la basura*
to put the dustbins out	*sacar los cubos de basura*
to take the bottles to a bottle bank	*llevar las botellas a un contenedor de cristales*
to recycle	*reciclar*

OFFERING TO HELP — *OFRECERSE PARA AYUDAR*

Can I help you with the…?	***¿Puedo ayudar con la...?***
cooking - See173-183	***comida (f)***
Shall we get ourselves a snack?	*¿Tomamos un aperitivo?*
Shall I cook my favourite recipe?	*¿Guiso mi plato favorito?*
Shall I make a cake?	*¿Hago un pastel?*
Shall I make some biscuits?	*¿Hago galletas? (f)*
housework - See 50-52	***los quehacéres de la casa***
Can I help you with the cleaning?	*¿Puedo ayudarte con la limpieza?*
ironing - See 49	***la plancha***
Would you like me to do the ironing?	*¿Quieres/quiere que haga la plancha?*
washing up - See40-41	***lavar los platos***
dusting - See 51	***pasar el polvo***
Shall I dust the living room?	*¿Paso el polvo en el cuarto de estar?*
shopping - See 20	***la compra***
Is there anything you want from the shops?	*¿Quieres algo de las tiendas?*
Do you want to give me a list?	*¿Puedes darme una lista?*

WOULD YOU LIKE ME TO...? *¿QUIERE QUE...*

post your letters - See 332-334	*eche tus cartas al buzón?*
dry the dishes - See 41	*seque los platos?*
lay / clear the table - See 34-35	*ponga / limpie la mesa?*
load / unload	*carge / descarge el lavaplatos? //*
the dishwasher - See 42	*llene / vacie el lavaplatos?*
make some toast - See 45	*haga más tostadas?*
make the beds - See 55	*haga las camas?*
put the kettle on - See 44	*ponga la olla de agua a hervir?*
tidy up	*recoja?*
vacuum - See 50	*pase la aspiradora?*
do the laundry - See 47-49	*lave la ropa?*
walk the dog - See 234	*pasee al perro?*
mow the lawn - See70	*corte el césped?*

THE BEDROOM *EL DORMITORIO*

Types of bed	***Tipos de cama***
a single bed	*una cama individual*
a double bed	*una cama doble*
bunk beds	*literas (f)*
to climb the ladder	*subir la escalera*
to get down	*bajar*
to choose	*elegir*
the top / bottom bunk	*la litera de arriba / de abajo*
a camp bed	*una cama plegable*
an inflatable mattress	*un colchon de aire*

THE BEDROOM — *EL DORMITORIO*

The bed linen	***El lino / la muda para la cama***
to make the beds	*hacer las camas*
to throw over	*estender / cubrir*
to put on	*poner*
to straighten	*estirar*
to tuck	*pillar / plegar*
to turn down	*doblar*
to change the bed	*cambiar las sábanas*
A sheet	***Una sábana***
the bottom / the top sheet	*la sábana de abajo / de arriba*
a single / double sheet	*una sábana simple / doble*
an undersheet	*una sábana protectora*
A pillow / a pillow case	***La almohada / la funda***
to plump up	*mullir*
Bed covers	***Cobertores (m) para las camas***
a duvet	*cobertor / edredón (m)*
a duvet cover	*una funda para el edredón*
a blanket	*una manta*
How many blankets do you like?	*¿Cuántas mantas quieres?*

BEDROOM FURNITURE — *EL MOBILIARIO EN LA HABITACION / EL DORMITORIO*

The bedside table	***La mesita de noche***
a bedside lamp	*la lámpara de la mesita de noche*
to turn on / off	*encender / apagar*
to need a new bulb	*necesitar una nueva bombilla*

THE BEDROOM cont. — *EL DORMITORIO cont.*

An alarm clock	***Un despertador***
to set the alarm	*poner el despertador*
to go off	*sonar la alarma*
to switch off the alarm	*apagar la alarma / parar la alarma*
What time shall I set the alarm?	*¿A qué hora pongo la alarma?*
What time do you want to get up tomorrow?	*¿A qué hora quieres levantarte mañana?*
Will you wake me, please?	*¿Puedes despertarme, por favor?*
to wind the clock	*dar cuerda al reloj*
to sleep through the alarm	*no escuchar la alarma / quedarse dormido*

The wardrobe	***El armario / guardaropas***
a double / single wardrobe	*un guardaropas de dos puertas / un guardaropas*
a hanger	*una percha*
a skirt hanger / a coat hanger	*una percha para falda / una percha para abrigos*
a rail	*una barra*
to hang up	*colgar*
full hanging / half hanging	*colgar / colgar doblado*

A chest of drawers	***Una cómoda***
the top / middle / bottom drawer	*el cajón de arriba / del medio / de abajo*
to open / to shut	*abrir / cerrar*

A dressing table / a stool / to sit	***Un tocador / un taburete / sentarse***
a mirror	*un espejo*
to look at one's reflection in	*mirarse*
to look good / to look terrible	*estar bien / tener mal aspecto*

THE BEDROOM cont. — *EL DORMITORIO cont.*

Doing one's hair	***Peinarse***
a hair brush	*cepillo (m)*
to do one's hair	*cepillarse / peinarse*
to brush one's hair	*cepillarse*
a comb	*un peine*
to comb one's hair	*peinarse*

THE WINDOW — *LA VENTANA*

to open / shut the window	*abrir / cerrar la ventana*
to air the room	*airear la habitación*
to draw / to open the curtains	*correr / abrir las cortinas*
to lower the blind	*bajar la persiana*
to raise the blind	*subir la persiana*

THE BATHROOM — *EL CUARTO DE BANO*

Having a bath	***Darse un baño / bañarse***
to get undressed	*vestirse*
to have a bath	*bañarse*
to put the plug in	*poner el tapón*
to run the bath	*llenar el baño*
to turn on the taps	*abrir el grifo / los grifos*
hot / cold / a mixer tap	*grifo (m) de agua caliente / fría / mezclador (m)*
to add bubble bath	*poner burbujas (f)*
bath oil / bath salts	*aceite de baño(m)/ sales de baño(f)*
essential oil	*poner aceite (m)de esencias (f)*
to get in the bath	*meterse en el baño*
to use a shower cap	*usar un gorro de baño*
to sit down / to lie down	*sentarse / tumbarse*
to immerse oneself	*meterse en el agua*

HAVING A BATH — *TOMANDO UN BAÑO / BAÑANDOSE cont.*

Washing oneself	***Lavándose***
soap	*jabón (m)*
a flannel	*una toallita de baño*
a loofah	*una esponja para la espalda*
a pumice stone	*una piedra pomez*
a back brush	*un cepillo para la espalda*
to have a long soak	*darse un buen remojón*

Staying in the bath too long	***Quedándose en el baño mucho tiempo***
to hurry up	*darse prisa*
How long are you going to be?	*¿Cuánto vas a tardar?*
I would like to use the bathroom soon.	*Me gustaría utilizar el baño pronto*

Getting out	***Saliendo***
to stand up	*levantarse*
to get out	*salir*
to pull out the plug	*quitar el tapón*
to wash out the bath	*limpiar el baño*
a bath mat	*alfombrilla (f) de baño*

Drying oneself	***Secándose***
to dry oneself	*secarse*
a towel	*una toalla*
a towel rail	*un toallero*
a heated towel rail	*un toallero eléctrico*
a bath towel / a hand towel	*una toalla de baño / una toallita*
dry / wet	*seco / mojado*
clean / dirty	*limpio / sucio*

USING THE BATHROOM cont. — *UTILIZANDO EL BAÑO cont.*

Talcum powder and deodorant	***Polvos de talco (m) y desodorante (f)***
a powder puff	*borla (f)*
to put on	*ponerse*
anti-perspirant	*desodorante (m)*
a spray	*un atomizador*
a roll-on	*un roll-on*
a gel	*un gel*

Getting dressed	***Vistiéndose***
to get dressed	*vestirse*
a bathrobe	*un albornoz*
a dressing gown	*una bata*

Using the basin	***Usando el lavabo***
to wash one's hands	*lavarse las manos*
to wash one's face	*lavarse la cara*
to open one's toiletry bag	*abrir el bolso de aseo*
to look in the mirror	*mirarse en el espejo*

Cleaning one's teeth	***Limpiarse los dientes***
to clean one's teeth	*limpiarse los dientes*
a tube of toothpaste	*un tubo de pasta de dientes*
to squeeze	*presionar*
a toothbrush	*un cepillo de dientes*
soft / medium / hard	*suave / medio / duro*
natural bristle / nylon	*cerdas / nailon (nylon)*
to brush	*cepillar*
to rinse out the mouth	*enjuagarse*
to gargle	*hacer gargaras*
to use mouthwash	*usar licor dentífrico*

USING THE BATHROOM cont. — *UTILIZANDO EL BAÑO cont.*

Shaving	***Afeitándose***
to shave	*afeitarse*
an electric razor	*una máquina eléctrica*
to plug in / to turn on / off	*enchufar/ encender / apagar*
a razor / a razor blade	*una maquinilla*
shaving soap / cream / brush	*jabón (m) / crema (f) / brocha de afeitar(f)*
to lather	*enjabonar*
to nick	*rasguñar*
to bleed / to stop bleeding	*sangrar / parar de sangrar*
to rinse off	*aclarar*
to use aftershave	*usar crema para después del afeitado*
to splash on	*echar agua (f)*
to trim one's beard	*recortarse la barba*

Having a shower	***Duchándose***
the shower	*la ducha*
to take a shower	*darse una ducha*
to shut the curtain	*cerrar la cortina*
to shut the shower door	*cerrar la puerta de la ducha*
to turn on the shower	*abrir la ducha*
to adjust the temperature	*ajustar la temperatura*
to wash oneself	*lavarse*

Washing one's hair	***Lavándose el pelo***
to wash one's hair	*lavarse el pelo*
shampoo	*champú*
for dry / normal / greasy hair	*para cabellos secos / normales / grasos*
dandruff shampoo	*champú para la caspa*
to apply / to rub in	*aplicar / frotar*
to lather / to rinse	*enjabonar / aclarar*
conditioner	*acondicionador (m)*

USING THE BATHROOM cont. — *UTILIZANDO EL BAÑO cont.*

Drying one's hair	***Secándose el pelo***
to dry one's hair	*secarse el pelo*
to rub with a towel	*restregar con la toalla / frotar con la toalla*
to put one's hair in a turban	*ponerse un turbante*
to use a hairdryer	*usar el secador*
to borrow a hairdryer	*tomar prestado el secador*
to put on mousse / spray	*poner espuma (f) / atomizador (m)*
firm / medium / light control	*duro / fuerte // medio // ligero*
to blow dry	*secar*
to straighten	*alisar*
to curl	*rizar*

Using the loo	***Usando el servicio***
the toilet	*el baño*
to need the loo	*necesitar el baño*
to go to the loo	*ir al servicio*
to put the seat up / down	*levantar / bajar el asiento*
loo roll	*papel higiénico (rollo de papel)(m)*
We have run out of loo roll.	*Nos hemos quedado sin papel higiénico*
Is there any more loo roll, please?	*¿Hay más papel higiénico, por favor?*
to flush the loo	*tirar de la cadena*
the bidet	*el bidet*

Other objects on the bathroom shelf	***Otros objetos en la estantería del baño***
cotton wool	*algodón (m)*
tissues	*pañuelos (m)*
cotton wool buds	*algodones (m)*

USING THE BATHROOM cont. — *UTILIZANDO EL BAÑO cont.*

FOR WOMEN — *PARA LA MUJER*

Perfume	***Perfume (m)***
to put on	*ponerse / echarse*
toilet water	*agua de colonia (f)*
a spray / an atomiser	*un atomizador / un vaporizador*
a bottle	*una botella*

Personal hygiene	***Higiene personal (f)***
sanitary towels	*toallitas / compresas (f)*
tampons	*tampones (m)*
depilatory cream	*crema depilatoria*

Make-up / cosmetics	***Maquillaje (m) / cosméticas (f)***
a make-up bag	*una bolsa de maquillaje*
to put on make-up	*ponerse maquillaje*

Make-up for the face	***Maquillaje para la cara (facial)***
foundation	*maquillaje (m)*
blusher	*brocha (f)*
concealer	*corrector (m)*
powder	*polvos (m)*
to dot / spread evenly / smooth	*repartir / estender uniformemente / suavizar*

For the lips	***Para los labios***
lipstick / a tube of lipstick	*pintalabios /una barra de labios*
a lip brush	*un pincel para los labios*
lip outliner	*un delineador para los labios*
lip gloss	*abrillantador*
a lip salve	*una manteca (f) de cacao*
a pencil	*un perfilador (m)*
to outline / to fill in	*perfilar / rellenar*

MAKE-UP cont. *MAQUILLAJE*

For the eyes	***Para los ojos***
eyeliner	*delineador (m)*
eyeshadow	*sombra de ojos (f)*
mascara	*máscarilla rímel (f)*

For the eyebrows	***Para las cejas***
a pair of tweezers	*pinzas de depilar(f)*
to pluck	*depilar(se las cejas)*
to shape	*dar forma*
to brush	*cepillar*

Taking make-up off	***Desmaquijándose***
to apply	*aplicar / ponerse*
make-up remover	*crema desmaquilladora*
cotton wool	*algodón (m)*
to wipe	*restregar*
to remove	*remover*
eye make-up remover pads	*algodones para remover maquillaje de los ojos*
to cleanse	*limpiar*
cleansing lotion	*loción tonificante (f)*
to tone	*tonificar*
to nourish	*nutrir*
cream	*crema (f)*
a night / day cream	*crema de noche / de día*

THE GARDEN
EL JARDIN

TYPES OF GARDEN — *TIPOS DE JARDIN*

a cottage garden	*un jardín de casa de campo*
a herb garden	*un jardín de hierbas aromáticos*
a kitchen garden	*un jardín de hortalizas o verduras*
an orchard	*un huerto*
a wild flower garden	*un jardín de flores salvajes (f)*
a public garden	*un jardín público*
a park	*un parque*

DESCRIBING GARDENS — *DESCRIBIENDO JARDINES*

large / small	*grande / pequeño(a)*
formal / wild	*formal / salvaje*
pretty	*bonito*
untidy	*desordenado / descuidado*
overgrown	*descuidado*

COMMON GARDEN CONTENTS — *COSAS COMUNES EN EL JARDIN*

A flower bed	***Una jardinera***
a flower	*una flor*
a bud	*un brote / un capullo*
a plant	*una planta*
a weed	*una mala hierba*

A lawn	***Un césped***
a border	*un borde*
a path	*un camino*
a seat	*un asiento*

GARDENS cont. — *JARDINES cont.*

Trees	***Arboles***
a tree	*un arbol*
a trunk	*un tronco*
a branch	*una rama*
a twig	*una ramita*
a leaf	*una hoja*
a bush	*un arbusto*

OTHER GARDEN FEATURES — *OTROS RASGOS DEL JARDIN*

a greenhouse	*un invernadero*
a conservatory	*un conservatorio*
a pond	*un estanque*
a fountain	*una fuente*
a wall	*una pared*
a fence	*una valla*
a hedge	*un seto*

COMMON FLOWERS (abc) — *FLORES MAS COMUNES*

carnation	*clavel (m)*	narcissus	*narciso (m)*
daffodil	*narciso (m)*	rose	*rosa (f)*
geranium	*geranio (m)*	snowdrop	*campanilla de invierno (m)*
lavender	*lavanda (f)*	tulip	*tulipán (m)*
lily of the valley	*lirio (m)*		

COMMON WILD PLANTS (abc) — *PLANTAS SALVAJES MAS COMUNES*

bluebell / buttercup	*campanátula azul(f) / ranúnculo(m)*
cowslip / daisy	*prímula (f) / margarita (f)*
dandelion	*diente de león (m)*
dock leaf	*acedera (f) / ramaza (f)*
nettle	*ortiga (f)*

GARDENS cont. — ***JARDINES cont.***

COMMON TREES AND BUSHES (abc) — ***ARBOLES (m) Y ARBUSTOS (m) MAS COMUNES***

ash	*fresno (m)*	hawthorn	*espino (m)*
beech	*haya (f)*	holly	*acebo (m)*
birch	*abedul (m)*	oak	*roble (m)*
chestnut	*castaño (m)*	privet	*alheña (f)*
elm	*olmo (m)*	sycamore	*sicomoro (m)*
fir	*abeto (m)*	yew	*tejo (m)*

COMMON ANIMALS (abc) — ***ANIMALES MAS COMUNES***

a bat	*un murcielago*	a molehill	*una topera*
a hedgehog	*un erizo*	a rabbit	*un conejo*
a mole	*un topo (topillo)*	a squirrel	*una ardilla*

COMMON INSECTS (abc) — ***INSECTOS MAS COMUNES***

an ant	*una hormiga*	a fly	*una mosca*
a bee	*una abeja*	a moth	*una polilla*
a butterfly	*una mariposa*	a spider	*una araña*
a caterpillar	*un gusano*	a wasp	*una avispa*

COMMON BIRDS (abc) — ***PAJAROS MAS COMUNES***

a bird table	*una plataforma para dar de comer a los pájaros*
a blackbird / a blue tit	*mirlo (m) / alionín (m)*
a crow / a dove	*un cuervo / una paloma*
a magpie / an owl	*una urraca / una lechuza*
a pigeon / a robin	*una paloma / un petirrojo*
a rook / a starling	*un grajo / un estornino*
a thrush	*un zorzal / un tordo*
a bird's nest	*un nido de pájaro*
an egg	*un huevo*

GARDENS cont. — *JARDINES cont.*

GARDEN FURNITURE — *MUEBLES DE JARDIN*

a garden seat	*una silla de jardín*
a sunbed	*una tumbona par tomar el sol*
a deckchair	*una butaca de tijera*
a hammock	*una hamaca*
a statue	*una escultura / una estatua*
an urn	*una urna*
a bird table	*una plataforma para dar de comer a los pájaros*

GARDEN ENTERTAINMENT — *ENTRETENIMIENTOS PARA EL JARDIN*

HAVING A BONFIRE — *HACIENDO UNA HOGERA*

to gather wood	*reunir leña (f)*
to find kindling	*encontrar astillas (f)*
to light	*encender*
to smoke / smoke	*fumar / humo (m)*
flames	*llamas (f)*
sparks	*chispas (f)*
to cook jacket potatoes	*hacer patatas rellenas al fuego*
the direction of the wind	*la dirección del viento*
to change	*cambiar*
to get out of control	*perder el control*
to put out	*apagar*
a bucket of water	*un cubo de agua*
a hose	*una mangera*

GARDEN ENTERTAINMENT - HAVING FIREWORKS	*ENTRETENIMIENTOS PARA EL JARDIN - LOS FUEGOS ARTIFICIALES*
to stand well clear	*estar en un buen sitio*
to watch from over there	*ver desde allí arriba*
to light	*encender*
a fuse	*una chispa*
a match	*una cerilla*
to go out	*subir / lanzar*
to leave it alone	*dejarlo tranquilo*
to have another	*tener otro*
a fireworks display	*un espectáculo de fuegos artificiales (m)*
Guy Fawkes' night	*La noche de Guy Fawkes*
The fifth of November	*El cinco de Noviembre*
a box of fireworks	*una traca*
a sparkler	*una bengala*
a catherine wheel	*torretas (f) / castillos de fuego (m)*
a rocket	*un cohete*
a Roman candle	*un candelabro romano*

BARBECUES	*BARBACOA (f)*
See "Food" 184-5, 313	

GARDEN GAMES	*JUEGOS DE JARDIN*
Playing mini golf	***Jugando al Mini-Golf***
a golf club	*un palo de golf*
a golf ball	*una pelota de golf*
a hole	*un aqüjero*
to pot the ball in one	*meterla a la primera*
clock golf	*golf a contra reloj*
to strike	*golpear*

GARDEN ENTERTAINMENT — *ENTRETENIMIENTOS PARA EL JARDIN*

Playing croquet	***Jugando al croquet***
a croquet mallet	*un mazo de croquet*
a hoop	*una argolla*
the central stick	*el palillo central*
to go straight through	*pasar*
to hit the hoop	*golpear la argolla*
to knock someone out of the way	*eliminar a alguien*

Playing bowls	***Jugando a los bolos***
to throw	*lanzar / bolear*
to roll	*rodar*
to hit	*golpear*
to miss	*no atinar*
to be the nearest	*ser el más cercano / estar más cerca que los demás*
to be hit out of the way	*eliminar*

Trampolining	***Tirándose desde el trampolín***
a trampoline	*un trampolín*
to bounce	*rebotar / dar un salto*

GARDENING — *JARDINERIA*

The equipment	***El equipo***
the garden shed	*la caseta*
a wheelbarrow	*la carretilla*
a spade / a fork	*una pala / rastrillo / un pincho*
a trowel	*una paletilla*
a hoe / a rake	*una azada / un rastrillo*
a pair of clippers	*un par de tijeras*
a hedge trimmer	*una cortadora de seto*
a broom	*un cepillo de cerdas para el jardín*
a dustbin	*un recogedor de basura*

GARDENING cont. — *JARDINERIA cont.*

Mowing the lawn	***Cortando el césped***
a lawn mower	*un corta césped*
an electric mower	*una cortadora de césped eléctrica*
a hand mower / a motor mower	*una cortadora de césped manual / una cortadora de gasolina*
to cut the grass	*cortar el césped*
to push / to pull	*empujar / traer (hacia si)*
to alter the setting	*alterar la organización*
to turn the corner	*dar la vuelta a la esquina*
straight lines	*lineas rectas*
to empty the box	*vaciar la cubeta / caja*
grass cuttings	*briznas (f) de césped*
The grass needs cutting.	*El césped necesita un corte.*

Doing the weeding	***Preparando el jardín /quitando las malas hierbas***
a weed	*una mala hierba*
to pull out	*arrancar*
to uproot	*arrancar de raiz / desrraigar*

Watering the garden	***Regando el jardín***
The garden needs watering.	*el jardín necesita agua.*
a watering can	*una regadera*
to fill	*llenar*
to spray	*esparcir*
a hose pipe	*una mangera*
a sprinkler	*un aspresor / una rociadera*
an automatic sprinkler	*una rociadera automática*
to turn on / off	*poner / quitar*

PETS
ANIMALES DE COMPANIA

A budgerigar	***Un periquito***
a cage	*una jaula*
a perch	*una barra*
a swing / to swing	*un columpio / columpiarse*
a mirror / to admire himself	*un espejo / mirarse a sí mismo*
a bell / to ring	*una campana / tocar*

A cat	***Un gato***
a kitten	*un gatillo / gatito*
a cat basket	*una cesta*

A dog	***Un perro***
a puppy	*el cachorro*
a dog kennel	*la perrera*
to take the dog for a walk - See 234	*pasear al perro*
to go to dog training classes	*llevar a entrenar al perro*

A dove	***Una paloma***
a dove cote	*un palomar*

A goldfish	***Un pez dorado/un pez de colores***
a goldfish bowl	*una pecera*
water	*agua*
to swim around	*nadar en círculos*
weeds	*plantas acuáticas*
pebbles	*grava (f) / piedras (f)*
to clean out the tank	*limpiar el tanque*

PETS cont. / *ANIMALES DE COMPAÑIA*

Other pets	***Otros animales de compañía***
a guinea pig	*un conejillo de indias*
a hamster	*un hámster*
a mouse	*un ratón / un ratonillo*
a parrot - to talk	*un loro / hablar*

Useful expressions	***Expresiones útiles***
Does it bite?	*¿muerde?*
Don't put your finger in the cage.	*No pongas el dedo en la jaula.*
I have to take it to the Vets.	*Tengo que llevarlo al veterinario.*

GAMES
JUEGOS

COMMON EXPRESSIONS — *EXPRESIONES COMUNES*

Would you like to play?	***¿Quieres jugar?***
What would you like to play?	*¿A qué quieres jugar?*
Do you like playing..?	*¿Te gustar jugar al...?*
Shall we have a game of..?	*¿Echamos una partida al...?*

How many can play?	***¿Cuántos juegan?***
It's a game for two people.	*Es un juego para dos personas.*
You need four people to play.	*Se necesitan cuatro personas.*
We haven't got enough people.	*No hay gente suficiente.*
We have too many people.	*Hay demasiado gente.*

You play in teams.	***Se juega en grupos / en equipos.***
How many are in each team?	*¿Cuántos hay en cada equipo?*
Will you be in my team?	*Estarás en mi equipo?*
I'll be in the other team.	*Voy con el otro equipo.*

What do you need to be able to play?	***¿Qué se necesita para jugar?***
You need paper and a pencil.	*Se necesita un papel y lápiz.*
This pencil is blunt.	*Este lápiz no tiene punta.*
My lead has broken.	*La mina se ha roto.*
Have you another pencil?	*¿Tienes otro lápiz?*
Could I have more paper, please?	*¿Tienes más papel, por favor?*

STARTING GAMES cont. *EMPEZAR LOS JUEGOS*

Where shall we play?	***¿Dónde jugamos?***
Shall we play in..?	*¿Jugamos en...?*
..my / your room	*...mi habitación / tu habitación*
..the living room?	*...en la sala de estar*
..on this table?	*...en esta mesa*
..on the floor?	*...en el suelo*

How long does a game take?	***¿Cuánto dura el juego?***
This game doesn't take long.	*No es muy largo.*
This game takes too long.	*Es muy largo.*
It takes at least an hour.	*Se tarda al menos una hora.*
This is a quick game.	*Es muy rápido.*

How do you play it?	***¿Cómo se juega?***
You have to..	*Tienes que...*
The object of the game is to..	*El objetivo del juego es...*
You start here.	*Se empieza aquí.*
You go this way round the board.	*Se va en esta dirección sobre el tablero.*

Choose a token	***Elige una ficha***
Which token would you like?	*¿Que ficha quieres ser?*
Which colour would you like to be?	*¿Que color te gustaría ser?*

What happens if you land here?	***¿Qué pasa si caes aquí?***
You get another turn.	*Tiras otra vez.*
You lose a turn.	*Pierdes un turno.*
You go back three spaces.	*Retrocedes tres espacios / casillas.*
You go forward two spaces.	*Avanzas dos espacios / casillas.*
You have to go back to the beginning.	*Tienes que volver a empezar.*

GAMES cont. — *JUEGOS cont.*

Where is the finish?	***¿Dónde está la meta?***
You finish here.	*La meta está aquí.*
The first person to finish wins.	*La primera persona en terminar gana.*

Pick up a card.	***Coge una carta / tarjeta***
What does the card say?	*¿Que dice la carta?*
I can't read what's on the card.	*No puedo leer lo que dice la tarjeta.*
What does that mean?	*¿Qué significa?*
Show me what I have to do now	*Dime lo que tengo que hacer ahora.*
You can keep the card till later.	*Puedes quedarte con la carta hasta luego.*

Money	***Dinero***
Who's going to be banker?	*¿Quién va a ser la banca?*
Can I be banker?	*¿Puedo ser la banca?*
Will you be banker?	*¿Quieres ser la banca?*
How much money do you start with?	*¿Con cuánto se empieza?*
You have twenty thousand pounds to start with.	*Tienes veinte mil libras para empezar.*
Each time you go round you get given..	*Cada vez que das una vuelta te dan...*

GAMES cont. *JUEGOS cont.*

Buying and selling	***Comprando y vendiendo***
You can buy a..	*Puedes comprar un/una...*
Do you want to buy it?	*¿Quieres comprarlo?*
I'd like to buy..	*Me gustaría comprar...*
I haven't got enough money.	*No tengo dinero suficiente.*
How much money do I have to pay?	*¿Cuánto dinero tengo que pagar?*
You have to pay..	*Tienes que pagar...*
Have you change for a fifty pound note?	*¿Tienes cambio de cincuenta libras?*
You didn't give me my change.	*No me diste el cambio.*
You have to give me / all the other players..	*Me tienes que dar / tienes que dar a todos los jugadores...*
You have to pay a fine.	*Tienes que pagar una multa.*
You pay ten times what's on the dice.	*Tienes que pagar diez veces lo que marque el dado.*

The rules	***Las reglas***
Can I read the rules, please?	*¿Puedo leer las reglas?*
It's against the rules.	*No está en las reglas.*
That's cheating.	*Estás haciendo trampas.*
You can't do that.	*No puedes hacerlo.*

Who starts?	***¿Quién empieza?***
The highest starts.	*El número más alto.*
The lowest starts.	*El número más bajo.*
You need a six to start.	*Necesitas un seis para salir.*
You need a double to start.	*Necesitas un doble para empezar / salir.*
Shall we toss a coin to see who starts?	*¿Echamos una moneda para ver quién empieza?*
Heads or tails? It's heads.	*¿Cara o cruz? Cara.*

GAMES cont. — *JUEGOS cont.*

Throw the dice.	***Lanza el dado.***
How many dice do you use?	*¿Cuántos dados se necesitan?*
You use two dice.	*Se necesitan dos dados.*
You only use one.	*Sólo se usa uno.*
Have you got a shaker?	*¿Tienes un cubilete?*
The dice rolled off the table.	*El dado se ha salido del tablero?*
The dice fell on the floor.	*El dado se ha caido al suelo?*
Shake again.	*Tira otra vez.*

What did you throw?	***¿Qué sacaste?***
I threw a..	*Saque / tengo un...*
..one / two / three	*...uno / dos / tres*
..four / five / six	*...cuatro / cinco / seis*
You have to throw a six.	*Tienes que sacar un seis.*
You have to throw a double.	*Tienes que sacar dobles.*
Throw again.	*Tira otra vez.*

Do you like this game?	***¿Te gusta este juego?***
This game is..	*Este juego es...*
..too difficult / too easy	*...demasiado dificil / fácil.*
..rather boring.	*muy aburrido.*
..excellent.	*estupendo.*

How do you win?	***¿Cómo se gana?***
The winner is the first person to finish.	*El ganador es la primera persona en finalizar.*
The winner is the person with the most..	*El ganador es la persona con más...*
..money.	*...dinero.*
..points.	*...puntos.*
Shall we see who's won?	*¿Veamos quién ganó?*
Count up your money.	*Cuenta tu dinero.*
How much money have you got?	*¿Cuánto dinero tienes?*
Add up your points.	*Suma tus puntos.*
How many points have you got?	*¿Cuántos puntos tienes?*

GAMES cont. / *JUEGOS cont.*

Who's won?	***¿Quién ha ganado?***
I've won / You've won.	*Yo gané / Tu ganaste.*
He's won / She's won.	*El ganó / Ella ganó.*
We've won / They've won.	*Nosotros ganamos / Ellos ganaron.*
Our team won.	*Nuestro equipo ganó.*
Their team won.	*Su equipo ganó.*
Well played!	*¡Genial! ¡Bien hecho!*
Bad luck!	*¡Mala suerte!*

Shall we stop now?	***¿Lo dejamos ya?***
Shall we have one more game?	*¿Echamos otra partida?*
Is there time for another game?	*¿Tenemos tiempo para otra partida?*
Shall we play the best of three?	*¿El mejor de tres?*
Shall we play something else?	*¿Jugamos a otra cosa?*
It's time to stop.	*Tiempo de parar. Se acabo.*
We'd better put it away.	*Vamos a guardarlo / vamos a dejarlo ya.*

MONOPOLY — *MONOPOLY / MONOPOLI*

THE BOARD — *EL TABLERO*

Go	***Salida***
to pass Go	*pasar 'Salida'*
I just passed Go.	*Acabo de pasar la Salida.*
Collect two hundred pounds salary as you pass Go.	*Page doscientas libras al pasar por la casilla de salida.*
Can I have my salary, please?	*¿Puedes darme mi dinero, por favor?*

In Jail	***En la cárcel***
Just Visiting	*De visita*
I am just visiting.	*Estoy de visita.*
In Jail.	*En cárcel.*
I am in jail.	*Estoy en la cárcel.*
I've been sent to jail.	*Me manda a la cárcel / tengo que ir a la cárcel.*
I have/haven't a card to get out of jail free.	*No tengo una tarjeta para salir de la cárcel.*
I threw doubles three times in succession so I have to go to jail.	*Saqué tres dobles seguidos así es que tengo que ir a la cárcel.*
You need to throw a double to get out.	*Tienes que sacar dobles para salir.*
Will you sell me your get out of jail free card?	*¿Me vendes tu tarjeta para salir de la cárcel?*
How much do you want for your get out of jail free card?	*¿Cuánto quieres por tu tarjeta para salir de la cárcel?*
I will pay the fifty pound fine now.	*Pago la multa de cincuenta libras para salir.*
I have to pay the fifty pound fine now.	*Tengo que pagar la multa de cincuenta libras ahora.*
I've missed three turns so I can come out this go.	*He perdido tres turnos, puedo salir ahora.*

MONOPOLY cont. — *MONOPOLY cont.*

Income Tax	***Tasas***
Pay two hundred pounds.	*Paga doscientas libras*
You pay all taxes to the Bank.	*Paga todas las tasas al banco.*
Super Tax	*Super Tasa*
Pay one hundred pounds.	*Paga cien libras.*

Other squares	***Otras casillas***
Free Parking	*No paga*
Go to Jail	*Ve a la cárcel*

The Properties	***Las propiedades***
a street	*una calle*
a road	*una carretera*
a square	*una plaza*

The Stations	***Las estaciones***
Rent	*La renta*
If two / three / four stations are owned..	*Si se posee dos / tres / o cuatro estaciones...*

The Utilities	***Las compañías***
The Waterworks	*La compañía de aguas*
The Electricity Company	*La compañía de electricidad*
If one utility is owned, rent is four times amount shown on one die.	*Si se posee una compañía se multiplica por cuatro el número del dado.*
If both utilities are owned, rent is ten times amount shown on one die.	*Si se posee ambas compañías, la renta se multiplica por diez veces el número que marque el dado.*

MONOPOLY cont. / *MONOPOLY cont.*

THE CARDS / *LAS CARTAS / LAS TARJETAS*

Property Cards	***Cartas / Tarjeta de propietario***
a site	*una propiedad*
a Title Deed	*Titulo de Propietario*
rent - site only	*propiedad*
rent with one / two / three / four houses	*alquiler de la propiedad con una / dos / tres o cuatro casas*
rent with a hotel	*propiedad con un hotel*
If a player owns all the sites of any colour group, the rent is doubled on unimproved sites in that group.	*Si un jugador posee todas las propiedades de un mismo color, el alquiler se duplica en propiedades sin edificar dentro del grupo.*
Cost of houses - one hundred pounds each.	*El precio por casa – cien libras cada una*
Cost of hotels - one hundred pounds plus four houses.	*El precio por hotel – cien libras más cuatro casas*
Mortgage value of site.	*Valor de la hipoteca de una propiedad.*

Chance	***La Suerte***
Pick up a Chance card.	*Coge una tarjeta de suerte.*
Take the top card.	*Coge la carta de arriba.*
Put the used card at the bottom of the pile.	*Pon la carta usada abajo del montón.*
What does it say?	*¿Qué dice?*
It says.. (abc)	*Dice...*
Advance to Go	*Ve a la salida*
Advance to Mayfair.	*Ve a Mayfair.*
Advance to Pall Mall - If you pass Go collect two hundred pounds.	*Ve a Pall Mall – si pasas la casilla de salida cobra doscientas libras.*
Bank pays you a dividend of fifty pounds.	*La banca arroja un dividendo de cincuenta libras a tu favor.*

MONOPOLY cont. ***MONOPOLY cont.***

Drunk in charge - Fine twenty pounds.	*Multa por conducir borracho – Veinte libras de multa.*
Get out of Jail free - This card may be kept until needed or sold.	*Sal de la cárcel directamente. Guarda esta tarjeta hasta que puedas utilizarla o venderla.*
Go back three spaces.	*Retrocede tres casillas.*
Go to Jail. Move directly to Jail. Do not pass Go. Do not collect two hundred pounds.	*Ve a la cárcel. Redirectamente a la cárcel sin pasar por la casilla de salida y sin cobrar las docientas libras.*
Make general repairs on your houses - for each house pay twenty five pounds.	*Reparaciones en casas – por cada casa paga veinticinco libras.*
Speeding fine - fifteen pounds.	*Multa por exceso de velocidad – paga quince libras.*
Take a trip to Marylebone Station and if you pass Go collect two hundred pounds.	*Ve a la estación del Norte y se pasas por la casilla de salida cobra doscientas libras.*
You are assessed for street repairs - forty pounds per house, one hundred and fifteen pounds per hotel.	*Reparaciones en tu propiedades – cuarenta libras por casa, ciento quince libras por hotel.*
Your building loan matures - Receive one hundred and fifty pounds.	*Intereses de prestamos en tus propiedades – Recibe ciento cincuenta libras.*
You have won a crossword competition - Collect one hundred pounds.	*Premio de palabra cruzadas – cobra cien libras.*

MONOPOLY cont. / *MONOPOLY cont.*

Community Chest	***Tarjetas de Comunidad***
What does it say? It says..(abc)	***¿Qué dice? Dice...***
Advance to Go.	*Ve a la salida*
Annuity matures - Collect one hundred pounds.	*Intereses anuales – cobra cien libras.*
Bank error in your favour - Collect two hundred pounds.	*Error del banco a tu favor – cobra doscientas libras.*
Doctor's fee - Pay fifty pounds.	*Factura del doctor - Paga cincuenta libras.*
From sale of stock - You get fifty pounds.	*Por inmueble – recibe cincuenta libras.*
Get out of Jail free - This card may be kept until needed or sold.	*Sal de la cárcel directamente – Esta tarjeta puede ser guardada hasta que sea necesitada o vendida.*
Go back to Old Kent Road.	*Retrocede a la Plaza de Lavapiés.*
Go to Jail. Move directly to Jail. Do not pass Go. Do not collect two hundred pounds.	*Ve a la cárcel. Ve directamente sin pasar por la casilla de salida y sin cobrar las doscientas libras.*
Income Tax Refund - Collect twenty pounds.	*Devolución de tasas – Cobra veinte libras de cada jugador.*
It is your Birthday - Collect ten pounds from each player.	*Es tu cumpleaños – Cobra diez libras de cada jugador.*
Pay a ten pound Fine or take a "Chance".	*Paga una multa de diez libras o toma una "tarjeta de suerte".*
Pay Hospital one hundred pounds.	*Paga al hospital cien libras.*
Pay your Insurance Premium - fifty pounds.	*Paga tu Seguro – cincuenta libras.*
Receive interest on seven per cent Preference Shares - twenty five pounds.	*Recibe un interés de siete por ciento en tus acciones – veinticinco libras.*
You have won Second Prize in a Beauty Contest - Collect ten pounds.	*Has ganado el Segundo Premio de Belleza – Cobra diez libras.*
You inherit one hundred pounds.	*Has heredado cien libras.*

MONOPOLY cont. / *MONOPOLY cont.*
The Play / *El Juego*

Choosing the pieces	***Eligiendo la piezas / fichas***
Which piece do you want to be?	*¿Qué ficha quieres?*
What colour do you want to be?	*¿Qué color quieres?*

Starting a game	***Empezando a jugar***
Shake two dice to start.	*Tira dos dados para empezar*
The player with the highest total starts.	*El jugador con el total más alto empieza.*
I start.	*Yo empiezo.*
You start.	*Tu empiezas.*
He / she starts.	*El / Ella empieza.*

Whose turn is it now?	***¿De quién es el turno ahora?***
It's my / your / his / her go.	*Es mío / tuyo / suyo / es mi / tu / su turno.*
We are playing clockwise / anticlockwise.	*Jugamos en la dirección de la manillas del reloj / en dirección contraria a las manillas del reloj.*
It's not your turn.	*No es tu turno.*
You went out of turn.	*Se te ha pasado el turno.*
You'd better miss your next go.	*Tienes que esperarte un turno.*

Throwing the dice	***Tirando los dados***
to throw a double	*Tirar un doble / doblete / doblarse*
I threw a double so I throw again.	*Saqué doble luego tiro otra vez.*
I threw three doubles so I have to go to jail.	*Saqué tres dobles luego tengo que ir a la cárcel.*
to throw two sixes	*tirar a sacar la mayor puntuación posible.*

MONOPOLY cont. / *MONOPOLY cont.*

Moving the tokens	***Mover las fichas***
I shook a three so I move three places.	*Saqué un tres así que me muevo tres espacios.*
We can both be on that space at the same time.	*Podemos estar en el mismo sitio a la vez.*
I have to advance to Go.	*Tengo que ir a la salida.*
I have to go directly to jail.	*Tengo que ir directamente a la cárcel.*

Landing on squares	***Cayendo en las casillas***
I hope you land on my property.	*Espero que caigas en mi casilla / propiedad.*
Oh no! I just landed on your property.	*¡Oh no! He caido en tu propiedad.*
Does anyone own the property I just landed on?	*¿Tiene alguien esta propiedad en que he caido?*
It's mine, so you owe me..	*Es mia, dame / me debes...*
How much do I have to pay you?	*¿Cuánto te tengo que pagar?*
You have to pay me twenty two pounds rent - site only.	*Me tienes que dar / pagar veinte dos libras de alquiler – sin edificar solo.*
I have three houses, so that's nine hundred pounds you owe me.	*Tengo tres casas, así que son novecientas libras a pagar.*
You have landed on my hotel.	*Has caido en mi hotel.*

Buying property	***Comprando propiedades / terrenos***
Do you want to buy that?	*¿Quieres comprar esa / ese?*
Yes, I'll buy it, please.	*Sí, lo compro, por favor.*
No, I don't think I'll buy it.	*No, no creo que quiero comprarlo.*
No, I haven't enough money.	*No, no tengo suficiente dinero.*
Have you any change?	*¿Tienes cambio?*

MONOPOLY cont.	*MONOPOLY cont.*
Selling property	***Vendiendo propiedades***
Would you like to sell me..?	*¿Quieres venderme...?*
I want to sell these houses back to the bank.	*¿Quiero vender estas casas a la banca?*
You only get half price if you sell property back to the Bank.	*Solo te devuelven la mitad del valor si vendes propiedades al banco / la banca.*

Putting houses on	***Poniendo casas / edificando***
Houses are green.	*Las casas son verdes.*
I want to put a house on here.	*Quiero poner casas aquí.*
I have two houses, so you have to pay me..	*Tengo dos casas, a pagarme...*
Could I buy a house, please?	*¿Puedo comprar una casa, por favor?*
I would like four houses, please.	*Quisiera cuatro casas, por favor?*
You have to put houses evenly over your properties.	*Tienes que colocar las casas claramente sobre tu propiedad / terreno.*
The bank has run out of houses, so you'll have to wait.	*El banco se ha quedado sin casas así es que tienes que esperar.*
The bank now has houses again - would you like to bid for them?	*La banca / el banco tiene casas ahora. ¿Quieres pujar por éstas?*

Putting a hotel on	***Edificando con hoteles***
Hotels are red.	*Los Hoteles son rojos.*
I want to buy a hotel now.	*Quiero comprar un hotel ahora.*
You can't put a hotel on until you have four houses on each site.	*No puedes edificar con hoteles hasta que tengas cuatro casas en cada terreno.*
You give the Bank the four houses and pay the difference for a hotel.	*Da las cuatro casas al banco y paga por la diferencia al poner el hotel.*
Here are the houses in exchange.	*Aquí tienes las casas por el cambio.*
I have to pay.....extra.	*Tengo que pagar...extra.*

MONOPOLY cont. | *MONOPOLY cont.*

The Banker	***El jugador o cargo de la banca***
Do you want to buy it?	*¿Quieres comprarlo?*
It costs..	*Vale / cuesta / son...*
You owe the Bank..	*Debes al banco...*
Does anyone want to bid for this property?	*¿Quiere alguien pujar por este terreno?*
You are the highest bidder.	*Tú eres el pujante más alto.*
I haven't got the right change.	*No tengo el cambio justo.*
Can someone change this note, please?	*¿Puede alguien dar cambio, por favor?*
The Bank has run out of money.	*La Banca no tiene dinero.*
The Bank will have to give you an I.O.U. (an I owe you).	*La Banca tiene que utilizar créditos.*

Mortgaging property	***Hipotecando propiedades***
I would like to mortgage this, please.	*Me gustaría hipotecar esto, por favor.*
The mortgage value is printed on each Title Deed.	*El valor de la hipoteca está señalado en los títulos de propiedad.*
Turn the card face down to show it's mortgaged.	*Da la vuelta a la tarjeta para ??? la hipoteca.*
There is no rent to pay because the property is mortgaged.	*No hay que pagar renta / alquiler porque la propiedad está hipotecada.*
You have to pay ten per cent when you lift the mortgage.	*Tienes que pagar el diez por ciento cuando quieres levantar la hipoteca.*
You can't mortgage houses or hotels.	*No se puede hipotecar casas ni hoteles.*
You can't build on mortgaged property.	*No se puede edificar en las propiedades hipotecadas.*
You have to pay off the mortgage first.	*Tienes que pagar la hipoteca primero.*

MONOPOLY cont. | *MONOPOLY cont.*

Being bankrupt	***Bancarrota***
I'm afraid I can't pay you.	*Me temo que no puedo pagarte.*
I haven't any money.	*No tengo dinero.*
I shall have to return my houses/hotels to the Bank.	*Tengo que devolver mis casas / hoteles a la banca.*
You only get half their value if you return them.	*Solo se te da la mitad al devolverlas.*
Will you take part cash and part property?	*¿Podría darte la mitad en efectivo y la otra mitad en propiedades?*

Seeing who has won	***Viendo quien ha ganado***
Shall we stop now and see who has won?	*¿Vamos a parar y ver quién ha ganado?*
Shall we leave the game here and carry on playing later?	*¿Por qué no lo dejamos aquí y seguimos jugando más tarde?*
Add up all your money.	*Suma todo tu dinero.*
Add up the value of your property.	*Añade el valor de la suma de todas.*
How much do you own?	*¿Cuanto tienes? Tus propiedades*
I own..	*Tengo*
You have won.	*He ganado.*
I think I've won.	*Creo que he ganado.*

CLUEDO | *CLUEDO*

THE OBJECT OF THE GAME | *EL OBJETIVO DEL JUEGO*

To solve by elimination and deduction the murder of Dr. Black, the owner of Tudor Close, whose body has been found at the foot of the stairs leading to the cellar at a spot marked "X". The winner is the first player to guess correctly:-	*Resolver por eliminación y deducción quién mató al Doctor Black, propietario de la casa Tudor, y cuyo cuerpo ha sido encontrado a los pies de las escaleras que van al sótano o en el sitio marcado con una "X". El ganador es el primer jugador en adivinarlo correctamente.*
• Who the murderer was.	• *¿Quién lo mató?*
• Which weapon was used.	• *¿Qué arma se utilizó?*
• The room in which the crime was committed.	• *La habitación en la que el crimen se produjo.*

The spot marked "X"	***El lugar marcado con una "X"***
the stairs leading to the cellars	*Las escaleras que llevan / van al sótano.*
the envelope marked "Murder Cards"	*El sobre que dice "Tarjetas del Crimen".*

The three "Murder Cards"	***Las Tres Tarjetas del Crimen***
the murderer	*el asesino*
the weapon	*el arma*
the room in which the crime was committed	*la habitación en la que se cometió el crimen / asesinato*

CLUEDO cont. — *CLUEDO cont.*

Selecting the three "Murder Cards"	***Seleccionando las Tres Tarjetas del Crimen***
Shuffle the nine room cards well.	*Baraja las nueve habitaciones muy bien.*
Shuffle the six weapon cards separately.	*Baraja las seis armas separadamente.*
Shuffle the six person cards too.	*Baraja las seis personas tambien.*
Cut the piles of cards.	*Corta el montón de tarjetas.*
Place the top card of each pile unseen into the Murder Envelope.	*Pon las tarjetas de arriba del montón dentro del sobre del Crimen.*
There should be a room card, a weapon card and a person card.	*Deben haber una tarjeta del lugar, de arma y de persona.*

The people and their pieces	***Las Piezas***
Colonel Mustard - Yellow	*Amarilla – El Coronel Mustard*
Professor Plum - Purple	*Violeta – El Profesor Plum*
The Reverend Green - Green	*Verde – El Reverendo Green*
Mrs. Peacock - Blue	*Azul – Mrs Peacock*
Miss Scarlett - Red	*Roja – Miss Scarlett*
Mrs. White - White	*Blanca – Mrs White*

The Board	***El Tablero***
the ground floor plan of Tudor Close	*la planta baja de la casa Tudor*
start	*la salida*
a square	*una casilla*
a door	*una puerta*

CLUEDO cont. / *CLUEDO cont.*

The rooms	***Las Habitaciones***
the lounge	*la sala de estar*
the dining room	*el comedor*
the kitchen	*la cocina*
the ballroom	*el salón*
the conservatory	*el conservatorio*
the billiard room	*la habitación de billar*
the library	*la librería*
the study	*el estudio*
the hall	*el hall*

The secret passages	***Los Pasadizos Secretos***
from the study to the kitchen and vice versa	*del estudio a la cocina y vice versa*
from the lounge to the conservatory and vice versa	*del salón al conservatorio y vice versa*
You can use a secret passage instead of throwing the dice.	*Puedes utilizar un pasadizo secreto en lugar de tirar los dados.*
Using a secret passage counts as one move.	*Cuando se usa un pasadizo secreto cuenta como un turno.*

The Weapons	***Las Armas***
The Candlestick	*El Candelabro*
The Dagger	*El Cuchillo / La Daga*
The Lead Piping	*El Atizador*
The Revolver	*El Revólver*
The Rope	*La Soga*
The Spanner	*La Llave Inglesa*
the tokens	*las armas*

CLUEDO cont. / *CLUEDO cont.*

"Detective Notes" cards	***"Tarjetas para las notas sobre la investigación"***
Suspected Persons	*Sospechosos*
Probable Implements	*Posibles armas del crimen*
Suspected Scene of Murder	*Posible escena del crimen*
Have you got some pencils?	*¿Tienes lapiceros?*
Could I have a pencil, please?	*¿Me puedes dar un lápiz por favor?*
to tick off	*marcar*
to cross off	*poner una cruz*
to make a note of	*tomar notas*
to record	*grabar*
to eliminate from your enquiries	*eliminar por deducción*
Using "Detective Notes" cards	***Usando tus cartas de investigación***
to query	*(para) preguntar*
to get confused	*confundirse*
to forget	*olvidar*
You asked me that before.	*Me preguntaste esto antes*

Playing	***Jugando***
Place the pieces on their starting squares.	*Poner las fichas a la salida.*
Put the weapons in different rooms.	*Poner las armas en habitaciones diferentes.*
Draw the three Murder Cards (see above).	*Escoge al azar las cartas del crimen. (véase arriba)*
Put the Murder Cards in the Murder Envelope.	*Pon las cartas del crimen en el sobre del crimen.*
Put the Murder Envelope on the spot marked "X".	*Pon el sobre del crimen en el lugar marcado con una "X".*
Shuffle all the cards together.	*Baraja todas las tarjetas juntas*

PLAYING CLUEDO cont.	***JUGANDO AL CLUEDO / INDICIO cont.***
Deal out the cards one at a time clockwise round the table.	*Reparte las cartas de una en una en la dirección de las manillas del reloj.*
Sometimes some players have more cards than others. It is easier for them.	*Algunas veces algunos de los jugadores tienen más cartas que otros. Es más fácil para ellos.*
Each player decides to be one of the murder suspects and uses their token.	*Cada jugador decide ser uno de los sospechosos y utiliza la ficha correspondiente.*
Miss Scarlett always moves first.	*Miss Scarlett siempre mueve la primera.*
Play in a clockwise direction.	*Juega en la dirección de las manillas del reloj.*
Shake the dice and move your token accordingly.	*Lanza los dados y mueve tu ficha de acuerdo al resultado.*
You may not move diagonally.	*No se puede mover en dirección diagonal.*
You have to enter and leave rooms through the doors or secret passages.	*Se tiene que entrar y salir de la habitaciones a través de las puertas o pasadizos secretos.*

Making a suggestion	***Haciendo sugerencias***
When you enter a room, you can make a "suggestion" by calling into that room any other person (who has to go immediately into the room) and any weapon (which is then placed in the room). You cannot use any other room in your suggestion, only the room you are in.	*Cuando entras en una habitación puede hacer una "sugerencia" eligiendo esa habitación, otra persona (que tiene que ir inmediatamente a esa habitación) y cualquier de las armas (que entonces se sitúa en esa habitación). No puedes usar una habitación distinta de la que estás en tu "atento", solo la habitación donde estás.*

CLUEDO cont.

CLUEDO cont.

A sample suggestion "I suggest that the murder was committed in the Lounge by the Reverend Green with the Spanner."	***Un ejemplo de sugerencia*** *"Sugiero que el asesinato fue cometido en el cuarto de estar por el Reverendo Green con la llave inglesa."*

After the suggestion The player who is making the suggestion, does so to the player on his / her left.	***Después de Sugerir*** *El jugador que hace la sugerencia, hace esta a el jugador de su izquierda.*
This player has to examine his / her cards and if he has one (or more) of the suggested cards he must show one (and one only) of them secretly to the other person. (He should not admit to having more than one of the requested cards.) If this player has none of the cards, the person to his left is then asked the same question.	*Este jugador tiene que mirar a sus cartas y ver si tiene una (o más) de las cartas sugeridas, mostrando una sola de ellas en secreto a la otra persona. No se debe decir si se tiene más de una de las cartas.* *Si el jugador no tiene ninguna de las cartas, la persona de su izquierda es preguntada la misma cuestión.*
As soon as someone has shown one of the suggested cards, that turn is ended and play passes to the next player to the left. Each person tries by a process of elimination to discover the three Murder Cards.	*Tan pronto como una persona haya mostrado una de las cartas, el turno se termina y el turno pasa al siguiente a la izquierda.* *Cada persona intenta por eliminación descubrir las tres cartas del crimen.*

CLUEDO cont.

CLUEDO cont.

Making an accusation	***Haciendo una acusación***
When a player think he knows what the three Murder Cards are, he can, provided it is his turn (even if he has just made a suggestion), make an Accusation by writing down what he thinks the three cards in the Murder Envelope are and checking with the contents of the Murder Envelope, taking care that no-one else sees the cards.	*Cuando un jugador piensa que sabe lo que dicen las tres cartas, el puede, si es su turno (incluso si acaba de hacer un sugerencia), hacer una acusación escribiendo lo que piensa que las tres cartas en el sobre del crimen dicen y verificándolo con el contenido del mismo, teniendo cuidado de que nadie más lo vea.*

If the player is not correct..	***Si el jugador no lleva razón..***
he cannot make any more accusations in the game. He should replace the three cards in the Murder Envelope so that the other players can continue the game. He still has to answer other players' suggestions.	*no puede incriminar más en el juego. Debe volver a meter las tres cartas en el sobre para que los demás jugadores continúen el juego. El todavía tiene que responder las preguntas de los otros jugadores.*

N.B. If a player says he does not hold any of the suggested cards when he in fact does hold one, this player has no further turns in the game.	*Si un jugador dice que no tiene una de las cartas solicitadas cuando en realidad la tiene. Este jugador pierde todos sus turnos en el juego.*

CARD GAMES / *JUEGOS DE NAIPES*

GENERAL EXPRESSIONS / *EXPRESIONES GENERALES*

Would you like to play cards?	***¿Te gustaría jugar a las cartas?***
What games do you know?	*¿Qué juegos conoces?*
What would you like to play?	*¿A qué quieres jugar?*
Can you play..?	*¿Puedes jugar a...?*
Shall we play..?	*¿Por qué no jugamos a...?*
I'd like to play..	*Me gustaría jugar a...*
I've forgotten how to play.	*Se me ha olvidado como jugar a...*
Can you remind me how to play?	*¿Dime como se jugaba otra vez?*
Can you teach me how to play?	*Me enseñas a jugar?*

A pack of cards	***El mazo de cartas / La baraja de Cartas***
Have you got a pack of cards?	*¿Tienes una baraja de cartas?*
I brought a pack of cards with me.	*He traido una baraja de cartas conmigo.*
I'll go and get them.	*Voy y la cojo.*

Is it a full pack?	***¿Está la baraja completa?***
Shall we check the pack?	*¿Comprueba si está completa?*
Are there any missing?	*¿Falta alguna?*
There is one missing.	*No, están todas / No, no falta ninguna*
Have you got another pack?	*¿Tienes otro mazo de cartas?*

The different suits English / Spanish	***Las distintas muestras / los distintos palos English / Spanish***
clubs / clubs	*tréboles / bastos*
diamonds / coins	*diamantes / oros*
hearts / cups	*corazones / copas*
spades / spades	*espadas / espadas*

CARD GAMES cont. — *JUEGOS DE NAIPES cont.*

The number cards	***Los números de los naipes***
ace	*el as / el uno / el triunfo*
ace high / ace low	*un triunfo major / un triunfo menor*
the ace of hearts	*el as de corazones*
two	*el dos*
the two of diamonds	*el dos de diamantes*
three / four / five / six	*el tres / cuatro / cinco / seis*
seven / eight / nine / ten	*siete / ocho / nueve / diez*

The face cards	***Las figuras***
Jack	*El Caballo*
Queen	*La Dama / La Reina*
King	*El Rey*
Joker	*La Sota / El comodín / Sota de oros*

PLAYING CARD GAMES — *JUGANDO A CARTAS*

Shuffling	***Barajando***
Shuffle the cards.	*Baraja las cartas*
I'll shuffle / you shuffle.	*Yo barrajo / tú barajas*
Give the cards a good shuffle.	*Barajea bien las cartas*
The cards aren't shuffled properly.	*Los naipes no están bien barajeados.*

Cutting	***Cortando***
to cut	*cortar*
You cut to me.	*córtame*
I'll cut to you.	*yo te corto*

CARD GAMES cont. / *JUEGOS DE NAIPES cont.*

Dealing	***Repartiendo***
It's your deal.	*Tú repartes*
You deal the cards face up / face down.	*Reparte boca arriba / boca abajo.*
You dealt two cards then.	*Has repartido dos cartas en una.*
You missed one out.	*Se te ha pasado una.*
I'm the dealer this time.	*Yo reparto esta vez.*
I've forgotten where I'm up to.	*Se me ha olvidado a quién reparto ahora.*
Count your cards.	*Cuenta tus cartas.*
I am one short.	*Me falta una.*
I have one extra.	*Tengo una demás.*
We'd better re-deal.	*Lo mejor es repartir otra vez.*

Assessing your hand	***Colocando las cartas en la mano***
I haven't sorted my hand yet.	*No me las he colocado todavía.*
Let me just arrange my cards.	*Dejame colocar las cartas.*
I've got a good hand this time.	*Tengo una buena mano esta vez.*
I've got a poor hand again.	*Tengo malas cartas otra vez.*

Leading	***Saliendo***
You lead.	*Tu sales.*
It's my / his / her / our / your / their lead.	*Me / Te / Se / Nos / Os / Les toca salir.*
She led the three of diamonds.	*Ella salió con el tres de diamantes.*
What did you lead?	*¿Con qué saliste?*

Playing one's hand	***Haciendo tú propio juego***
He played an ace.	*El juega con su as.*
What did he play?	*¿Con qué juega?*
I don't know what to play.	*No sé que echar.*

CARD GAMES cont. / *JUEGOS DE NAIPES cont.*

Following suit	***Arrastrando a un palo***
You must follow suit if you can.	*Tienes que arrastrar si tienes palo.*
I can't follow suit.	*No puedo arrastrar.*
A strong suit	*una baza fuerte / una mano buena*
a weak suit	*una baza floja / una mano mala*

Trumping	***Arrastrando***
What are trumps?	*¿Cuál es la muestra?*
Spades are trumps.	*Las espadas son muestra.*
The three of trumps.	*El tres es la muestra.*
I haven't got any trumps.	*No tengo muestra.*
He was holding all the trumps.	*Me he quedado con todas la muestras.*

Throwing away cards	***Desbarajándose***
to discard	*descartar*
the stock pile	*el montón para descartar*
I need to throw one away.	*Necesito quitarme de una.*
I don't know which to throw away.	*No sé cuál debo quitarme.*

Picking up cards	***Cogiendo Cartas / Robando Cartas***
Have you picked up yet?	*¿Has robado ya?*
Pick one up off the pile.	*Roba una del montón.*
What did you pick up?	*¿Qué has robado?*

Putting cards down	***Ocultando Cartas / Deshacerse de una Carta***
to put a card face down	*deshacerse de una carta*
to put a card face up	*mostrar una carta*
What did she put down?	*¿De qué se ha deshecho?*

CARD GAMES cont. — *JUEGOS DE NAIPES cont.*

Missing a turn	***Pasando un turno***
I missed my turn.	*Se me ha pasado mi turno.*
You missed your turn.	*Se te ha pasado el turno.*
You have to miss a turn.	*Tienes que esperarte hasta el próximo turno.*

Passing	***Pasando***
I can't play anything.	*No tengo cartas.*
I shall have to pass.	*Tengo que pasar.*
I pass.	*Paso.*
She passed.	*Ella pasó.*

Winning tricks	***Bazas Ganadas***
How many tricks have you won?	*¿Cuántas manos has ganado?*
Well done!	*¡Bien hecho!*
I just won that trick.	*Acabo de ganar esa baza.*
I don't think I'm going to win many.	*No creo que vaya a ganar muchas bazas.*
We only need to win another one.	*Sólo necesitamos ganar otra baza.*
We need to win seven tricks.	*Necesitamos ganar siete bazas.*

Losing tricks	***Bazas Perdidas***
How many tricks can we afford to lose?	*¿Cuántas bazas podemos permitirnos perder?*
How many tricks have we lost?	*¿Cuántas bazas hemos perdido?*
Sorry!	*¡Lo siento!*

CARD GAMES cont. — *JUEGOS DE NAIPES cont.*

Cheating	***Haciendo trampas***
Did you cheat?	*¿Has hecho trampas?*
I never cheat.	*Nunca hago trampas.*
You shouldn't cheat.	*No deberías hacer trampas.*
Don't look at my cards.	*No mires mis cartas*
I can see your cards.	*No puedo ver tus cartas.*

Memorising cards	***Memorizando las cartas***
to remember	*recordar*
to forget	*olvidar*
to count	*contar*
I can't remember if the Ace has gone.	*No recuerdo si el as ha salido.*
I have forgotten how many..	*He olvidado cuántos...*
How many trumps have gone?	*¿Cuántas muestras han salido?*
Try to remember the tricks.	*Intenta recordar las bazas.*
Count the aces / the trumps.	*Cuenta los ases / las muestras.*
Have all the hearts gone?	*¿Han salido todos los corazones?*

WHIST

WHIST

You need:	*Se necesita:*
A fifty two card pack	*Una baraja de cincuenta y dos cartas*
Four people (two pairs of partners)	*Cuatro personas (dos parejas)*

The Object of the Game	*El Objetivo del Juego*
To win as many of the thirteen available tricks as possible.	*Ganar el mayor número de bazas posibles de las trece que se pueden ganar.*

HOW TO PLAY

COMO JUGAR

• The dealer deals out all the cards one by one and face down to each player in turn so that each has thirteen cards.	• *El que reparte da todas las cartas de una en una a cada jugador repartiendo trece a cada uno en total.*
• He should start by dealing to the person on his left so that the last card is dealt to himself.	• *Se debe empezar repartiendo a la primera persona a la izquierda para que la última carta vaya a quien reparte.*
• This last card is dealt face up and determines what trumps are.	• *La última carta se pone boca arriba y ésta es la muestra.*
• The player to the dealer's left starts the play with any card.	• *La persona a la izquierda del que reparte es mano.*
• The other players have to follow suit if they can but can trump the trick if they cannot.	• *Los otros jugadores tienen que tirar el mismo palo si tienen, pero pueden fallar con muestra si no tienen ese palo.*
• If more than one trump is played, the higher trump wins the trick.	• *Si entran en juego más de una muestra la más alta gana la baza.*

HOW TO PLAY WHIST cont. / *COMO JUGAR WHIST cont.*

• If no trumps are played, the highest card of the suit wins with ace counting high.	• *Si no hay muestras, la más alta de las cartas del mismo palo gana. Siendo el as el más alto.*
• The person who wins the trick leads the first card in the next round.	• *La persona que gana la baza sale a continuación.*

Scoring	***Marcando / Contando puntos***
• Each trick over six won by either pair of players counts as one point.	• *Cada baza a partir de seis ganadas por cualquiera de las parejas puntúa como una partida.*
• A game is won when seven points have been won.	• *Una partida entera se gana cuando se consiguen siete partidas (parciales).*

RUMMY / *RUMMY*

You need:	***Se necesita:***
A fifty two card pack	*Una baraja de cincuenta y dos cartas.*
Any number of players from two to six.	*Un número de jugadores de dos a seis.*

The Object of the Game Rummy	***El Objetivo del Rummy es:***
To get rid of all your cards by laying them down on the table in front of you.	*Deshacerse de todas tus cartas echándolas boca abajo en la mesa en frente de tí.*

RUMMY cont.	*RUMMY cont.*
Players try to collect and arrange cards in the following ways:	*Los jugadores toman y colocan las cartas de las siguientes:*
• Three of a kind or four of a kind - e.g. three Aces or four Sixes	• *Tres de un mismo tipo o cuatro de una misma clase: por ejemplo tres ases o cuatro seises.*
• A sequence of three or more cards of the same suit - e.g. Two, Three, Four, Five of Spades.	• *Una secuencia de tres o más cartas del mismo palo – por ejemplo dos, tres, cuatro, cinco de espadas.*

HOW TO PLAY RUMMY	*COMO JUGAR AL RUMMY*
Cut for dealer who deals to each player:	*Corta al que reparte y repartir las cartas a los jugadores:*
• ten cards each if there are two players	• *diez cartas para cada uno si hay dos jugadores.*
• seven cards each if there are three or four players	• *siete cartas para cada uno si hay tres o cuatro jugadores.*
• six cards each if there are five or six players	• *seis cartas para cada uno si hay cinco o seis jugadores.*
Place remaining cards face down on the table to form a stock pile.	*Pon las cartas sobrante boca arriba en la mesa formando un montón de robo.*
Turn up the top card of the stock pile and lay it face up beside the stock pile to form a waste pile.	*Da la vuelta a la última carta del montón de robo y situarla al lado formando un montón de descarte.*
The player on the dealer's left starts the game.	*El jugador a la izquierda del que reparte empieza el juego.*
Players look at their hands for the beginnings of any of the above groups or sequences of cards.	*Los jugadores miran a sus manos y buscan grupos o el comienzo de una escalera o secuencia.*

HOW TO PLAY RUMMY cont.	***COMO JUGAR AL RUMMY cont.***
If you are lucky enough to have any group or sequence you can lay it on the table in front of you.	*Si eres afortunado en tener un grupo o escalera, puedes dejarlo sobre la mesa en frente de tí.*
If not, you can either pick up the turned-up waste card or take one from the stock pile.	*Si no, puedes coger una del robo o coger la carta que está en el montón de descarte boca arriba.*
You have to throw one card away - either the one you have just picked up or one from your existing hand.	*Tienes que dejar una carta – la que acabas de coger o una de las que tenías originalmente en la mano.*
Players can also add cards to any other player's cards already laid on the table.	*Los jugadores pueden también dejar cartas con las de los otros jugadores que están sobre la mesa.*
You win when you are the first person to get rid of all your cards.	*Se gana cuando eres la primera persona en deshacerse de todas las cartas*

SCORING	***PUNTUANDO***
When someone has won the game, all other players add up the points they still hold in their hand as follows:-	*Cuando alguien gana la partida, todos los demás jugadores se apuntan tantos números como cartas tienen en sus manos todavía.*
• Aces count low as one.	• *Los ases valen uno.*
• Number cards count their number value.	• *Las cartas con número valen el número que tengan.*
• Jacks, Queens and Kings count ten each.	• *Las figuras valen diez cada una.*

RUMMY - SCORING cont.	***RUMMY - PUNTUANDO cont.***
The winner is awarded the total number of points held by all other players.	*El ganador gana el total resultante de la suma de todos los puntos de los demás concursantes.*
If the winner was able to put all his cards straight down on the table on his first go then he is said to have "gone rummy" and gets awarded double the other players' total points.	*Si el jugador que sale se las manejó para poner todas sus cartas sobre la mesa al principio de la partida, se dice "rummy" y se le da el doble de puntos del total final puntuado por todos los jugadores.*
The overall winner can be the first one to reach five hundred points or some other pre-determined score.	*El ganador final puede acordarse como aquél que puntúa quinientos puntos en primer lugar. O otra puntuación previamente acordada.*

PONTOON

LAS VEINTIUNA / EL PONTON

You need:	***Se necesita:***
A fifty two card pack	*Una baraja de cincuenta y dos cartas*
Dead matchsticks or counters for laying bets.	*Cerillas usadas o fichas para apostar*
Someone to be banker / dealer.	*Una banca / el que reparte (repartidor)*

Scoring	***Puntuando***
• Kings, Queens & Jacks count as ten each.	• *Los Reyes / Reinas (damas) / Sotas valen diez cada uno.*
• Aces count 'low' as one or 'high' as eleven - whichever is convenient at the time.	• *Los ases pequeños o grandes valen uno o once respectivamente, dependiendo de lo que convenga en la situación.*
• All the number cards have their ordinary value.	• *Las cartas numeradas tienen su valor numérico.*

PONTOON cont.	*LAS VEINTIUNA / EL PONTON cont.*
How to Play	*¿Cómo se juega?*
• Choose someone to be dealer who in the game of Pontoon is called the banker.	• *Se toma a alguien como repartidor de las veintiuna. Se le llama la banca.*
• Players can take turns to be banker.	• *Los jugadores toman turnos para ser la banca.*
• The banker plays against the other players.	• *La banca juega contra los otros jugadores.*
• Any reasonable number of people can play.	• *Cualquier número de jugadores puede jugar siendo un número razonable.*
• All suits are ignored.	• *Los palos no cuentan en este juego.*
• The banker shuffles the cards (which are not shuffled again until a new banker takes over).	• *La banca baraja las cartas (que no se vuelven a barajar hasta que otro jugador tiene la banca).*

THE RULES OF PONTOON	*REGLAS DE LAS VEINTIUNA*
• The banker deals one card face down to each player, including himself.	• *La banca da una carta boca arriba a cada jugador, incluido a él mismo.*
• The other players look at their own card, keeping it secret, but the banker cannot look at his own card yet.	• *Los otros jugadores miran a sus cartas sin decir lo que tienen, pero la banca no puede ver la suya.*
• Each player then makes a bet with counters or matchsticks, putting a lot on if they think their card is good and only one counter if not. Each has to bet something.	• *Cada jugador hace una apuesta con las fichas o las cerillas poniendo muchas si piensa que su carta es buena y solo una si no es buena. Cada jugador tiene que apostar algo.*

THE RULES OF PONTOON cont.	*REGLAS DE LAS VEINTIUNA cont.*
• The banker then deals a second card to each player.	• *La banca reparte otra carta a cada jugador.*
• The aim of the game is to score twenty one exactly, or as close to twenty one as possible.	• *El objetivo del juego es puntuar veintiuna exactamente, o quedarse lo más cerca posible a veintiuna.*
• Players add up their score.	• *Los jugadores suman sus puntos.*
• The banker then asks each player in turn if they want to "stick" (i.e. not take any more cards) or if they want to "twist" (i.e. be dealt another card but this time face up).	• *La banca entonces pregunta a cada jugador por turno si quieren "quedarse" (por ejemplo ¿otra carta?) o si quieren otra descubierta (repartir otra carta pero esta vez boca arriba)*
• Players can twist up to three times (making a maximum total of five cards).	• *Los jugadores pueden pedir cartas descubiertas, tres veces (sumando un máximo total de cinco cartas por jugador.)*
• If the total score in a player's hand exceeds twenty one then that player is "bust" and puts his cards down on the table.	• *Si la suma total de la mano de un jugador es superior a veintiuna, el jugador se ha "pasado" y pone sus cartas sobre la mesa boca abajo.*
• When all players have decided either to stick or are bust, the banker turns his cards over for everyone to see and proceeds to stick or twist like everyone else.	• *Cuando todos los jugadores se han "plantado" ("quedado") o se han "pasado", la banca da la vuelta a su carta enfrente de los demás jugadores y procede a "puntarse" o "pedir cartas descubiertas".*
• The banker takes all the counters bet by players who either went bust or scored lower than himself or the same as himself.	• *La banca toma todas las fichas apostados por jugadores que se han pasado o que tienen menos puntuación que ella o la misma puntuación que la banca.*

THE RULES OF PONTOON cont. / *REGLAS DE LAS VEINTIUNA cont.*

• He has to pay players who scored higher than he did himself the same number of counters as they bet.	• *Tiene que pagar a aquellos jugadores que consiguieron una puntuación superior a la suya dándoles la misma cantidad de fichas apostadas .*
• If the banker scores twenty one made with an Ace together with any King, Queen or Jack he calls "Pontoon" and receives double stakes from each player, unless one of the players has a five card trick (which beats Pontoon) or a "Royal Pontoon" which consists of three sevens and beats everything.	• *Si la banca puntúa veintiuna con un Rey, Dama (Reina) o Sota y un as. Dice "veintiuna" y recibe el doble de cada apuesta de los jugadores, a no ser que un jugador tenga una baza de veintiuna con cinco cartas (que gana a las veintiuna de figura y as) o una "veintiuna" de tres sietes que gana a todo.*
• A player with a Royal Pontoon receives treble stakes. If the banker has a Royal Pontoon it only counts as an ordinary Pontoon.	• *Un jugador con veintiuna de tres sietes recibe el triple de la apuesta. Si la banca levanta veintiuna de tres sietes solo se cuenta como una normal.*

BRIDGE

BRIDGE

Counting the points in your hand	***Contando los puntos en tu mano***
ALLOW:	***DA:***
• four points for an Ace	• *cuatro puntos por un as*
• three points for a King	• *tres puntos por un rey*
• two points for a Queen	• *dos puntos por una dama*
• one point for a Jack	• *un punto por una sota*

PLUS	***MAS:***
Either:	***O Bien:***
• one point for each trump over four trumps	• *un punto por cada cinco muestras*
• one point for each card over three in each side suit	• *un punto por cada carta superior o tres dentro de un palo.*

Or:	***O:***
• one point for each suit with two cards in it	• *un punto por cada dos cartas de un mismo palo*
• two points for each singleton	• *dos puntos por cada carta simple*
• three points for each void suit	• *tres puntos por la ausencia de cartas de un palo*

Who is bidding?	***¿Quién apuesta?***
Who's turn is it to bid first?	*¿A quién le toca apostar primero?*
It's my / your / his / her / our / their bid.	*Me toca apostar a mí / a tí / a ella / a él / a nosotros / a vosotros / a ellas / a ellos*
Are you ready to bid?	*¿Estás listo(a) para hacer tu apuesta?*
Are you going to bid?	*¿Vas a apostar?*
To open the bidding	*hacer una apuesta*

BRIDGE cont.	***BRIDGE cont.***
What are you bidding?	*¿Qué apuestas?*
No bid.	*No apuesto nada.*
One club/diamond/heart/spade.	*Un trébol / un diamante / un corazón / una espada*
One no-trump.	*Una carta de otro palo distinto a la muestra.*
Two clubs / diamonds / hearts / spades	*Dos de trébol / de diamantes / de corazones / de espadas*
An opening bid of two of a suit.	*Una apuesta de salida de dos de un palo / salida con dos de un palo.*
He / she did not bid.	*El/Ella no apuesta (no va).*
I did not bid.	*No apuesto (no voy)*
My partner did not bid.	*Mi pareja no va.*

The type of bid	***Tipos de apuestas***
A forcing bid.	*Una apuesta forzada.*
A weak / strong bid	*Una apuesta débil / fuerte.*
A raising bid.	*Una apuesta mayor.*
A no-trump bid.	*Una apuesta sin muestra.*
A pre-emptive bid.	*Una apuesta prioritaria.*
A re-bid.	*Un desdoble*

The responses	***Las respuestas***
Pass / No bid / to re-bid.	*Paso / No voy / doblar la apuesta.*
to raise the bidding..	*subir la apuesta / apostar más...*
..in your partner's suit	*...en la baza de mi compañero*
..in your own suit.	*...en mi baza / juego*
A single raise / double raise.	*Subo / Doblo.*
to jump	*Saltar / pasar el turno*
to keep on bidding	*continuar apostando / seguir apostando*
to continue bidding	*continuar apostando*
a biddable / rebiddable suit	*un palo en el que se puede hacer una apuesta / volver a apostar*
to force to game	*hacer juego*

BRIDGE cont. | *BRIDGE cont.*

Scoring	***Marcando***
Who is going to keep the score?	*¿Quién se va a encargar del marcador?*
I'll score.	*Yo me encargo del marcador.*
Will you score?	*¿Te encargas de llevar los puntos?*
What's the score at the moment?	*¿Cuánto va? ¿Qué puntuación tenemos?*

Necessary numbers	***Números necesarios***
ten / twenty / thirty / forty / fifty	*diez / veinte / treinta / cuarenta / cincuenta*
sixty / seventy / eighty / ninety	*sesenta / setenta / ochenta / noventa*
one hundred	*cien*
one hundred and ten / twenty etc.	*ciento diez / veinte etc...*
two hundred / three hundred etc	*doscientos / trescientos etc...*
one thousand	*mil*
one thousand, five hundred and fifty	*mil quinientos cincuenta*

The tricks	***Las bazas***
the first trick	*la primera baza*
subsequent tricks	*las bazas siguientes*
an undertrick	*un desquite*
an overtrick	*una baza para desquite*

Doubling	***Doblándose***
doubled / undoubled / redoubled	*doblo / desdoblo / redoblo*

Vulnerable	***Vulnerable***
not vulnerable	*seguro*

Above the line	***Sobre la línea***
below the line	*por debajo de la línea*

BRIDGE cont. / *BRIDGE cont.*

Slams	***Slams***
a small slam	*un slam*
a grand slam	*un gran slam*

Honours	***Créditos***
four trump honours	*crédito de cuatro triunfos*
five trump honours	*crédito de cinco triunfos*
four aces in one hand	*cuatro ases en una mano*

Rubbers	***Partidas***
a two / three game rubber	*una partida de dos / tres juegos*
an unfinished rubber	*una partida sin terminar*

Games	***Juegos / Partidas***
for one game	*por una partida / un juego*
for part score in unfinished game	*por puntuación parcial en una partida a medias.*

CHESS / *EL AJEDREZ*

The Chessboard	***El Tablero***
portable	*portátil*
electronic	*electrónico*
a black square	*una casilla negra*
the white squares	*las casillas blancas*
the right / left corner	*la esquina derecha / izquierda*
opposite	*opuesto(a)*
diagonal	*diagonal*

CHESS cont. — *EL AJEDREZ cont.*

The pieces	***Las piezas de ajedrez***
The King	*El Rey*
The Queen	*La Reina*
The Bishop	*El Alfil*
The Knight	*El Caballo*
The Rook	*La Torre*
The Pawns	*El Peón*

Common words (abc)	***Palabras comunes***
back	*detrás / hacia atrás*
behind	*atrás / detrás*
black	*negro(a)*
to capture	*comer*
to castle	*enrocarse*
"check"	*"jaque"*
to check	*hacer "jaque"*
checkmate	*hacer jaque mate*
a draw	*tablas*
defensive	*defensivo*
forward	*hacia delante*
in front of	*enfrente de*
lined up	*a la altura de*
mate	*mate*
a move	*un movimiento*
my / your move	*mi / tu turno*
to move	*mover*
occupied	*cogido*
opposite	*opuesto*
powerful	*fuerte / poderoso*
protected	*protegido*
to remove	*remover*
safe	*a salvo*

CHESS cont. / *EL AJEDREZ cont.*

COMMON WORDS (ABC) cont. / *PALABRAS COMUNES cont.*

to take	*tomar*
shielded	*defender*
taken	*tomado*
threatened	*amenazado(a)*
unoccupied	*libre*
unprotected	*desprotegido*
white	*blanco(a)*

DRAUGHTS / *DAMAS*

The Pieces	***Las piezas***
black	*negra(o)*
white	*blanca(o)*
red	*roja(o)*

Rules for Draughts	***Reglas de las Damas***
• A game for two players	• *Juego para dos*
• Each player has twelve pieces.	• *Cada jugador tiene doce piezas.*
• One player has all white pieces.	• *Uno de los jugadores mueve blancas.*
• The other player has all black pieces.	• *El otro mueve negras.*
• Both players move only on the black squares.	• *Ambos jugadores deben mover sobre las casillas negras.*
• Black always starts.	• *Las negras empiezan a mover.*

RULES FOR DRAUGHTS cont.	***REGLAS DE LAS DAMAS cont.***
• The pieces move forwards diagonally one square at a time.	• *Las piezas se mueven hacia delante diagonalmente de una en una casilla.*
• A player can take his opponent's pieces by jumping over them provided there is an empty square to land on.	• *Un jugador puede comer las piezas del otro saltando sobre ellas, siempre que se quede en una casilla vacia / libre.*
• A player can capture more than one of his opponent's pieces at once.	• *Un jugador puede comer más de una pieza en un turno.*
• When a piece reaches the opposite side of the board it is made into a king (by placing a second piece on top of the first).	• *Cuando un jugador pone una de sus piezas en el otro lado del tablero ésta se convierte en una reina (y así lo indica con una segunda ficha colocada encima de la primera).*
• A king can move backwards as well as forwards one square at a time.	• *Una reina puede moverse hacia atrás y hacia delante de una casilla en cada movida.*
• The winner is the one who takes all his/her opponent's pieces or who immobilizes his/her opponent's pieces.	• *El ganador es aquél que se come todas las piezas del rival, o aquél que inmoviliza todas las piezas de su rival.*

DOMINOES *DOMINO*

The Pieces	***Las Piezas***
a blank	*una blanca*
a double blank	*una doble blanca*
a spot / a pip	*una simple / el pito / el punto*
one/two/three spots	*una simple / dos/ tres simple*
four/five/six spots	
a piece with a six and a five	*seis – cinco*
a double six	*doble seis*
face up / face down	*hacia arriba / hacia abajo*
One end is a..	*un lado es un...*
The other end is a..	*el otro es un...*

Playing dominoes	***Jugando al Domino***
• Shall we play dominoes?	• *¿Jugamos al dominó?*
• Have you got a set of dominoes?	• *¿Tienes un juego de dominó?*
• Is it a full set of twenty eight?	• *¿Tienes todas las fichas? ¿las veinte ocho fichas?*
• Turn the pieces face downwards.	• *Pon las fichas boca abajo.*
• Mix the pieces up.	• *Mezclalas / mezcladas*
• Any number of people can play.	• *Se puede jugar con cualquier número de jugadores.*
• Draw a piece to see who starts.	• *Coge una ficha al azar para ver quién empieza.*
• The player who draws the highest domino is the first to play.	• *El jugador que coge la más alta empieza a jugar.*
• Each player then takes it in turn to select one domino until all the dominoes are used up.	• *Entonces los jugadores por turnos seleccionan fichas de dominó hasta que todas han sido utilizadas.*

PLAYING DOMINOES cont. / *JUGANDO AL DOMINO cont.*

• Each player sets his dominoes on edge so that his opponent cannot see his dominoes.	• *Cada jugador pone sus fichas de pie en frente de sí misma para evitar que los otros jugadores véan su juego.*
• The first player places a domino face up on the table.	• *El primer jugador pone una ficha de dominó boca arriba sobre la mesa.*
• The second player then has to add one of his dominoes to form a match - i.e. if the first domino played was one with three spots at one end and four spots at the other, the second player must put down a domino with either three or four spots on one side.	• *El segundo jugador entonces tiene que poner al lado una ficha suya que haga juego - p.e. si la primera era el tres / cuatro / el segundo jugador necesita poner una ficha con un tres o con un cuatro en uno de los lados y el otro puede ser cualquiera.*
• The dominoes are laid short end to short end unless a double is played. Doubles are placed crosswise at right angles to the line of dominoes.	• *Las fichas se tiran y colocan unidas por el lado pequeño, pero si es un doble que se sitúa a través de la línea de principal de orden del dominó.*
• If a player has no domino that matches either end of the line he has to miss his go.	• *Si un jugador no tiene ficha que poner, dice "paso".*
• The game ends when one player manages to play all his dominoes.	• *El fuego termina cuando uno de los jugadores coloca todas sus fichas.*

PLAYING DOMINOES cont. / *JUGANDO AL DOMINO cont.*

• If at any stage no player can play a domino, everyone counts up the number of spots on their remaining dominoes and the winner is the player with the fewest spots.	• *Si sucede que ningun jugador tiene fichas que hagan juego, todos cuentan el número de puntos en sus respectivas fichas sobrantes, y el ganador es el juego con menos puntuación.*
• If there is a draw between two players with the same number of spots, the winner is the person with the fewest dominoes.	• *Si hay tablas con uno de los jugadores, el ganador se determina por el número de fichas sobrantes. Aquél que tenga menos.*

JIGSAW PUZZLES / *ROMPECABEZAS / PUZ(Z)LES*

Types of jigsaws	***Tipos de rompecabezas***
a one hundred piece puzzle	*un rompecabezas de cien piezas*
a five hundred piece puzzle	*un rompecabezas de quinientas piezas*
a one thousand piece puzzle	*un rompecabezas de mil piezas*
an easy one	*un rompecabezas fácil*
a difficult one	*uno difícil*
a pretty one	*uno bonito*

JIGSAW PUZZLES cont. / *ROMPECABEZAS / PUZ(Z)LES cont.*

Choosing and starting a jigsaw	***Escogiendo y empezando un rompecabezas***
Would you like to do a jigsaw?	*¿Te gustaría hacer un rompecabezas?*
Shall we do a jigsaw together?	*¿Podemos hacer un rompecabezas juntos?*
Which one would you like to do?	*¿Cuál quieres hacer?*
Where shall we do it?	*¿Dónde lo hacemos?*
Have you got a tray to do it on?	*¿Tienes una bandeja en dónde hacerlo?*
Can we use this table?	*¿Podemos utilizar esta mesa?*
Turn over all the pieces.	*Da la vuelta a las piezas.*
face up / face down	*pon las boca arriba / boca abajo*
Shall we sort out all the edge pieces first?	*¿Hacemos los bordes del rompecabezas primero?*
Have we got the four corner pieces?	*¿Tienes las piezas de las cuatro esquinas?*
Here is..	*Aquí hay...*
..one corner piece	*...una esquina*
Here is another corner piece.	*Aquí hay otra pieza de otra esquina.*
Here's the last corner piece.	*Aquí está la última.*
Shall we sort the pieces out into colour groups?	*¿Agrupamos las piezas en colores?*
There is one piece missing.	*Falta una pieza.*

Finding particular pieces	***Buscando piezas en particular***
Have you seen the piece that goes here?	*¿Has visto la pieza que va aquí?*
It has two tabs and one indent.	*Tiene dos dientes y un hueco.*
It has one straight edge.	*Tiene un lado recto*
Have you seen a sky piece?	*¿Has visto una pieza del cielo?*
Have you seen a piece with yellow flowers on?	*¿Has visto una pieza con flores amarillas?*

JIGSAW PUZZLES cont. / *ROMPECABEZAS / PUZ(Z)LES cont.*

FINDING PARTICULAR PIECES cont. / *BUSCANDO PIEZAS EN PARTICULAR*

I'm looking for a mainly green piece with a bit of red on it.	*Estoy buscando una pieza casi toda verde, con un poco de rojo.*
Try this one.	*¿Qué tal ésta? prueba ésta.*
This might fit.	*Esta puede valer.*
It fits.	*vale / encaja*
It doesn't fit.	*no encaja / vale*

Useful verbs (abc)	***Verbos útiles***
to break it up	*deshacerlo*
to carry on	*seguir*
to collect together	*amontonar / agrupar*
to find	*encontrar*
to finish	*finalizar / terminar*
to get it out	*sacarlo(a)*
to leave it	*dejarlo*
to look at the picture	*mirar al cuadro*
to look for	*buscar*
to put it away	*quitarlo(a)*
to put a piece on one side	*dejar una pieza aparte*
to search for	*buscar*
to sort	*clasificar*
to start	*empezar*
to stop	*parar*
to try	*intentar*
to turn over	*remover / dar la vuelta*

SHORTER GAMES — *JUEGOS CORTOS*

SNAP — *SNAP*

You need:	***Se necesita:***
A pack of fifty two cards for two to five players.	*Una baraja con cincuenta y dos cartas para un grupo de dos a cinco jugadores.*
Two packs of cards for more than five players.	*Dos barajas de cartas para más de cinco jugadores.*

The Object of the Game	***El objetivo del Juego***
To win all the cards.	*Ganar todas las cartas.*

How to Play	***Cómo Jugar***
• Deal out all the cards face down equally between all players.	• *Reparte todas las cartas boca abajo entre los jugadores.*
• Players must not look at their cards but should keep them in a pile face down in front of them.	• *Los jugadores no deben mirar a sus cartas, deben dejarlas en un montón en frente de ellos.*
• The first player turns over the top card of his pile and places this face up in the middle of the table.	• *El primer jugador da la vuelta a la carta de arriba del montón y la pone boca arriba en el medio de la mesa.*
• The next player does the same.	• *El siguiente jugador hace lo mismo.*
• If any of the players notice that the second card is of the same rank as the one underneath they can shout "Snap!".	• *Si un jugador se da cuenta de que la segunda carta tiene el mismo número que la de abajo, grita "snap".*

SNAP cont. / *SNAP*

• The first person to shout "Snap!" picks up the central pile of cards and adds them, face down, to the bottom of his pile. He then turns over his top card and the game proceeds as before.	• *La primera persona en gritar "snap" recoge las cartas del centro de la mesa y las añade a su montón boca abajo. Entonces levantando la carta de arriba y se comienza el proceso de nuevo.*
• If you lose all your cards you are out of the game.	• *Si pierdes todas tus cartas, has perdido.*

BEETLE / *UN ESCARABAJO*

You need:	*Se necesita:*
Paper and pencils.	*Papel y lápices.*
A dice and a shaker.	*Un dado y un cubilete.*
Any number of people can play.	*Juegan todos los que quieran.*

How to Play	***Cómo Jugar***
• The object of the game is to draw a complete beetle.	• *El objetivo del juego es conseguir un escarabajo completo.*
• The players take it in turns to throw one dice.	• *Los jugadores tiran el dado en turnos.*
• Each person has to throw a six to start because a six means that you can draw the beetle's body.	• *Cada persona sale con un seis para empezar. El seis es el cuerpo del escarabajo.*
• Throwing a five means that you can add a head to the body.	• *Un cinco significa que puedes poner la cabeza al escarabajo.*

BEETLE cont. ***UN ESCARABAJO***

• Throwing a four gives your beetle a leg (a complete beetle needs six legs).	• *Un cuatro te da una pata para el escarabajo. (un escarabajo necesita seis patas)*
• Throwing a three gives your beetle an eye (two eyes needed).	• *Un tres te da un ojo para el escarabajo (necesitas dos)*
• Throwing a two gives your beetle an antenna (two needed).	• *Un dos te da las antenas para el escarabajo (necesitas dos)*
• Throwing a one gives your beetle a tail.	• *Un uno te da una cola para el escarabajo.*
• Eyes and antennae cannot be drawn without first getting a five for a head.	• *Los ojos y las antenas no pueden dibujarse sin sacar un cinco para la cabeza primero.*
• The first person to complete their beetle wins the game.	• *La primera persona en completar su escarabajo gana el juego.*

I SPY / *VEO, VEO*

How to Play	***Cómo Jugar***
• Any number can play.	• *Pueden jugar tantas personas come se quiera.*
• The first person says:	• *La primera persona dice:*
"I spy with my little eye something beginning with…."	***"Veo, veo...***
• He/she then adds the first letter of an object they can see.	• *Entonces el jugador dice la primera letra con la que comienza el objeto que ve.*
• The other people have to guess what the word is by asking:	• *El resto tienen que adivinar la palabra preguntando:*
"Is it a…..?"	***¿es un(una) ...?***
• and then adding a word beginning with the chosen letter.	• *y entonces diciendo una palabra que empiece por esa letra.*
• The person who guesses the object correctly takes over and becomes the next person to spy a new object.	• *La persona que adivina el objeto correctamente pasa a ser la persona que plantéa la adivinanza del nuevo objeto.*

NOUGHTS AND CROSSES — *LAS TRES EN RAYA*

You need	***Se necesita:***
Paper and two pencils.	*Papel y dos lápices.*
Two people to play.	*Se juega con dos personas.*

Useful expressions	***Expresiones útiles***
Draw a noughts and crosses frame.	*Dibuja un cuadro para las tres en raya.*
Are you going to be noughts?	*¿Vas a ser los círculos?*
I'll be noughts.	*Soy círculos.*
You can be crosses.	*Tú eres las cruces.*
You start.	*Tú empiezas.*
It's my turn to start.	*Es mi turno de empezar.*
You have to get three noughts or three crosses in a row.	*Tienes que poner tres cruces o tres círculos en una linea.*
The rows can be horizontal, vertical or diagonal.	*Las líneas pueden ser horizontales, verticales o diagonales.*
I've won / You've won.	*He ganado / Has ganado.*
to win	*ganar*
to lose	*perder*
Shall we play again?	*¿Jugamos otra?*
Shall we play the best of three?	*¿Al mejor de tres?*

OUTDOOR GAMES *JUEGOS DE EXTERIOR*

SKIPPING	***SALTAR A LA COMBA***
to skip	*saltar*
a skipping rope	*una comba*

HOP SCOTCH	***JUGAR A LA PIEDRA***
to hop	*saltar*
to turn around	*dar la vuelta*

HIDE AND SEEK	***ESCONDITE***
Cover your eyes.	*Tápate los ojos.*
Don't peep.	*No mires.*
Count to a hundred.	*Cuenta hasta cien.*
Coming ready or not.	*Estaís preparados o no.*
to hide / to look for / to find	*esconderse / buscar / encontrar*

A TREASURE HUNT	***LA BUSCA DEL TESORO***
Divide into teams.	*Formar equipos.*
Will you be on my team?	*¿Quieres venir con mi equipo?*
Do it in pairs.	*Hacerlo en parejas.*
Here is a clue.	*Aquí hay una pista.*
Read the clue.	*Lee la pista.*
What does it say?	*¿Qué dice?*
What does that mean, do you think?	*¿Qué significa? ¿Qué piensas?*
To look for	*buscar*
to find	*encontrar*
to be unable to find	*no ser capaz de encontrar*
to win	*ganar*
to get the prize	*conseguir un premio.*

OUTDOOR GAMES — *JUEGOS DE EXTERIOR*

ROLLER SKATING	*PATINES DE RUEDAS*
a pair of roller skates	*un par de patines de ruedas*
roller boots	*botas de patinar*
roller blades	*patines de cuchilla*
Have you got any roller skates?	*¿Tienes un par de patines?*
May I borrow your roller skates?	*¿Puedes prestarme tus patines?*
to put on	*ponerse*
to lace up	*abrocharse / atarse*
to adjust	*ajustar*
to balance	*mantener el equilibrio*
to hold on to something	*sujetarse a algo*
to fall over	*caerse*
to take off	*empezar a patinar*

FLYING A KITE	*JUGAR CON LA COMETA*
a kite	*una cometa*
a string	*una cuerda*
to hold on to	*sujetar*
to rise up	*elevar*
to fall	*dejar caer*
to swoop	*hacer una calada*
the wind	*el viento*
There isn't enough wind.	*no hay suficiente viento*
It's too windy.	*Hay demasiado viento.*

OTHER ACTIVITES	*OTRAS ACTIVIDADES*
to do cartwheels	*jugar*
to do handstands	*hacer el pino*
to climb trees	*subir árboles*

PUTTING A TENT UP	*LEVANTAR UNA TIENDA DE CAMPANA*
Have you got a tent?	*¿Tienes una tienda?*
Shall we try to put it up?	*¿Ponemos la tienda de campaña?*
Can you remember how to do it?	*¿Te acuerdas cómo se hace?*
Would your mother / father help?	*¿Le preguntamos a tu padre / madre si puede ayudarnos?*
to put up the tent pole	*levantar el mástil de la tienda*
to put the frame together	*poner el armazón*
to throw over the canvas	*poner la lona*
to hammer in the pegs	*clavar los ganchos*
to tighten the guy ropes	*tensar las sogas*
to put down a ground sheet	*extender la loneta sobre el suelo*
to do up the zip	
to unzip the door flap	*abrir la cortinilla*
to spend a night in the tent	*pasar la noche en la tienda de campaña*
a torch	*una linterna*
to switch on / switch off	*encender / apagar*
to get cold	*pasar frío*
to go inside	*ir dentro*

GARDEN PLAY EQUIPMENT — *JARDIN – RECREO JUEGOS DE JARDIN*

SWINGING	*COLUMPIANDOS*
a swing	*un columpio*
to swing	*columpiarse*
to give someone a push	*dar impulso / empujar*
Will you push me, please?	*¿Me puedes dar un empujón?*
Do you want a push?	*¿Quieres que te empuje?*
To stand up	*levantarse*
to sit down	*sentarse*
to go very high	*subir muy alto*
to jump off	*saltar / tirarse*

GARDEN PLAY EQUIPMENT cont. — *JARDIN – RECREO JUEGOS DE JARDIN*

A SEE-SAW	***BALANCIN***
to see-saw	*balancearse*
to go up and down	*subir y bajar*
to balance	*equilibrar*
to bump	*chocar*

A SLIDE	***TOBOGAN***
to climb the ladder	*subir la escalera*
to sit down	*sentarse*
to slide down	*escurrirse / dejarse caer por el tobogán*
feet first / head first	*de piés / de cabeza*
to have another go	*tirarse otra vez*

A CLIMBING FRAME	***LAS ESTRUCTURA / LAS CASITAS***
a ladder	*la escalera (una)*
to climb	*subir*
a monkey bar	*una barra para dejarse caer*
to hang from	*colgarse*
to hang upside down	*colgarse boca abajo*

COMPUTERS
ORDENADORES

TYPES OF COMPUTER	***TIPOS DE ORDENADORES***
a personal computer	*un ordenador personal*
a desktop computer	*un ordenador*
a laptop computer	*un ordenador portátil*
a network computer	*una computadora*

HARDWARE	***HARDWARE / PARTES PRINCIPALES***
the monitor	*el monitor*
the screen	*la pantalla*
the keyboard (see below for details)	*el tablero (véase detalles abajo)*

THE MOUSE	***EL RATON***
to click	*apretar / pulsar*
to double-click	*pulsar dos veces*
to right click / to left click	*pulsar a la derecha / a la izquierda*
a mouse mat	*superficie para el ratón*
a joystick	*un joystick*

A TOWER	***UNA TORRE***
the CD-ROM drive	*una unidad de CD-ROM*
the floppy disk drive	*una unidad para discos blandos*
the tape drive	*una unidad para cintas*

A MODEM	***UN MODEM***
a fax	*un fax*
e mail	*correo electrónico*
an e mail address	*un apartado para el correo electrónico*
to send	*enviar*
to receive	*recibir*

COMPUTERS cont. — *ORDENADORES cont.*

THE SPEAKERS	*LOS ALTAVOCES*
multi-media	*multi-media*
to turn up / down	*subir / bajar*

THE PRINTER	*LA IMPRESORA*
a colour printer	*la impresora a color (una)*
a black and white printer	*la impresora en blanco y negro (una)*
a print preview	*en ensayo de impresión*
to zoom in / out	*aumentar / disminuir (reducir)*
to print out	*imprimir*
all pages	*todas las páginas*
odd / even pages	*páginas*
the current page	*la página corriente*
selected pages	*páginas escogidas*
three copies	*tres copias (f)*

THE MEMORY	*LA MEMORIA*
ROM	*ROM*
RAM	*RAM*
How much memory does your computer have?	*¿Cuánta memoria tiene tu ordenador?*
My computer doesn't have enough memory.	*Mi ordenador no tiene suficiente memoria.*

THE SOFTWARE	*EL SOFTWARE*
system software	*sistema de software*
application software	*paquete de aplicaciones*
a floppy disk	*un disco blando*
a CD-ROM	*un CD-ROM*
a programme	*un programa*

COMPUTERS - THE SOFTWARE cont. | *ORDENADORES - EL SOFTWARE cont.*

a computer game (See 139-144)	*una consola de juegos*
educational software	*paquete de programas educativos*
word processing software	*procesador software*
database software	*base de datos software*
desktop publishing software	*software de publicación*
draw / paint software	*software para dibujos y gráficos*
a typing course	*un curso de mecanografía*
an encyclopaedia	*una enciclopedia*
art gallery software	*un paquete de aplicaciones para museos*

THE KEYBOARD | *EL TECLADO*

TYPING	*ESCRIBIENDO / TECLEANDO*
to touchtype	*escribir / teclear*
speed	*velocidad*
to be slow	*ser lento*
to be quick	*ser rápido*
accuracy	*corrección*
to make mistakes	*equivocarse / tener faltas*
to be very accurate	*no tener faltas*
to type with two fingers	*escribir con dos dedos*

THE KEYS | *LAS TECLAS / LOS BOTONES*

The Alphabet	***El Alfabeto***
capital letters	*las mayúsculas*
lower case letters	*las minúsculas*
caps lock	*techa de las mayúsculas*

THE KEYBOARD — *EL TECLADO*

Punctuation	***Puntuación***
a full stop	*un punto y final*
a comma	*una coma*
a semi-colon	*un punto y coma*
a colon	*dos puntos*
an exclamation mark	*una exclamación*
a question mark	*un interrogación*
inverted commas	*comillas (f.pl)*
an apostrophe	*un apóstrofe*
brackets	*paréntesis (m)*

Numeric keys	***Teclas para los números***
addition	*suma*
subtraction	*resta*
multiplication	*multiplicación*
division	*división*
brackets	*paréntesis*
a decimal point	*un punto decimal*
the equals sign	*resultado / igual*
the ampersand	*el signo & ("y")*

The function keys	***Las funciones***
the enter key	*el botón / la tecla de enter*
the return key	*el botón / la tecla de return*
the tab key	*el tabulador*
the shift key	*la tecla para cambiar la dirección*
the caps lock key	*la tecla para las mayúsculas*
the number lock key	*la tecla para los números*
control	*el control*
alt	*alto*
escape	*salida*

THE KEYBOARD cont. / *EL TECLADO cont.*

The edit keys	***Funciones para la impresión***
scroll up / down	*desplazar hacia arriba / hacia abajo*
scroll left / right	*desplazar hacia la izquierda / hacia la derecha*
delete	*borrar*
insert	*insertar*
home	*volver al punto de partida / punto inicial*
end	*finalizar*
page up / down	*page up / page down*
print screen	*imprimir en pantalla*

WORD PROCESSING / *EL PROCESAMIENTO DE TEXTOS / PROCESANDO TEXTOS*

Entering text	***Metiendo el texto***
a cursor	*un cursor*
to type	*escribir a máquina*
to enter	*entrar / enter*
to insert	*insertar / meter / insert*
to overwrite	*escribir encima*

Editing	***Impresión***
to edit	*imprimir*
to cut	*cortar*
to paste	*empastar / imprimir / paste*
to copy	*copiar*
to delete	*borrar*
to spell-check	*corregir*
to indent	*introducir espacios / sangrar*
word-wrap	*salto de línea automático*
to sort text alphabetically	*ordenar el texto alfabéticamente*

WORD PROCESSING cont. / *EL PROCESAMIENTO DE TEXTOS cont.*

Formatting	***Formato***
to format	*arreglar*
the font	*la primera plana*
font style / font size	*estilo / tamãno formato*
colour / italics	*color / itálica (cursiva)*
bold / underlined	*negrita / subrayado*
highlighted	*resaltado / resaltar*

The page set-up	***El arreglo de la página***
a page break	*un límite de página*
page layout view	*cuadrícula de página*
to set the margins	*poner los márgenes*
headers and footers	*cabeceras y pies de página*

Paragraphs	***Párrafos***
single / double line spacing	*simple / doble espacio de línea*
left / right indents	*sangría a la izquierda / a la derecha*
to align / the tabs	*alinear / los tabuladores*

Justification	***Margen de error / justificación***
right / left justification	*sobremargen derecho / izquierdo*
to justify both sides	*poner sobre margen en ambos márgenes*
justification on / off	*sobremargen conectado / sin conectar*
to centre	*centrar*

The tools	***Las Herramientas / tools / extras***
a tool bar	*una barra de herramientas*
to word count	*contar palabras*
a dictionary / a thesaurus	*un diccionario / un thesaurus*
the spell-checker	*un corrector de faltas*

WORD PROCESSING cont. — *EL PROCESAMIENTO DE TEXTOS cont.*

File management	***El uso de ficheros***
a file	*un fichero*
to open	*abrir*
to close	*cerrar*
to save	*salvar*
to name	*poner un nombre*
to re-name	*cambiar el nombre*

THE INTERNET — *EL INTERNET*

The Superhighway	*El Superhighway*
The World Wide Web	*La Red Internacional*

Getting on to the Internet	***Conectando Internet***
an access provider	*un proveedor del servicio de Internet*
an online service provider	*un proveedor de línea*
an e mail address	*una dirección para el correo electrónico*
a joining fee	*una tasa de afiliación*
to pay a subscription	*pagar subscripción*
a subscriber / to register	*un subscriptor / registrar*

Browsing	***Echando una ojeada / hojear***
to log in	*entrar en el sistema / acceder*
to use your password	*usar una palabra secreta / password*
to browse	*echar una ojeada / hojear*
a web browser / to surf	*un globo / pasar*
an interest group	*un paquete de actividades*
a newsgroup	*un paquete de noticias*
an information source	*un fuente de información*

THE INTERNET — *EL INTERNET*

Browsing cont.	***Echando una ojeada / hojear cont.***
hypertext	*hipertexto*
to click on	*apretar / hacer clic*
to return to the home page	*volver al menú principal*
to download information	*descargar información*
to join a mailing list	*unirse a una lista de propaganda comercial*
to prepare a message	*preparar un mensaje*
on-line	*conectado*
off-line	*desconectado*

Internet jargon	***Argot de la Red de Internet***
Gopher	*Gopher*
Archie	*Archie*
a lurker	*un lurker*
netiquette	*netiquette*
virtual reality	*realidad virtual / efecto real*
a Cyber café	*un Café Cibernético*
a Cyber pub	*un Bar Cibernético*
Cyberspace	*Espacio Cibernético*
Sig (Signature file)	*Firma / Firma de archivo*
Usenet	*Usuario de Red Informática*
Winsock	*Winsock*

Smileys	***Gráficos de caras***
a smiley / an emoticon	*un gráfico de cara sonriendo / un emoticón*
☺ happy	*contento*
;-) winking	*guiñando el ojo*
:-p tongue in cheek	*sacando la lengua*

COMPUTER GAMES
JUEGOS DE ORDENADOR

GENERAL EXPRESSIONS	*EXPRESIONES GENERALES*
Would you like to play on the computer?	*¿Quieres jugar con el ordenador?*
Do you have any good computer games?	*¿Tienes juegos de ordenador buenos?*
I have a Game Gear.	*Tengo un Game Gear.*
I have a Super Nintendo.	*Tengo un Super Nintendo.*
Does it run on batteries or mains?	*¿Funciona con batería o electricidad?*
Have you a mains adaptor?	*¿Tienes un adaptador de electricidad?*
May I have a turn now?	*¿Puedo intentarlo ahora?*
You've had a long go.	*Venga, llevas mucho rato.*
How many can play at once?	*¿Cuántos pueden jugar a la misma vez?*
This game is for one / two players only.	*Este juego es sólo para uno / sólo para dos jugadores.*
I'd like to get it - was it expensive?	*Me gustaría tenerlo / adquirirlo - ¿Fue caro?*

STARTING A GAME	*EMPEZANDO A JUGAR*
Where is the on / off button?	*¿Dónde esta el botón para encenderlo / apagarlo?*
How do you load the game?	*¿Cómo se carga el juego?*
You type in the word…	*Tienes que escribir una palabra...*
Then you press this..	*Entonces se pulsa aquí.*
What's the password?	*¿Cuál es la palabra clave?*
The password is..	*La clave es...*
What's the aim of the game?	*¿Cuál es el propósito del juego?*
Explain to me what happens.	*Explícame que es lo que pasa.*
Are there any secret passageways or hidden rooms?	*¿Hay algún pasadizo secreto o habitaciones ocultas?*

COMPUTER GAMES cont. / *JUEGOS DE ORDENADOR cont.*

THE CONTROLS	***LOS CONTROLES***
Do you use a joystick or a mouse or special keys?	*¿Utilizas un joystick (mando), un ratón o botones especiales?*
You right click / left click the joystick / the mouse.	*Pulsas el botón de la izquierda / de la derecha del mando / joystick o del ratón.*
You shoot with the joystick.	*Se dispara con el joystick.*
Which keys do you use?	*¿Qué botón se usa?*
What do the different keys do?	*¿Para qué sirven los diferentes botones?*
These keys make you go up / down.	*Estos botones son para ir hacia arriba / abajo.*
These keys make you go right / left.	*Estos botones son para ir a la derecha / izquierda.*
What does the space bar do?	*¿Para que sirve el espaciador?*
The space bar makes you jump.	*El espaciador te permite saltar.*
Can you pause this game?	*¿Puedes parar el juego?*
You pause it like this..	*Se detiene haciendo esto.*

The Volume	***El Volumen***
How do you turn the volume up / down?	*¿Cómo se sube / se baja el volumen?*
You increase / decrease the volume like this.	*El volumen se sube / se baja haciendo esto.*
It's a bit loud.	*Está un poco alto.*
It's disturbing people.	*Está molestando a la gente.*
It's too quiet.	*Está demasiado bajo.*
I can't hear it properly.	*No puedo oirlo bien.*

COMPUTER GAMES cont. / *JUEGOS DE ORDENADOR cont.*

SCORING / *MARCANDO PUNTOS / PUNTUANDO*

Lives and bonus points	***Vidas y bonos***
How many lives do you have to start with?	*¿Cuántas vidas te dan al principio?*
I've just lost a life.	*Acabo de perder una vida.*
I've got three lives left.	*Me quedan tres vidas.*
How do you get bonuses?	*¿Cómo se consiguen bonos?*
You have to pick up these things to score extra.	*Se tiene que coger estas cosas para obtener puntuación extra.*

Time limits	***Los Límites de Tiempo***
Is there a time limit?	*¿Hay un tiempo límite?*
No, there's no need to hurry.	*No, no tienes que darte prisa.*
Yes, the time limit is five minutes.	*Sí, el tiempo límite es cinco minutos.*

Level of difficulty	***Niveles de dificultad***
Have you ever managed to finish this game?	*¿Has acabado este juego alguna vez?*
No, it's very difficult.	*No, es muy difícil.*
Yes, but it takes a lot of practice.	*Sí, pero se necesita mucha práctica.*
What level have you got to?	*¿Hasta que nivel has llegado?*
I've got to the first / second / third level.	*Estoy en el nivel uno / dos / tres.*
I've got to the last / next to the last level.	*Estoy en el último nivel / cerca del último nivel*

COMPUTER GAMES cont. — *JUEGOS DE ORDENADOR cont.*

Level of difficulty cont.	***Niveles de dificultad cont.***
Does it speed up at each level?	*¿Aumenta la velocidad en cada nivel?*
It gets much quicker at the next level.	*En el siguiente nivel va más rápido.*
You get a bonus life at each level.	*Te dan una vida extra en cada nivel.*

What's your score?	***¿Cuál es tu marcador?***
What's your total now?	*¿Cuál es tu total?*
What did you score last time?	*¿Qué puntuaste la última vez?*
What's the best you've ever scored?	*¿Cuál es tu record?*

USEFUL VERBS (abc)	***VERBOS UTILES***
to accelerate	*acelerar*
to attack	*atacar*
to avoid	*evitar*
to chase	*perseguir*
to click	*pulsar*
to climb	*escalar / subir*
to collect	*coger*
to concentrate	*concentrar*
to decrease	*disminuir*
to defend	*defender*
to die	*morir*
to duck	*esquivar / agachar la cabeza*
to enter	*entrar*
to exit	*salir*
to fly	*volar*
to follow	*seguir*
to get a bonus	*conseguir un bono*

COMPUTER GAMES - USEFUL VERBS (abc) cont.	*JUEGOS DE ORDENADOR - VERBOS UTILES cont.*
to hide	*esconderse*
to increase	*aumentar*
to insert	*meter*
to jump	*saltar / dar un salto*
to kill	*matar*
to leave	*dejar*
to live	*vivir*
to load	*cargar*
to lose	*perder*
to lose concentration	*perder concentración*
to pause	*parar / detenerse*
to press	*presionar*
to print	*imprimir*
to remember	*recordar*
to score	*marcar / puntuar*
to shoot	*disparar*
to slow down	*reducir la velocidad/ ir más despacio*
to speed up	*aumentar la velocidad / ir más rápido*
to surprise	*sorprenderse*
to switch on / off	*encender / apagar*
to take	*tomar*
to throw	*lanzar*
to turn around	*dar la vuelta*
to type	*marcar*
to win	*ganar*

DIRECTION WORDS	*PALABRAS PARA DAR DIRECCIONES*
in / on	*en / sobre*
over / under	*sobre / debajo de*
round / through	*al rededor / a través*
up / down	*arriba / abajo*
before / after	*antes / después*
left / right	*a la izquierda / derecha*
near / far away	*cerca / lejos*

COMPUTER GAMES cont. / *JUEGOS DE ORDENADOR cont.*

DESCRIPTIVE WORDS (abc)	*PALABRAS PARA DESCRIBIR*
clumsy	*torpe*
complicated	*complicado(a)*
correct	*correcto(a)*
dangerous	*peligroso(a)*
difficult	*difícil*
easy	*fácil*
exposed	*expuesto(a)*
false	*falso(a)*
flashing	*intermitente*
hidden	*escondido(a)*
highest	*el más alto(a)*
long	*largo(a)*
lowest	*el más bajo(a)*
quick	*rápido(a)*
round	*redondo(a)*
safe	*seguro(a)*
secret	*secreto*
short	*corto(a)*
skilful	*habilidoso(a)*
slow	*lento(a)*
tense	*tenso(a)*
vulnerable	*vulnerable*

TELEVISION, VIDEO & RADIO

TELEVISION, VIDEO Y RADIO

BASIC VOCABULARY	*VOCABULARIO BASICO*
a television	*una televisión*
the remote control	*el mando / el control remote*
to point	*apuntar*
a video player	*un video*
a video cassette	*un videocaset*
a video game	*un video juego*
a radio	*una radio / un aparato de radio*

WATCHING TELEVISION	*VIENDO TELEVISION*
Would you like to watch T.V.?	*¿Te gustaría ver la tele?*
What's on the television at the moment?	*¿Qué echan ahora?*
Is there anything good on the television?	*¿Hay algo que merezca la pene en tele?*
What's on the other channels?	*¿Qué hay en los otros canales?*
Shall we turn over?	*¿Cambiamos?*
We have this programme in my country.	*Tenemos este programa en mí país.*
Do you like..?	*¿Te gusta...?*
Shall we stop watching television?	*¿Apagamos la tele?*
My family want to watch something else now.	*Mí familia quiere ver algo distinto ahora.*
Shall we do something else instead?	*¿Quieres que hagamos algo distinto?*

TELEVISION cont. / *TELEVISION cont.*

THE CONTROLS FOR T.V., VIDEO AND RADIO (abc)	*LOS CONTROLES DE LA TELE, VIDEO Y RADIO*
the aerial point	*la antena*
a channel	*un canal*
a counter	*un contador*
counter reset	*contador visual*
eject / to eject	*eject / sacar*
fast forward / to fast forward	*echar hacia delante / pasar*
indicator light / to flash	*indicador / lucir*
on / off	*on / off*
pause / to pause	*pausa / parar*
play / to play	*play / enchufar (dar marcha)*
to press a button	*pulsar un botón*
programme / to programme	*programa / programar*
record / to record	*grabar / grabar*
to repeat	*repetir*
to reset	*programar / reset*
rewind / to rewind	*rebobinado / rebobinar*
search	*buscar*
slow	*lento*
the speed	*rápido*
a switch / to flick a switch	*un enchufe / enchufar*
the timer	*el contador*
to tune	*conectar / entonar*
to use the remote control	*usar el mando*
video / to insert	*video / meter*
video in / video out	*video dentro / fuera*

TELEVISION cont. / *TELEVISION cont.*

USEFUL EXPRESSIONS / *EXPRESSIONES UTILES*

Turning it on and off	***Enchufando / desenchufando (encendiendo / apagando)***
How do you turn it on / off?	*¿Cómo se enchufa / apaga?*
You turn it on / off here.	*Se enchufa / apaga aquí.*

Volume control	***El botón para el volumen***
It's a bit too loud.	*Está un poco alto.*
How do you turn it up / down?	*¿Cómo se sube / baja de volumen?*
I can't hear it properly.	*No lo puedo oir bien.*

Playing a video	***Pasando el video***
How do you insert the video?	*¿Cómo se mete el video?*
The video needs rewinding.	*El video no está rebobinado.*
How do you rewind it ?	*¿Cómo se rebobina?*
How do you fast forward it?	*¿Cómo se pasa rápidamente?*
Can you pause it for a moment, please?	*Puedes pararlo por un momento, por favor?*
How do you pause / eject it?	*¿Cómo se para / saca?*

Recording	***Grabando***
How do you record something?	*¿Cómo se graba?*
Is it recording properly?	*¿Se está grabando bien?*
Are you sure you are recording the right programme?	*¿Estás seguro que estás grabando el programa que quieres?*
Can you programme the video to record while we are out?	*¿Puedes programar el video para grabar cuando estemos fuera?*
Shall we record it and watch it some other tine?	*¿Por qué no lo grabamos y vemos en otro momento?*
Would you like to watch that programme we recorded?	*¿Quieres ver el programa que grabamos?*

RECORDING ON VIDEOS — GRABANDO CON VIDEOS

How does the remote control work?	***¿Cómo se usa el control remote?***
Do you have Video Plus programming?	*¿Tienes la programación de video codificado?*
The tape has come to an end.	*La cinta se ha acabado.*
Have you got another tape?	*¿Tienes otra cinta?*

TUNING THE RADIO	*ENCENDIENDO LA RADIO*
How do you tune the radio?	*¿Cómo conecto la radio? ¿Cómo busco las emisoras?*
Can you find me the local radio station?	*¿Puedes encontrar la radio local?*
Which is the best pop music programme?	*¿Cuál es el mejor programa de música pop?*
What wavelength do you tune it to?	*¿Qué honda es para encontrarlo?*

DIFFERENT TYPES OF T.V. PROGRAMMES	*DIFERENTES TIPOS DE TELEPROGRAMAS*
an advertisement	*un anuncio / un comercial*
a cartoon	*los dibujos animados*
a chat show	*un show de debate / charla coloquio*
a discussion programme	*un programa de debate*
a documentary	*un documental*
an education programme	*un programa educativo*
a film	*una película*
a party political broadcast	*una retransmisión de un partido político*
a quiz	*un concurso*
a report	*un reportaje*
a situation comedy	*una comedia*
a sports programme	*un programa de deportes*
a thriller	*un thriller / una película de miedo*

DIFFERENT TYPES OF T.V. PROGRAMMES cont. / *DIFERENTES TIPOS DE TELEPROGRAMAS cont.*

Soap operas	***Las telenovelas***
Which soaps do you have in your country?	*¿Qué telenovelas tienes en tu país?*
We watch this at home.	*Vemos ésta en casa.*
We are further behind / ahead of you.	*Nosotros no hemos llegado aquí / llegamos aquí hace tiempo.*

The news	***Las noticias***
the news headlines	*los titulares*
I'd like to watch the headlines, please.	*Me gustaría ver los titulares.*
Did you see the news?	*¿Viste las noticias?*
What was on the news?	*¿Qué dijeron en las noticias?*
Was there any news about..?	*¿Dijeron algo sobre...?*
I didn't hear the news today.	*No he visto las noticias hoy.*
The news was boring / depressing / appalling.	*Las noticias eran aburridas / deprimentes / malísimas.*
What has happened?	*¿Qué ha pasado?*
Was there anything interesting on the news?	*¿Dijeron algo interesante en las noticias?*

DIFFERENT TYPES OF T.V. PROGRAMMES cont. — *DIFERENTES TIPOS DE TELEPROGRAMAS cont.*

The weather forecast	***El tiempo***
Did you hear the weather forecast?	*¿Qué hay del tiempo?*
It's going to be….(abc)	*Va a ...*

breezy	*haber brisas*	rainy	*llover*
cloudy	*estar nublado*	showery	*haber lloviznas*
cold	*hacer frio*	snowy	*nevar*
freezing	*escarchar*	sunny	*hacer sol*
hot	*hacer calor*	thundery	*haber tormentas*
icy	*granizar*	windy	*hacer viento*
minus five	*estar a menos 5 grados*		

When?		*¿Cuándo?*	
later	*más tarde*	overnight	*por la noche*
this morning	*esta mañana*	tomorrow	*mañana*
this afternoon	*esta tarde*	the day after	*el día después / mañana*
this evening	*esta noche*	next week	*la próxima semana*
tonight	*esta noche*	soon	*pronto*

THE VIDEO HIRE SHOP
LA TIENDA DE ALQUILER DE CINTAS DE VIDEO

USEFUL EXPRESSIONS	*EXPRESIONES UTILES*
Shall we go and get a video out?	*¿Vamos y alquilamos un video?*
Have you got your ticket?	*¿Tienes tu tiquet?*
You have to show your ticket.	*¿Tienes que enseñar la tiquet?*
Can you get any film out on your ticket?	*¿Puedes sacar videos con tu tiquet?*
Are there some films you can't get out on your ticket?	*¿Hay películas que puedas sacar con tu tiquet?*
How much does it cost to hire this video?	*¿Cuánto cuesta alquilar un video?*
When does it have to be back by?	*¿Cuándo tiene que estar de vuelta?*
How many videos can we get out?	*¿Cuántos videos podemos sacar?*
What do you want to watch?	*¿Qué quieres ver?*
I'd like to see this one.	*Me gustaría ver éste.*
Is this one good?	*¿Está éste bien?*
Is it very frightening?	*¿Da mucho miedo?*
Where is the comedy / thriller / cartoon / horror section?	*¿Dónde está la sección de comedias / películas de suspense (miedo) / películas de miedo?*
Where are the new releases?	*¿Dónde están las nuevas adquisiciones?*
Is it out on video yet?	*¿Ha salida ya en video?*
When is it going to be out on video?	*¿Cuándo vais a tener el video?*
I've got that one on video at home.	*Tengo ésta en video en casa.*

MUSIC
LA MUSICA

LISTENING TO MUSIC — *ESCUCHANDO MUSICA*

HI FI STEREO SYSTEM — *CADENA DE ALTA FIDELIDAD*

A Compact Disc (C.D.) player	***Un disco compacto***

A tape deck	***Una cinta cubierta***
a cassette tape	*una cinta de caset*
to record on	*grabar*
to record over	*grabar encima*
to erase	*limpiar*
to rewind	*rebobinar*
to fast forward	*pasar hacia delante*
to pause	*parar*

A record turntable	***Un tocadiscos***
a record / a single	*un disco / un single*
a short playing record	*un disco de 45 revoluciones*
a long playing record (an L.P.)	*un LP ("el pi") / un disco de larga duración*
a track	*una banda sonora*
a stylus	*una aguja / un estilo*
a scratch	*un arañazo*
an old seventy eight	*un disco de setenta ocho revoluciones*

LISTENING TO MUSIC cont. / *ESCUCHANDO MUSICA cont.*

SOUND REPRODUCTION	*LA REPRODUCCION DEL SONIDO*
the amplifier	*un amplificador*
the speakers	*los altavoces*
the headphones	*los auriculares*
the sound quality	*la cualidad del sonido*
to adjust	*ajustar*
the volume	*el volumen*
the bass / the treble	*los graves / los agudos*
the balance	*el equilibrador*
poor	*pobre*
good	*bueno*
excellent	*excelente*
stereophonic	*estereofónico*
quadrophonic	*cuadrofónico*

AM / FM RADIO	*AM / FM RADIO*
the tuner	*el sincronizador*
to tune in	*sincronizar*
to be out of tune	*no estar bien sincronizado*
to retune	*volver a sincronizar*
to crackle	*hacer ruido*
the band	*la banda*
the wavelength	*la frecuencia de honda*

LISTENING TO MUSIC cont. — *ESCUCHANDO MUSICA cont.*

USEFUL VERBS AND COMMANDS (abc)	***VERBOS Y ACCIONES UTILES***
to adjust the controls	*ajustar los controles*
to decrease	*bajar*
to erase	*limpiar*
to fast forward	*pasar hacia delante*
to increase	*aumentar*
to listen	*escuchar*
to pause	*hacer una pausa*
to play	*play ???*
to programme	*programar*
to record	*grabar*
to record on	*grabar en*
to record over	*grabar sobre*
to repeat	*repetir*
to replay	*pasar de nuevo*
to retune	*volver a sincronizar*
to rewind	*rebobinar*
to skip a track	*pasar una banda sonora*
to switch off	*apagar / desenchufar*
to tune in	*sincronizar*
to turn down	*bajar el volumen*
to turn on	*enchufar*
to turn up	*subir el volumen*

LISTENING TO MUSIC	***ESCUCHANDO MUSICA***
Would you like to listen to some music?	*¿Quieres escuchar música?*
Shall we go and listen in my room?	*¿Quieres que escuchemos música en mi habitación?*
What sort of music do you like?	*¿Qué tipo de música te gusta?*

LISTENING TO MUSIC cont. / *ESCUCHANDO MUSICA cont.*

What would you like to listen to?	*¿Qué quieres escuchar?*
What's your favourite group?	*¿Qué es tu grupo favorito?*
Who's your favourite singer?	*¿Cuál es tu cantante favorito?*
What's number one in your country at the moment?	*¿Cuál es el número uno en tu país ahora?*
Did this stereo system cost a lot?	*¿Te costó mucho el estéreo?*
It's very good reproduction.	*Es una copia muy buena.*
The quality of this recording isn't all that good.	*La calidad de ésta grabación no es tan buena.*
It was recorded live.	*Se grabó en vivo.*
Is this group popular in your country?	*¿Es éste un grupo popular en tu país?*
I've never heard of them before.	*Nunca he escuchado su música antes.*
I play in a group.	*Toco en un grupo.*
I'm the lead singer / guitarist / drummer.	*Soy el cantante / el guitarrista / el batería.*
We formed a group a year ago.	*Formamos un grupo el año pasado.*

I LIKE..		***ME GUSTA...***	
classical	*la música clásica*	pop	*pop*
folk	*la música folk*	rap	*el rap*
inde	*el indi*	reggae	*el reggae*
jazz	*el jazz*	soul	*la música soul*
New Age	*la música New Age*		

MUSIC LESSONS AND PRACTICE
LECCIONES DE MUSICA Y PRATICAS

MUSIC LESSONS	*LECCIONES DE MUSICA*
a music teacher	*un profesor de música*
a piano lesson	*una lección de piano*
How long have you had piano lessons?	*¿Cuánto tiempo has estado yendo a lecciones de piano?*
I am only a beginner.	*Soy sólo un principiante.*
I've been learning for three years.	*He estado yendo tres años.*

THE PIANO	*EL PIANO*
an upright piano	*piano vertical o recto*
a grand piano	*un piano de cola*
Would it be O.K. if I played your piano?	*¿Te importa si toco tu piano?*
Am I disturbing anyone?	*¿Estoy molestando a álguien?*
to put on the practice pedal	*presionar el pedal de práctica*
the loud pedal	*pedal fuerte*
the soft pedal	*sordina*
the piano stool	*el taburete de piano*
Is the stool the right height?	*¿Está el taburete a tu altura?*
How do you make it a little higher / lower?	*¿Cómo lo subo un poco / cómo lo bajo un poco?*
to raise	*subir*
to lower	*bajar*
to adjust	*ajustar*
a metronome	*metrónomo*

MUSIC LESSONS AND PRACTICE cont. — *LECCIONES DE MUSICA Y PRATICAS cont.*

THE VIOLIN	*EL VIOLIN*
a violin case	*la funda del violin (una)*
a bow	*un arco*
a string	*una cuerda*
to tune the violin	*afinar el violín*
It sounds a bit out of tune.	*suena desafinado*
Can you help me to tune it properly?	*¿Puedes ayudarme a afinarlo bien?*
to break a string	*romper una cuerda*
a music stand	*un trípode*
a music case	*una partitura*

MUSIC PRACTICE	*PRACTICAS*
to practise	*practicar*
to practise the piano	*practicar el piano*
to practise one's pieces	*practicar piezas*
to practise one's scales	*practicar las escalas*
Do you mind if I do my piano practice now?	*¿Te importa sí practico / toco piano ahora?*
I haven't done enough practice.	*No lo he tocado mucho.*
I am supposed to do half an hour a day.	*Debería hacer media hora al día*

EXAMINATIONS	*EXAMENES*
Do you take music exams?	*¿Tienes exámenes de música?*
What grade are you up to now?	*¿Qué curso estás haciendo ahora?*
Which grade are you taking next?	*¿Qué curso haces el próximo año?*
I failed my last exam.	*No pasé mí último examen.*
I got a pass / merit / distinction.	*Saqué aprobado / saqué nota / saqué MH. Con distinción.*

READING
LEYENDO

BOOKS *LIBROS*

TYPES OF BOOKS	*TIPOS DE LIBROS*
a hardback	*un libro de pastas duras / publicación de lujo*
a paperback	*una publicación normal*
a best seller	*un best seller*
a prize winner	*un libro ganador de un premio literario*
a novel	*una novela*
a book of poetry	*un libro de poesía*
a play	*una obra de teatro*

FICTION	*LA FICCION*
a thriller	*la novela detectivesca o de suspense*
a romance	*una novela romántica*
a mystery	*una novela de misterio*
science fiction	*una novela de ciencia-ficción*
a horror story	*una novela de miedo / horror*
a series	*una serie de novelas*
a sequel	*???*

NON-FICTION	*SENERO REALISTA*
biography	*biografía*
autobiography	*autobiografía*
historical	*novela histórica*
faction (mixture of fact and fiction)	*novela factual*

READING cont. ***LEYENDO cont.***

REFERENCE BOOKS	*LIBROS DE REFERENCIA*
a dictionary	*un diccionario*
to look a word up	*buscar una palabra*
alphabetical order	*orden alfabético*
an atlas	*un atlas*
an encyclopaedia	*una enciclopedia*

CHILDREN'S BOOKS	*LIBROS PARA NINOS*
a fairy tale	*un cuento de hadas*
a picture book	*un libro illustrado / de imágines*
a cartoon	*un libro de dibujos*

THE WRITERS OF BOOKS	*LOS ESCRITORES DE LIBROS*
an author	*un autor(a)*
a biographer	*un biógrafo(a)*
a poet	*un poeta*
a playwright	*un dramaturgo(a)*

READING	*LEYENDO*
to read	*leer*
Do you mind if I read for a while?	*¿Te importa sí leo un ratito?*
I am in the middle of a really good book at the moment.	*Estoy en el medio de un libro my interesante en este momento.*
Do you feel like reading for a bit?	*¿Te apetece leer un ratito?*
Would you like to see what books I have?	*¿Te gustaría echar un vistazo a los libros que tengo?*
What is this book like?	*¿Qué tal está este libro?*
This book is excellent.	*Este libro está fenomenal.*
Where are you up to?	*¿Por dónde vas?*
What has just happened?	*¿Qué ha pasado?*

READING cont. / *LEYENDO cont.*

My sister / brother has some books you might like to read.	*Mí hermana(o) tienen libros que al lo mejor te gustan.*
I love reading.	*Me encanta leer.*
I like to read in bed before I go to sleep.	*Me gusta leer en la cama antes de dormirme.*
I don't read much.	*No leo mucho.*
She is a real bookworm.	*Ella debora libros.*
to use a bookmark	*Usar una señal / un separador*

NEWSPAPERS / *LOS PERIODICOS*

TYPES OF NEWSPAPERS	*TIPOS DE PERIODICOS*
a daily newspaper	*un diario*
a weekly newspaper	*un periódico semanal*
a national newspaper	*un periódico nacional*
a local newspaper	*un periódico local*
the gossip columns	*una columna de cotilleos*
the gutter press	*la prensa sensacionalista / prensa amarilla*

SECTIONS OF A NEWSPAPER	*SECCIONES DE LOS PERIODICOS*
the headlines	*los titulares*
a leading article	*el artículo principal*
a report	*un reportaje*
a letter	*una carta*
the sports pages	*las páginas deportivas*
the fashion pages	*las páginas sobre moda*
the weather forecast	*el tiempo*
Births, Marriages and Deaths	*Nacimientos, Bodas y Defunciones*
a crossword	*los pasatiempos*
the horoscope (See page 165-166)	*el horóscopo*

READING cont. — *LEYENDO cont.*

PRODUCERS OF NEWSPAPERS	*LOS ARTIFICES DEL PERIODICO*
the editor	*el editor*
the sub-editor	*el sub-editor*
the journalists	*el periodista*
the foreign correspondent	*el corresponsal en el extranjero*
a freelance journalist	*el periodista independiente*
the photographer	*el fotógrafo*
the press	*la prensa*
the paparazzi	*el paparazzi*

MAGAZINES — *REVISTAS*

TYPES OF MAGAZINES	*TIPOS DE REVISTAS*
a glossy magazine	*una revista elegante*
a monthly	*una revista mensual*
a weekly	*una revista semanal*
an expensive magazine	*una revista cara*
a fashion magazine	*una revista de moda*
a music magazine	*una revista de música*
a specialist magazine	*una revista especializada*
children's magazines	*revistas para niños*
comics	*comic*

LENDING AND BORROWING BOOKS — *COGIENDO Y DEJANDO LIBROS PRESTADOS*

LENDING AND BORROWING BOOKS	*COGIENDO Y DEJANDO LIBROS PRESTADOS*
to lend	*prestar*
to borrow	*pedir prestado*
This book is a good one.	*Este libro es bastante bueno.*
I can lend it to you if you like.	*Te lo puedo prestar sí quieres.*
Would you like to borrow a book?	*¿Te gustaría sacar un libro?*

BORROWING BOOKS cont. / *TOMANDO LIBROS PRESTAODS*

Don't forget to return it, will you?	*No olvides devolverlo, ¿de acuerdo?*
I'll write my name in it.	*Voy a escribir mi nombre en él.*
You can take it back home with you if you want and post it back to me.	*Te lo puedes llevar a casa sí quieres y mandarlo por correo de vuelta.*

THE LIBRARY	***LA BIBLIOTECA***
a public library	*una biblioteca pública*
the librarian	*el bibliotecario*
a library ticket	*un pase de biblioteca*
to take out a book	*sacar un libro*
Would you like to take out a book on my ticket?	*¿Quieres sacar un libro con mi pase?*
How many books may I borrow at once?	*¿Cuántos libros puedo sacar al mismo tiempo?*
It has to be back by 3rd November.	*Tienes que devolverlo el 3 de Noviembre.*
My library books are due back today.	*Tengo que devolver los libros a la biblioteca hoy.*
My books are overdue.	*El plazo de prestamo de mi libro se ha pasado.*
How much is the fine?	*¿Cuánto es la multa?*
Can you also borrow films / cassettes?	*¿Se pueden sacar películas y cintas en préstamo?*

READING cont. / *LEYENDO cont.*

BUYING BOOKS AND MAGAZINES	***COMPRANDO LIBROS Y REVISTAS***
a book shop	*una librería*
a second-hand book shop	*una librería de segunda mano*
a bookstall	*un tenderete de libros*
a news stand	*un puesto de periódicos*
Where can I buy English books and newspapers?	*¿Dónde puedo comprar libros y periódicos en inglés?*
I have got a book token.	*Tengo un tiquet de descuento para libros.*
Can I use this token here?	*¿Puedo utilizar el tiquet de descuento aquí?*
May I pay (partly) with this book token, please?	*¿Puedo pagar la diferencia con este tiquet de descuento, por favor?*
How much extra do I owe?	*¿Cuánto más debo?*

DESCRIBING BOOKS		***DESCRIBIENDO LIBROS***	
The plot is…		*El argumento es sobre...*	
This book is about…		*El libro es sobre...*	
The characterisation is..		*Los personajes son...*	
The language / setting is...		*El lenguaje / la presta en escena es...*	
boring	*aburrido(a)*	poetic	*poético(a)*
clever	*inteligente*	predictable	*previsible*
concise	*conciso*	pretentious	*pretencioso(a)*
contrived	*retraído(a)*	romantic	*romántico(a)*
different	*diferente*	sad	*triste*
difficult	*difícil*	sarcastic	*sarcástico(a)*
easy to read	*fácil de leer*	slow	*lento(a)*
exciting	*emocionante*	surprising	*sorprendente*
fast	*rápido*	tense	*tenso(a)*
funny	*divertido/ gracioso(a)*	typical	*típico(a)*
		unexpected	*inesperado(a)*
gripping	*apasionante*	untypical	*atípico(a)*
hysterical	*histérico(a)*	unusual	*inusitado(a)*
long-winded	*entramado(a)*		

HOROSCOPES
SIGNOS ZODIACALES / LOS HOROSCOPOS

THE SIGNS OF THE ZODIAC	*LOS SIGNOS DEL ZODIACO*
• Aries (The Ram)	• *Aries (El Venado)*
• Taurus (The Bull)	• *Tauro (El Toro)*
• Gemini (The Twins)	• *Géminis (Los Gemelos)*
• Cancer (The Crab)	• *Cáncer (El Cangrejo)*
• Leo (The Lion)	• *Leo (El León)*
• Virgo (The Virgin)	• *Virgo (La Virgen)*
• Libra (The Balance)	• *Libra (La Balanza)*
• Scorpio (The Scorpion)	• *Escorpio (El Escorpión)*
• Sagittarius (The Archer)	• *Sagitario (El Centauro con el Arco)*
• Capricorn (The Goat)	• *Capricornio (La Cabra)*
• Aquarius (The Water Bearer)	• *Acuario (Los Acuáticos)*
• Pisces (The Fishes)	• *Piscis (Los Peces)*

THE HEAVENLY BODIES	*LOS ASTROS DEL CIELO*
the Sun	*el sol*
the Moon	*la luna*
the Planets	*los planetas*
• Mercury	• *Mercurio*
• Venus	• *Venus*
• Mars	• *Marte*
• Jupiter	• *Júpiter*
• Saturn	• *Saturno*

HOROSCOPES cont. — *LOS HOROSCOPOS cont.*

USEFUL EXPRESSIONS	*EXPRESIONES UTILES*
What does your horoscope say?	*¿Qué dice tu horóscopo?*
My horoscope sounds interesting.	*Mi horóscopo suena bien.*
My horoscope sounds terrible.	*Mi horóscopo es malo.*
Listen to what my horoscope says.	*Escucha lo que mi horóscopo dice.*
Read me my horoscope.	*Léame mi horóscopo.*
What sign are you?	*¿Qué signo eres?*
I am a Gemini.	*Soy Géminis.*
I was born under the star sign of Aries.	*Nací bajo el signo de Aries.*
What time of day were you born?	*¿A qué hora naciste?*
Where were you born?	*¿Dónde naciste?*
in conjunction with….	*en conjunción con...*
under the influence of…	*bajo la influencia de...*
on the cusp	*entre medias de / entre signos (del horóscopo)*
position	*posición (f)*
house	*casa (f)*
Do you believe in horoscopes?	*¿Crees en los horóscopos?*
I think they're rubbish.	*No creo nada.*
I think they are very accurate.	*Creo que son muy buenas.*
Let me guess what star sign you are.	*Déjame que adivine tu horóscopo.*
Are you a Capricorn?	*¿Eres Capricornio?*

FOOD
COMIDA

MEALS , COURSES & SNACKS	*COMIDA, PLATOS Y APERATIVOS*
early morning tea	*el té por la mañana temprano*
breakfast	*el desayuno*
elevenses	*el almuerzo / la comida*
lunch	*la comida*
afternoon tea	*la merienda*
dinner	*la cena*
supper	*la cena*
a snack	*un aperitivo*
the first course / a starter	*el primer plato / los entremeses*
the fish course	*el plato de pescado*
the main course	*el plato principal / el segundo plato*
the dessert	*el postre*
cheese and biscuits	*queso y galletas*
coffee and mints	*café y pastas*

SEATING ARRANGEMENTS	*SENTANDOSE*
Would you like to sit here?	*¿Quieres sentarte aquí?*
Sit next to me.	*Siéntate junto a mí.*
Sit opposite me.	*Siéntate en frente de mí.*
Sit anywhere.	*Siéntate en cualquier sitio.*

FOOD PREFERENCES — *COMIDA FAVORITAS*

LIKES	*GUSTOS*
I thought that was..	*Me parece que fue...*
gorgeous / delicious / really good	*magnífico / delicioso / muy bueno*
How did you make it?	*¿Cómo lo hiciste?*
Would you give me the recipe?	*¿Quieres darme la receta?*
Is it difficult to cook?	*¿Es difícil de hacer?*

FOOD PREFERENCES cont. — *COMIDA FAVORITAS cont.*

LIKES cont.	***GUSTOS cont.***
Shall we cook a meal for you tomorrow?	*¿Qué tal si cocinámos para tí mañana?*
I love cooking.	*Me encanta cocinar.*
Would you like some more?	*¿Quieres más?*
Would you like a second helping?	*¿Quieres repetir?*
Only if no-one else wants it.	*Sólo sí nadie va a comer más.*

DISLIKES	***COSAS QUE NO GUSTAN***
Is there anything you don't like eating?	*¿Hay algo que no te guste?*
Just say if you don't like it.	*Sí no te gusta dilo.*
I am just not very hungry.	*No tengo mucha hambre.*
I'm afraid I don't eat…	*Lo siento pero no como...*
I'm sorry but….disagrees with me.	*Lo siento pero... no me va bien.*
I can get you something else.	*Puede darte algo distinto.*
What do you feel like eating?	*¿Qué te apetece comer?*
Have you any…?	*¿Tienes...?*

EXPERIMENTING WITH FOOD	***PROBANDO COMIDA***
This is typically English / French.	*(Esto) es típico de Inglaterra / España*
Have you ever tried this before?	*¿Lo has probado antes?*
Can I try just a little bit, please?	*¿Puedo probar un poquito sólo, por favor?*
What do you think of it?	*¿Qué te parece?*
How do you cook this?	*¿Cómo se hace / guisa?*
How do you prepare this?	*¿Cómo se prepara?*

FOOD cont. — *COMIDA cont.*

EATING	*COMIENDO*
to eat	*comer*
to drink	*beber*
to bite	*morder*
to chew	*masticar*
to taste	*probar*
to swallow	*tragar*
to digest	*digerir*
to choke	*atragantarse*
to burn your mouth	*quemarse (uno) la boca*

DIFFERENT DIETS	*DISTINTAS DIETAS*
I am vegetarian.	*Soy vegetariano(a)*
I am a vegan.	*Soy vegetariano(a) estricto(a)*
I am diabetic.	*Soy diabético(a)*
I like junk food.	*Me gusta la comida rápida*
I am allergic to…	*Soy alérgico(a) a...*
I am trying to lose weight.	*Estoy intentando perder peso / kilos.*
I am trying to gain weight.	*Estoy intentando poner peso / kilos..*
I am trying to count my calories.	*Estoy intentando prestar atención al consumo de calorías.*
How many calories does this have?	*¿Cuántas calorías tiene esto?*
I don't eat starch with protein.	*No mezcla productos feculentos con proteínas.*
I prefer my vegetables raw.	*Prefiero la verdura sín cocinar.*
I am on a low fat diet.	*Estoy a dieta / tengo una dieta baja en grasas.*
I can't eat fried food.	*No puedo comer fritos.*

TYPICALLY BRITISH FOOD	*COMIDA TIPICAMENTE INGLESA*
Bangers and mash - sausages and mashed potatoes.	***Salchichas con patata*** – *salchichas y patatas cocidas en masa.*
Shepherd's pie - minced beef and onion, topped with mashed potato.	***Tarta del pastor*** – *ternera molida con cebolla y cubierta de patata cocida en masa.*
Cornish pasty - an individual pie containing potatoes, vegetables and minced meat, typical of Cornwall.	***Tarta individual con patata*** – *vegetables y carne molida. Comida típica de Cornwall.*
A full English breakfast - fried eggs, bacon, sausage, grilled tomato, mushrooms, fried bread and sometimes black pudding.	***Desayuno Inglés completo*** – *huevos fritos, bacon, salchicha, tomate frito, champiñones, pan frito y morcilla de arroz a veces.*
Porridge - oats or oatmeal simmered with water and/or milk which the Scots eat with salt not sugar.	***Porridge*** – *Avena o harina de avena con agua o leche que los escoceses comen con sal, sin azúcar.*
Yorkshire pudding - made from batter and traditionally eaten with roast beef for Sunday lunch.	***Yorkshire Pudding*** – *hecho a partir de una pasta para rebozar con ternera asada. Se come tradicionalmente los domingos a la hora de la comida.*
Fish and chips - fish deep fried in batter with chips.	***Pescado y patatas*** */ Fish y Chips – pescado frito con gabardina y patatas fritas.*

TYPICALLY BRITISH FOOD cont.	*COMIDA TIPICAMENTE INGLESA cont.*
A hot cross bun - a small bread like bun with currants in and a cross marked on top eaten on Good Friday.	***Bollo pequeño*** *que lleva pasas y decorado con dos rallas en forma de cruz, y se toma en semana Santa.*
Cheddar - a common British cheese often known as 'mousetrap'.	***Cheddar*** *– queso típico inglés conocido normalmente como "la trampa" para ratones.*
Lardy cake - a bread made with lard and dried fruit topped with a sticky sugary mixture.	***Un pan*** *hecho con manteca de cerdo y frutos secos y lleva una capa de azúcar pegajosa.*
Bakewell tart - a tart filled with almond paste and jam created in Bakewell in Derbyshire.	***Un pastel*** *relleno de crema de almendra y mermelada* típico *de Bakewell en Derbyshire*
Christmas pudding - a rich pudding made with a variety of dried fruit which can be kept for over a year.	***Pastel de Navidad*** *- un pastel enriquezido por una variedad de frutas secas, y que se puede conservar hasta más de un año.*

TYPICALLY SPANISH FOOD	*COMIDA TIPICA ESPANOLA*
Black pudding	***Morcillas de Burgos***
Spiced sausage	***Chorizo***
Parma Ham	***Jamón Serrano***
Spanish omelette - ingredients: potatoes, onions, eggs, olive and salt.	***Tortilla Española*** *- ingredientes: patatas, cebolla, huevos, aceite de oliva y sel.*
Paella - a sea food dish - ingredients: rice, chicken, pork, mussels, clams, mixed herbs and saffron.	***Paella*** *- ingredientes: arroz, pollo, cerdo, calamares, almejas, especias y azafran.*
Manchego's broth - ingredients: a pumpkin, an onion, green peppers, tomatoes, white pepper, white wine, olive oil and salt.	***Pisto Manchego*** *- ingredientes - calabacnes, cebolla, pimientos verdes, tomates, pimienta blanca, vino blanco, aceite y sel.*
Asturian casserole - ingredients: white beans, spiced sausage, black pudding, potatoes, pork and turnip.	***Fabada Asturiana*** *- ingredientes: alubias blancas, chorizo, morcilla, patatas, carne de cerdo y nabo.*
Andalucian soup - ingredients: a slice of day old bread, tomatoes, green peppers, onions, boiled eggs, olive oil and salt.	***Gazpacho Andaluz*** *-ingredientes: pan del dia anterior, tomate, pimiento verde, cebolla, huevos duros, aceite y sal.*

COOKING *COCINANDO*

Cookery books	***Libros (m) de cocina***
a recipe / to follow / to look up	*una receta / seguir / mirar a*
instructions	*las instrucciones*
method / ingredients	*método (m) / los ingredientes*
cooking time	*tiempo de cocion / preparación (f)*
Serves three to four people.	*Se sirve para tres o cuatro personas*
an illustration	*una foto / una ilustración*

COOKERY TERMS (abc)		***TERMINOS CULINARIOS***	
to add	*añadir*	to grate	*rayar*
to arrange	*arreglar / alinear*	to grill	*hacer en el gril*
to bake	*cocer al horno*	to grind	*moler*
to blend	*triturar*	to heat up	*calentar*
to boil	*hervir*	to incorporate	*poner*
to casserole	*hacer a la cacerola*	to knead	*amasar*
to chop	*cortar en trozos*	to liquidize	*hacer puré*
to combine	*combinar*	to mash	*hacer masa / amasar*
to cool	*dejar enfriar*	to measure	*medir*
to cover	*cubrir*	to melt	*derretir*
to crimp	*rizar / mover*	to mince	*triturar*
to cut into	*cortar en*	to peel	*pelar*
cubes	*cuadrados*	to pour	*echar*
to divide	*dividir / cubos*	to press	*presionar*
to drain	*escurrir*	to rise	*subir*
to flip over	*dar la vuelta*	to roast	*asar / hornar*
to fold	*doblar*	to roll out	*enrollar*
to fold in	*meter*	to season	*condimentar*
to fry	*freír*	to sift	*tamizar*
to garnish	*guarnecer*		

COOKERY TERMS (abc)	*TERMINOS CULINARIOS*
to simmer	*hervir a baja temperatura*
to skewer	*ensartar (en un pincho)*
to slice	*cortar en rodajas*
to sprinkle	*echar una pizca de*
to steam / to stir	*hacer al vapor / mover*
to strain	*escurrir*
to taste / to test // to time	*probar // tomar el tiempo*
to toss	*sacudir, agitar*
to turn down	*poner boca abajo*
to turn out	*sacar*
to turn up	*poner boca arriba*
to whisk	*batir*

COOKING MEASURES	*MEDIDAS DE COCINAR*
a teaspoonful	*una cucharadita*
a quarter / half a teaspoonful	*un cuarto / media cucharadita*
three quarters of a teaspoonful	*tres cuartos de una cuchara pequeña*
a dessertspoonful	*una cucharada de postre*
a tablespoonful	*una cucharada*
a cupful / half a cupful	*una taza / media taza*
a pinch of	*una pizca de*

COOKING INGREDIENTS (AND HOW TO PREPARE THEM) — *INGREDIENTES PARA COCINAR (Y COMO PREPARARLOS)*

DAIRY PRODUCTS	*PRODUCTOS LACTEOS*
Milk	***Leche (f)***
whole milk	*leche entera*
semi-skimmed / skimmed milk	*semi desnatada / desnatada*
long life milk / powdered milk	*leche pasteurizada/ leche en polvo*
a milk bottle / a carton	*una botella / un cartón de leche*
a milk jug / to pour	*una jarra de leche / echar*
a drink of milk	*un vaso de leche*

COOKING INGREDIENTS cont. — *INGREDIENTES PARA COCINAR cont.*

DAIRY PRODUCTS cont. — *PRODUCTOS LACTEOS*

Cream	***Crema (f)***
double cream	*crema doble*
single cream	*crema*
clotted cream	*nata cuajada*
whipped cream	*nata montada*
soured cream	*crema amarga*
a jug of cream	*una jarra de crema*
to whisk / to whip	*montar / batir*

Butter, margarine etc.	***Mantequilla, margarina etc.***
salted / unsalted butter	*mantequilla salada / sín sal*
margarine	*margarina*
soft / hard	*blanda / dura*
suet / lard / dripping	*sebo / manteca de cerdo / pringue (grasa)*
a butter dish	*un plato para la mantequilla*
a butter knife	*un cuchillo para la mantequilla*
to spread	*extender*
to butter	*echar mantequilla*

Yoghurt	***Yogur / yogurt (m)***
set yoghurt	*paquete de yogur variado*
natural yoghurt	*yogur(t) natural*
low fat yoghurt	*yogur(t) bajo en calorías*
fruit yoghurt	*yogur(t) de frutas*
a pot of yoghurt	*yogur(t) en tarrina*

COOKING INGREDIENTS cont. — *INGREDIENTES PARA COCINAR*

DAIRY PRODUCTS cont. — *PRODUCTOS LACTEOS cont.*

Cheese	***Queso (m)***
hard / soft cheese	*queso fuerte / blando*
cream cheese	*queso cremoso*
cottage cheese	*queso campero*
goat's cheese	*queso de cabra*
Parmesan cheese	*parmesano*
cheese biscuits	*galletas (f) para tomar con queso*
a cheese board / a cheese knife	*una tabla para partir el queso / un cuchillo para cortar queso*
to cut	*cortar / partir*
a cheese grater	*un rayador*
to grate	*rayar*

EGGS — *HUEVOS*

EGGS	*HUEVOS*
a hen's egg	*un huevo de gallina*
a quail's egg	*un huevo de codorniz*
brown / white	*moreno / blanco*
fresh / old	*fresco / no fresco*
large / medium / small	*grande / mediano / pequeño*
size one / two / three etc.	*extra / normal / pequeño (o primera / segunda / tercera categoría*
free range eggs	*huevos de granja*
farmyard / battery	*granja / huevos de batería*
a dozen / half a dozen	*una docena / media docena*
an egg box	*una caja / cartón de huevos*
the shell	*la cáscara*
to crack / to break	*cascar / romper*
the yolk / the white	*la yema / la clara*

COOKING INGREDIENTS cont. — *INGREDIENTES PARA COCINAR cont.*

Cooking eggs	***Huevos para cocinar***
a boiled egg	*un huevo cocido*
hard boiled / soft boiled	*muy cocido / poco hecho (pasado por agua)*
cooked for four / five / six minutes	*cuatro / cinco / seis minutos de cocción*
an egg cup	*una huevera*
soldiers	*soldaditos*
to take the top off the egg	*cortar la parte de arriba del huevo*
scrambled egg	*huevos revueltos*
poached egg	*huevo escalfado*

Preparing eggs	***Preparando huevos***
to separate the whites from the yolks	*separar la yema de la clara*
to whisk the whites / an egg whisk	*montar nata / nata montada*
an electric beater	*una batidora eléctrica*
stiffly beaten	*un batido a mano*
soft peaks	*blando por arriba*

BREAD	***PAN***
wholemeal / organic	*pan integral / orgánico*
brown / white / large / small	*moreno / blanco / largo / pequeño*
round / oblong	*un pan redondo / un pan rectangular*
unsliced / sliced	*entero / en rebanadas*
thick / medium / thin sliced	*rebanadas gordas/ medianas/finas*
a bread bin	*una panera*
a bread board / a bread knife	*una tabla de pan / un cuchillo para cortar pan*
to cut / to slice	*cortar / cortar en rebanadas*
a slice	*una rebanada*
to make breadcrumbs	*hacer migas de pan*

COOKING INGREDIENTS cont.	*INGREDIENTES PARA COCINAR cont.*

OTHER TYPES OF BREAD AND BAKED GOODS	***OTRO TIPO DE PAN Y REPOSTERIA***
a French stick	*una barra francesa*
a roll	*una ballena*
Ciabatta / pitta bread	*una ciabatta / pan de pita*
crumpets	*bollo o hojuela (para tostar)*
muffins	*mojicones*
tea cakes	*pastas de té*

COFFEE, TEA AND OTHER DRINKS	*CAFE, TE Y OTRAS BEBIDAS*

Coffee	***Café***
Do you like black or white coffee?	*¿Te gusta el café negro o con leche?*
instant coffee	*café instantáneo*
decaffeinated coffee	*café descafeinado*
coffee beans	*granos de café (m)*
full / medium / light roast	*bien / medio / ligeramente tostado*
to grind	*moler*
a coffee grinder	*un molinillo*
fine / medium / coarse ground	*fino / medio / granulado*

Tea	***Té***
a tea pot	*una tetera*
to warm the pot	*una tetera templada*
to let it brew	*dejar que se haga*
to pour / to strain	*echar / colar*
tea bags / tea leaves	*bolsitas de té / hojas de té*
an infuser / a tea strainer	*un infusor / un colador de té*
Do you like your tea with milk and sugar?	*¿Quieres el té con leche y azúcar?*
Milk and no sugar, please.	*Con leche y sín azúcar, por favor.*
No milk and no sugar, please.	*Sín nada, por favor.*

COOKING INGREDIENTS cont. — *INGREDIENTES PARA COCINAR cont.*

OTHER DRINKS		*OTRAS BEBIDAS*	
tonic water / soda water		*tónica / soda*	
ginger ale		*cerveza gaseosa / de jengibre*	
lemonade		*limonada / gaseosa*	
coca cola		*coca cola*	
squash / to dilute / water		*concentrado / diluir / agua*	
strong / weak / average		*fuerte / flojo / medio*	
Fruit juice / freshly squeezed		***Zumo (m) de frutas / recién exprimido***	
orange	*naranja*	tomato	*tomate*
grapefruit	*pomelo*	vegetable	*vegetables*
pineapple	*piña*	tropical juice	*frutas tropicales*
Additions to drinks		***Para poner con las bebidas***	
ice cubes		*cubitos (m) de hielo*	
a slice of lemon		*una rodaja de limón*	
a cherry		*una cereza*	

ALCOHOLIC DRINKS — *BEBIDAS ALCOHOLICAS*

cider	*sidra (f)*	rosé	*rosado*
beer	*cerveza (f)*	sparkling	*espumoso*
lager	*cerveza rubia*	Champagne	*Champán*
bottled	*en botella*	**Spirits**	***Bebidas Alcohólicas***
draught	*de tonel / a presión*	gin	*ginebra*
		whisky	*whisky / whiski*
canned	*en lata*	brandy	*brandy / brandi*
Wine	***Vino (m)***	vodka	*vodka*
a glass of	*un vaso de*	rum	*ron*
half a bottle of	*media botella de*	a single	*solo*
red	*tinto*	a double	*doble*
white	*blanco*		

COOKING INGREDIENTS cont. — *INGREDIENTES PARA COCINAR cont.*

MEAT — *CARNE*

How do you like your meat cooked?	*¿Cómo quieres la carne?*
rare / medium rare	*cruda / un poco cruda*
well done / crispy	*muy hecha / en supunto*

TYPES OF MEAT — *TIPOS DE CARNE*

beef	***carne de vaca***	Parma ham	*jamón de Parma*
a steak	***un filete***	**veal**	***lechal***
pork	***cerdo***	**lamb**	***cordero***
bacon	*beicon (m) / pancete (f)*	**offal**	***asadura / menudillos***
smoked	*ahumado*	liver	*el hígado*
unsmoked	*sín ahumar*	kidney	*un riñón*
streaky	*tocino*	sweetbreads	*mollejas*
ham	*jamón (m)*	**sausages**	***salchichas (f)***

POULTRY AND GAME — *AVES Y AVES DE CAZA*

a chicken	*un pollo*	a guinea fowl	*una gallina de guinea*
a duck	*un pato*	a pheasant	*un faisán*
a goose	*un ganso*	a hare	*una liebre*
a turkey	*un pavo*	a rabbit	*un conejo*
venison	*carne de venado*		

COMMON FRUITS — FRUTAS CORRIENTES

apple	*manzana (f)*	orange	*naranja (f)*
apricot	*albaricoque (m)*	peach	*melocotón (m)*
banana	*plátano (m)*	pear	*pera (f)*
grapefruit	*pomelo (m)*	pineapple	*piña (f)*
grapes	*uvas (f)*	plum	*ciruela (f)*
lemon	*limón (m)*	raspberry	*frambuesa (f)*
lime	*lima (f)*	satsuma	*mandarina (f)*
melon	*melón (m)*	strawberry	*fresa (f)*

COOKING INGREDIENTS cont. — *INGREDIENTES PARA COCINAR cont.*

PREPARING FRUIT — *PREPARANDO FRUTA*

to peel	*pelar*
the peel	*la peladura*
the pith	*el meollo*
to quarter	*partir en gajos*
to remove the pips	*quitar las pepitas*
to take out the stone	*quitar el hueso*

VEGETABLES & SALAD — *VEGETALES & ENSALADA*

aubergine	*berenjena*	mushroom	*champiñón*
avocado	*aguacate*	onion	*cebolla*
broad beans	*haba gruesa*	Spring onion	*cebolleta*
French beans	*alubias*	parsnip	*chirivía*
green beans	*judías verdes*	peas	*guisantes*
runner beans	*trepadoras*	red pepper	*pimiento rojo*
beetroot	*remolacha*	green pepper	*pimiento verde*
broccoli	*brécoles*	potato	*patata*
Brussels sprouts	*coles de Bruselas*	jacket potato	*patata cocida/ patata al horno*
cabbage	*repollo / berza*	boiled	*cocida*
carrot	*zanahoria*	mashed	*masa de patata*
cauliflower	*coliflor*	roasted	*asadas*
celeriac	*apio-nabo*	chips	*patatas fritas*
celery	*apio*	spinach	*espinaca*
courgette	*calabacín*	swede	*nabo sueco*
cress	*berro*	sweetcorn	*mazorca*
cucumber	*pepino*	radish	*rábano*
garlic	*ajo*	tomato	*tomate*
leek	*puerro*	turnip	*nabo*
lettuce	*lechuga*	watercress	*berro*

COOKING INGREDIENTS cont. — *INGREDIENTES PARA COCINAR cont.*

SUGAR, HONEY & JAM — *AZUCAR, MIEL Y MERMELADA*

SUGAR, HONEY & JAM	*AZUCAR, MIEL Y MERMELADA*
white sugar / granulated sugar	*azúcar / azúcar granulada*
castor sugar / icing sugar	*azúcar extrafino / azúcar de alcorza*
lump sugar / to sweeten	*terrón de azúcar / endulzar*
brown sugar	*azúcar morena fina*
syrup / golden syrup	*jarabe / melaza dorada*
black treacle / molasses	*melaza negra / melaza*
honey / runny honey	*miel / miel fina*
honeycomb	*una bandeja de miel / una tira de miel*
jam	*melaza negra*
orange / ginger marmelade	*mermelada de naranja / jenjibre*

FLOUR etc. — *HARINA*

FLOUR etc.	*HARINA*
plain flour / self-raising flour	*harina / harina de repostería*
white flour / wholemeal flour	*harina blanca / harina integral*
buckwheat flour	*alforfón / harina de trigo sarraceno*
cornflour / baking powder	*harina de maíz/ levadura en polvo*
bicarbonate of soda	*bicarbonato*
cream of tartar	*crémor tartárico*
arrowroot	*???*
gelatine / yeast	*gelatina / levadura*

PREPARING NUTS — *PREPARANDO NUECES / FRUTOS SECOS*

PREPARING NUTS	*PREPARANDO NUECES / FRUTOS SECOS*
to crack the shell	*romper / partir la cáscara*
nutcrackers	*el cascanueces*
whole nuts / chopped nuts	*nuez / partidas nueces*
ground nuts	*fruto seco molido*
salted / unsalted nuts	*frutos secos salados / sín sal*
roasted nuts	*frutos secos tostados*

COOKING INGREDIENTS cont. — *INGREDIENTES PARA COCINAR cont.*

SALT AND PEPPER — *SAL Y PIMIENTA*

table salt	*sal de mesa (f)*
sea salt	*sal gorda de mar*
crystal rock salt	*cristales (m) de sal*
celery salt	*sal de apio*
a salt mill	*un molinillo de sal*
to grind	*moler*
to season	*alinear*
to sprinkle	*echar*
a pinch of salt	*una pizca de sal*
peppercorns	*pimientas (f)*
black / white / green	*negras / blancas / verdes*
a pepper mill	*un molinillo de pimienta / pimentero*
to grind	*moler*
to fill	*llenar*

BARBECUES
BARBACOAS

SHOULD WE HAVE A BARBECUE?	***¿HACEMOS UNA BARBACOA?***
Should we eat outside?	*¿Por qué no comemos fuera?*

LIGHTING THE BARBECUE — *ENCENDIENDO LA BARBACOA*

Have we got..?	*¿Tenemos...*
• aluminium foil	• *papel (m) de aluminio / papel reynols ®*
• charcoal	• *carbón (m)*
• lighter fluid	• *líquido (m) para encender*
to squirt	*lanzar / echar (un liquido) / empapar / mojar*
to pour over	*echar*
to soak	*empapar*
to light	*encender*
a match	*una cerilla*
to stand back	*retirarse*
to get going well	*salir bien / prender bien*
to go out	*salir*

COOKING ON A BARBECUE — *COCINANDO EN UNA BARBACOA*

to be ready to cook	*estar listo(a) para cocinar*
to barbecue	*hacer en la barbacoa*
to grill	*hacer en el gril*
tongs	*tenazas / tenacillas*
skewers	*pincho / broqueta / brocheta*
to turn over	*dar la vuelta*

BARBECUES cont. / *BARBACOAS cont.*

FOOD / *COMIDA*

sausages	*salchichas (f)*
bacon	*beicon / bacon (m) / panceta (f)*
steaks	*filetes (m)*
chops	*chuletas (f)*
kebabs	*kebabs*
chicken drumsticks	*muslos de pollo (m)*
spare ribs	*costillas sueltas (f)*
marinade	*adobo (m)*
sauce	*salsa (f)*
to brush over	*impregnar con un pincel*
marshmallows	*malvaviscos (m)*

COMMON EXPRESSIONS FOR BARBECUES / *EXPRESIONES COMUNES PARA BARBACOAS*

Is it ready yet?	*¿Está listo(a) ya?*
Are they ready yet?	*¿Están listos(as) ya?*
They won't be long now.	*No les queda mucho.*
Another few minutes.	*Unos minutos más.*
This isn't cooked properly.	*Esto no esta hecho del todo*
I'm afraid this is a bit burnt.	*Me temo que esto se ha quemado un poco.*

EATING AT McDONALD'S — *COMIENDO EN McDONALD'S*

A HAMBURGER	***UNA AMBURGUESA DE CARNE***

A FILLET O' FISH	***UNA AMBURGUESA DE PESCADO***

A CHICKEN STEAK	***UN BOCADILLO DE POLLO***

CHICKEN McNUGGETS Chicken in breadcrumbs. Variety of sauces:- • mustard sauce • sweet and sour sauce • barbecue sauce • curry sauce	***McNUGGETS DE POLLO*** *Pollo con pan rallado. Salsas variadas:-* • *salsa de mostaza* • *salsa agridulce* • *salsa de barbacoa* • *salsa de especias curry*

EATING AT McDONALD'S cont.	***COMIENDO EN McDONALD'S cont.***
CHIPS	***PATATAS FRITAS***
A MILK SHAKE • vanilla • strawberry • banana • chocolate	***UN BATIDO DE LECHE*** • *vainilla* • *fresa* • *plátano* • *chocolate*
AN ORANGE JUICE	***UN ZUMO DE NARANJA***
TEA AND COFFEE	***TE*** (m) ***Y CAFÉ (m)***
APPLE PIE	***UN PASTEL DE MANZANA***
DOUGHNUTS	***DONUTS***

CINEMA & THEATRE
CINE & TEATRO

THE CINEMA — *EL CINE*

USEFUL EXPRESSIONS — *EXPRESIONES UTILES*

Would you like to go to the cinema..?	*¿Quieres ir al cine?*
• this afternoon?	• *¿esta tarde?*
• this evening?	• *¿esta noche?*
• tomorrow?	• *¿mañana?*
• one day?	• *¿uno de estos días?*
• while you are here?	• *¿mientras que estés aquí?*
There's a very good film on at the moment.	*Hay una película muy buena en este momento.*
It starts at…	*Empieza a las...*
It ends at…	*Termina a las...*
Is there a supporting film first?	*¿Hay nodo al principio?*
Is there an interval?	*¿Hay intermedio?*
Who's in the film?	*¿Quiénes son los actores?*
The star of the film is..	*La estrella / el protagonista es...*
It's starring…	*...Tiene el papel principal*
It's that man who was in..	*Es el hombre que hizo / que sale en...*
Wasn't she in..?	*¿No es ella la que hizo / sale en...?*
Who is the director?	*¿Quién es el director?*

THE CINEMA cont. — *EL CINE cont.*

BUYING TICKETS AND GOING IN — *COMPRANDO LAS ENTRADAS / LOS TICKETS Y YENDO AL CINE*

Could we have two tickets, please?	*¿Dos entradas, por favor?*
Can you reserve seats?	*¿Se pueden hacer reservas?*
Do you give a reduction to students?	*¿Hay descuentos para estudiantes?*
We are .....years old.	*Somos...*
Would you like some pop corn?	*¿Quieres palomitas de maíz?*
Would you like an ice cream or a drink?	*¿Quieres un helado o algo de beber?*
Do you want to go to the loo first?	*¿Quieres ir al servicios antes de que empiece?*
Where are the toilets?	*¿Dónde están los servicios?*
We'd better hurry - the film's just starting.	*Vamos a darnos prisa, la película acaba de empezar.*
Where would you like to sit?	*¿Dónde te gustaría sentarte?*
Do you like to be near the front or not?	*¿Te gustaría cerca de la pantalla?*
Can you see O.K.?	*¿Ves bien?*
I can't see because of the person in front of me.	*No puedo ver bien con la persona que tengo delante.*
Can we try to sit somewhere else?	*¿Podemos cambiar de sitio? / ¿Te importa sí cambiamos de sitio?*

FOLLOWING THE PLOT — *SIGUIENDO EL ARGUMENTO*

Does it have subtitles?	*¿Tienes subtítulos?*
It has subtitles / It's dubbed.	*Tiene subtítulos. Está doblada.*
Can you understand what's going on?	*¿Entiendes de qué va?*
I don't understand it.	*No me entero de lo que va.*
What just happened?	*¿Qué pasa?*
What did he say?	*¿Qué dijo?*

THE THEATRE — *EL TEATRO*

BOOKING SEATS — *RESERVANDO SITIOS / ASIENTOS*

the booking office	*La taquilla de reservas*
to reserve seats	*reservar sitios*
Which performance?	*¿Qué espectáculo? ¿Qué pase?*
The matinée	*la matinée / por la mañana*
the evening performance	*el pase de noche*
Where do you want to sit?	*¿Dónde quieres sentarse?*
In the stalls	*en las butacas*
in the circle	*en el anfiteatro*
What seats are available?	*¿Qué sitios hay disponible?*
How much are the seats?	*¿Cuánto valen los sitios?*

BUYING A PROGRAMME — *COMPRANDO EL PROGRAMA*

to buy a programme	*comprar el programa*
to look at the programme	*mirar al programa*
to see who is in the play	*ver quién está en la obra / quién actúa*
to study the plot	*estudiar el argumento / leer el argumento*
to read about the actors' backgrounds	*leer sobre la carrera artística de los actores*

HAVING SOMETHING TO EAT OR DRINK — *COMIENDO O BEBIENDO*

the bar	*el bar*
the restaurant	*el restaurant*
to have a drink	*tomar una copa*
before the performance	*antes de la representación*
in the interval	*en el intermedio / intervalo*
to book a table	*reservar una mesa*

THE THEATRE cont. — *EL TEATRO cont.*

THE AUDITORIUM — *EL AUDITORIO*

THE AUDITORIUM	*EL AUDITORIO*
an aisle	*el pasillo*
a box	*un palco*
the toilets	*los servicios*
a fire exit	*la salida de emergencia*
the acoustics	*la acústica*

THE SEATING — *SENTANDOSE / ACOMODANDOSE*

THE SEATING	*SENTANDOSE / ACOMODANDOSE*
to show your ticket	*enseñar / mostrar la entrada*
row A, B etc.	*fila A, B etc.*
an usher	*un acomodador*
to be shown to your seat	*mostrar a alguien su sitio*
the stalls	*las butacas*
the circle	*el anfiteatro*

BEFORE THE PERFORMANCE — *ANTES DE LA ACTUACION*

BEFORE THE PERFORMANCE	*ANTES DE LA ACTUACION*
to read the programme	*leer el programa*
to have a chocolate	*tomarse un chocolate / un dulce*
to let someone past	*dejar pasar a alguien*
to stand up	*levantarse*
to sit down	*sentarse*
to take your coat off	*quitarse el abrigo*
to get a good view	*conseguir un buen lugar / una buena vista*
to be able to see	*ser capaz de ver / poder ver*
to use the opera glasses	*usar prismáticos*
to insert a coin	*insertar una moneda*
to borrow	*pedir prestado*

THE THEATRE cont. — *EL TEATRO cont.*

THE STAGE — *EL ESCENARIO*

THE STAGE	EL ESCENARIO
a theatre in the round	*un anfiteatro*
a raised stage	*un escenario elevado*
the wings	*los lados*
the scenery	*el decorado*
a scene-change	*un cambio de escenario*
the props	*los accesorios*
to make an entrance	*hacer una entrada / entrar en escena*
to come on stage	*entrar en escena*
to exit	*salir*
to leave	*salir*

THE LIGHTING — *LA ILUMINACION*

THE LIGHTING	LA ILUMINACION
spotlights	*focos / reflectores (m)*
floodlights	*focos (m)*
coloured	*de colores*
to dim	*controlar la intensidad*
to go down	*bajar*
to go off	*apagarse*
to come back on	*volverse a encender*
the lighting effects	*los efectos luminotécnicos*

THE CURTAIN — *EL TELON*

THE CURTAIN	EL TELON
to open	*abrir*
to shut	*cerrar*
to raise	*elevar*
to fall	*caer*
a safety curtain	*un telón de seguridad*

THE THEATRE cont. / *EL TEATRO cont.*

THE PERFORMERS / *LOS ACTORES / EL ALENGO / EL REPARTO*

the cast	*el reparto*
the lead	*el papel principal*
the star	*la estrella*
the hero / the heroine	*el héroe / la heroína*
the villain	*el malo*
the actors / the actresses	*los actores las actrices*
the understudy	*el suplente*

THE WRITERS / *LOS ESCRITORES*

the playwright	*el escritor*
the composer	*el compositor*
the librettist	*el adaptador de escena*
the choreographer	*el coreógrafo*
the musical director	*el director musical*

THE TECHNICAL STAFF / *EL PERSONAL TECNICO / LOS TECNICOS*

the stage manager	*el director de escena / el jefe de escena*
the technical director	*el director técnico*
the lighting technicians	*los técnicos de iluminación*

THE PLAY / *LA OBRA*

a Shakespeare play	*una obra de Shakespeare*
a play by Pinter	*una obra escrita por Pinter*
a comedy / a farce	*una comedía / una farsa*
slapstick	*una comedia / una bufonada*
a tragedy / a history	*una tragedia / una obra histórica*
a thriller	*una obra de suspense*
a whodunnit	*una novela policíaca*
a romance	*un romance*
a pantomime	*una pantomima*
the plot	*el argumento / la trama*

THE THEATRE cont. — *EL TEATRO cont.*

REHEARSALS — *LOS ENSAYOS*

to rehearse	*ensayar*
to have a dress rehearsal	*un ensayo general*
a final rehearsal	*un ensayo final*

THE SET DESIGN — *EL DISENO ESCENICO*

abstract	*abstracto*	functional	*funcional*
artistic	*artístico*	eccentric	*excéntrico*
realistic	*realista*	unusual	*inusual*

THE COSTUME DESIGN — *EL DISENO DEL VESTUARIO*

historical	*histórico*	masked	*enmascarado*
period costume	*vestuario del periodo*	bold	*llamativo / atrevido*
contemporary	*contemporáneo*	extravagant	*extravagante*
imaginative	*imaginativo*		

THE MAKEUP — *EL MAQUILLAJE*

to be made up	*ser maquillado*	to emphasize	*enfatizar*
to exaggerate	*exagerar*	to remove	*quitar*
to conceal	*ocultar / disimular*	greasepaint	*maquillaje*
to distort	*cambiar*		

THE SPECIAL EFFECTS — *LOS EFECTOS ESPECIALES*

sound effects	*efectos de sonido*	battle noises	*ruidos de batalla*
music	*música*	lighting effects	*efectos luminotécnicos*
thunder	*trueno*	smoke	*humo / niebla*

THE THEATRE cont. — *EL TEATRO cont.*

THE PARTS OF THE PLAY — *PARTES DE LA OBRA*

THE PARTS OF THE PLAY	PARTES DE LA OBRA
a scene / the first scene	*una escena / la primera escena*
the second / third scene	*la segunda / tercera escena*
a change of scene	*un cambio de escena*
an act	*un acto*
the last act	*el último acto / el acto final*
a speech / a soliloquy	*un discurso / un soliloquio*
an aside	*aparte*

THE INTERVAL — *EL INTERMEDIO / EL INTERVALO*

THE INTERVAL	EL INTERMEDIO / EL INTERVALO
a brief interval	*un intermedio corto*
a long interval	*un intermedio largo*
to go to the bar	*ir al bar*
a long queue	*una fila larga / una cola larga*
to go to the toilet	*ir a los servicios*
to ring the bell	*tocar la campanilla*
to return to your seat	*volver a tu sitio*

THE END OF THE PLAY — *EL FINAL DE LA OBRA*

THE END OF THE PLAY	EL FINAL DE LA OBRA
to applaud / the applause	*aplaudir / el aplauso*
to clap	*dar palmas*
a standing ovation	*una ovación de pie*
to give a curtain call	*dar una llamada a escena*
to bow / to curtsy	*hacer una reverencia / hacer una reverencia*
to be given a bouquet	*entregar / dar un ramo de flores*

AFTER THE PLAY — *DESPUES DE LA OBRA*

AFTER THE PLAY	DESPUES DE LA OBRA
to go to the stage door	*ir a la salida del escenario*
to try to get an autograph	*intentar conseguir un autógrafo*
a signature	*una firma*
to sign an autograph book	*firmar un libro / libreto de autógrafos*

THE THEATRE cont. / *EL TEATRO cont.*

DISCUSSING THE PERFORMANCE (abc) / *CHARLANDO SOBRE LA OBRA / DISCUTIENDO SOBRE LA OBRA*

amateur	*amateur*	realistic	*realista*
convincing	*convincente*	sad	*triste*
excellent	*excelente*	sensitive	*sensible*
funny	*divertida*	spectacular	*espectacular*
hysterical	*graciosísima*	tense	*tensa*
imaginative	*imaginativa*	terse	*lacónica / sucinta*
impressive	*muy buena / impresionante*	theatrical	*teátrica*
ironic	*irónica*	tragic	*trágica*
moving	*emotiva*	true to life	*real*
professional	*profesional*	unconvincing	*no convincente*
psychological	*psicológica*		

OPERA / *LA OPERA*

TYPES OF OPERA / *TIPOS DE OPERA*

an opera	*una opera*	a comic opera	*una ópera bufa / una zarzuela*
an operetta	*una opereta / operetta*	a rock opera	*un musical*

TYPES OF SONG / *TIPOS DE CANCIONES*

a solo	*un solo*	an aria	*un aria*
a duet	*un duo*	a recitative	*un recitativo*
a chorus	*un coro*		

OPERA cont. — ***LA OPERA cont.***

THE SINGERS — ***LOS CANTANTES / LAS VOCES***

soprano / contralto	*la soprano / contralto*
alto / tenor	*alto / tenor*
falsetto	*falsete / de falsete*
baritone	*barítono*
bass	*bajo*
a prima donna	*una prima donna*

THE MUSIC — ***LA MUSICA***

the score	*la partitura de música*
the libretto	*el libreto*
the overture	*la obertura*

THE BALLET — *EL BALLET*

THE DANCERS etc. — ***LOS BAILARINES etc.***

a ballerina	*una bailarina*
a prima ballerina	*la bailarina central / la primera bailarina*
the corps de ballet	*el ballet / el cuerpo de bailarines*
the choreographer	*el coreógrafo / la coreógrafa*
the composer	*el compositor*

GETTING READY TO DANCE — ***PREPARANDOSE PARA BAILAR***

to do exercises at the barre	*hacer ejercicios de barra*
to warm up	*calentar*
to limber	*desentumecer*
to stretch the muscles	*estirar los musculos*
to loosen the joints	*relajar las articulaciones*

THE BALLET cont. — *EL BALLET cont.*

THE POSITIONS — *LAS POSICIONES*

the position of..	*la posición de...*	third position	*posición tercera*
the head	*la cabeza*	fourth position	*posición cuarta*
the arms	*los brazos*	fifth position	*posición quinta*
the body	*el cuerpo*	turned out	*presentación*
the legs	*las piernas*	in line	*en línea*
the feet	*los pies*	in the air	*en el aire*
first position	*posición primera*	pointed	*de puntillas*
second position	*posición segunda*		

THE MOVEMENTS — *LOS MOVIMIENTOS*

to jump	*saltar*
to leap	*saltar / dar un salto / elevar*
to turn	*dar la vuelta*
to beat the feet	*marcar el compás con movimiento de pies*
to change the leg position	*cambiar la posición de la pierna*
to do pointe work	*andar de puntillas*
to mime	*hacer mimo*
to gesture	*hacer gestos / gesticular*
an arabesque	*un arabesco*
a pirouette	*una pirueta*
a fouetté	*una Fouetté*
an entrechat	*un Entrechat*
a jeté	*una Jeté / a Jeté*
a pas de deux	*a Pas de Deux*
to partner	*bailar en pareja / hacer de pareja de baile*
a partner	*una pareja de baile*

THE BALLET cont. — *EL BALLET cont.*

BALLET CLOTHES etc. — *ROPA DE BALLET*

ballet shoes	*las zapatillas de baile*
blocked shoes	*zapatillas cerradas (f)*
to darn	*zurcir*
tights	*medias (f)*
a tutu	*el Tutu*
a hair net	*la redecilla para el pelo*
to put one's hair up	*hacer un moño*
to tie one's hair back	*hacer una coleta*
to plait one's hair	*trenzar el pelo*

THE BALLET ITSELF — *EL BALLET EN SI MISMO*

the music	*la música*
the composer	*el compositor*
the steps	*los pasos*
the choreographer	*el coreógrafo / la coreógrafa*
the conductor	*el director de orquesta / el maestro de orquesta*
the plot	*la trama*
the libretto	*el libreto*
the scenario	*el escenario*
the orchestra	*la orquesta*
the pit	*la platea*

PARTIES & CLUBS
FIESTAS Y BARES

GETTING IN	*ENTRANDO EN*
a nightclub	*un bar*
a bouncer	*un gorila*
How old do you have to be to get in?	*¿Qué edad tienes que tener para entrar?*
Have you got an identity card?	*¿Tienes algún tipo de identificación?*
Have you got anything that proves your age?	*¿Tienes algo para probar tu edad?*
How much does it cost to get in?	*¿Cuánto cuesta entrar?*

PARTIES	*FIESTAS*
Have you got an invitation?	*¿Tienes invitación?*
I am / am not invited.	*Estoy / no estoy invitado*
a gatecrasher	*un colón / un caradura / una persona que se cuela*
to give a party	*dar una fiesta*
to draw up a list of people to invite	*hacer una lista de gente a quien quieres invitar*
to take a bottle	*llevar una botella*

THE MUSIC	*LA MUSICA*
What's the music like?	*¿Cómo es la música?*
It's just a disco.	*Es una discoteca.*
There's live music.	*Hay música en vivo.*
The group is good.	*El grupo es bueno.*
What sort of music do you like?	*¿Qué tipo de música te gusta?*
This music isn't my sort of thing.	*Esta música no me va.*
I prefer…	*Prefiero...*
Which groups do you like?	*¿Qué grupos te gustan?*
Should we ask them to play..?	*¿Les pedimos que pongan...?*

PARTIES & CLUBS cont. / *FIESTAS Y BARES cont.*

INTRODUCTIONS	***PRESENTANDOSE***
What nationality are you?	*¿De qué nacionalidad eres?*
Are you English / French / German / Spanish?	*¿Eres inglés / francés / alemán / español?*
Can you speak English?	*¿Hablas inglés?*
What are you called? I'm called..	*¿Cómo te llamas? Me llamo...*
What's your name? My name is..	*¿Cómo te llamas? Me llamo...*
This is my friend….	*Este / esta es mi amigo(a)...*
Where do you live?	*¿Dónde vives?*
Where are you staying?	*¿Dónde te alojas?*
How old are you?	*¿Cuántos años tienes?*
I'm sixteen.	*Tengo dieciséis.*
Have you been here before?	*¿Has estado aquí antes?*
Are you at school / college / working?	*¿Estás en un escuela / un colegio / trabajando?*
Which school / college do you go to?	*¿A qué escuela / colegio vas?*
Where do you work?	*¿Dónde trabajas?*
What do you do?	*¿Qué haces?*
Do you know those people over there?	*¿Conoces a esa gente de allí?*
How old are they?	*¿Qué edad tienen?*
What's he / she like?	*¿Qué te parece él/ella? / Cómo es él/ella?*
Shall we go and talk to …?	*¿Por qué no vamos y hablamos a...?*
Do you like dancing?	*¿Te gusta bailar?*
She's a really good dancer.	*Ella baila muy bien.*
The music is so loud.	*La música está muy alta.*
I can't hear what you're saying.	*No puedo oír lo que dices.*

PARTIES & CLUBS cont. DRINKS	*FIESTAS Y BARES cont.* *BEBIDAS*
Shall we go to the bar?	*¿Vamos al bar?*
Which bar shall we go to?	*¿A qué bar podemos ir?*
Would you like a drink?	*¿Quieres beber algo?*
What would you like to drink?	*¿Qué quieres beber?*
I'd like a coke / a beer.	*Quiero una coca-cola / una cerveza.*
I'll have what you're having.	*Quiero tomar lo que tú tomes.*
You have to be eighteen.	*Tienes que tener dieciocho años.*
The drinks are very expensive.	*Las bebidas son muy caras.*

GETTING HOME AFTERWARDS	*YENDO A CASA DESPUES*
What time do you have to leave?	*¿A qué hora tienes que irte?*
What time does the club shut?	*¿A qué hora cierra el bar?*
What time does the party finish?	*¿A qué hora se termina la fiesta?*
Are you being picked up?	*¿Te van a recoger?*
Yes, I'm being picked up at one.	*Sí, me van a recoger a la una.*
How are you getting home?	*¿Cómo vas a ir a casa?*
Do you want a lift with us?	*¿Quieres que te acerque yo?*
Could I possibly have a lift in your car?	*¿Me podeis llevar en tu coche? Podríais acarrearme en su coche?*
Should we share a taxi?	*¿Compartimos un taxi?*
Which bus / train are you getting?	*¿Qué autobús / tren vas a coger?*
Can I see you again sometime?	*¿Nos podemos ver en otra ocasión?*
Should we go somewhere together tomorrow night?	*¿Quieres que salgamos juntos mañana por la noche?*
Would you like to go to the cinema with us tomorrow?	*¿Quieres venir al cine con nosotros mañana?*
Shall we go and get something to eat?	*¿Vamos y tomamos algo de comer?*

FAIR, CIRCUS & ZOO
FERIA, CIRCO & ZOO

THE FAIR — *LA FERIA*

USEFUL EXPRESSIONS — *EXPRESIONES UTILES*

There is a fair on - would you like to go?	*Hay una feria – ¿Quieres que vayamos?*
What rides do you like?	*¿Qué atracciones te gustan?*
Which rides would you like to go on?	*¿En qué atracciones quieres montar?*
How much money have you got to spend?	*¿Cuánto dinero puedes gastar?*
How much is it to go on the dodgems?	*¿Cuánto cuesta montar en los coches de choque?*
Should we have another go on that?	*¿Montamos otra vez en eso?*
What would you like to go on next?	*¿En qué montamos después?*
What time do we have to be home by?	*¿A qué hora tenemos que estar de vuelta en casa?*
If we get separated, shall we meet by the big wheel?	*Sí nos perdemos, nos encontramos cerca de la noria.*

THE RIDES — *LAS ATRACCIONES*

The Ferris Wheel	***La Noria***
Shall we sit together?	*¿Nos sentamos juntos?*

FAIRGROUND RIDES cont. ***APARATOS DE FERIA cont.***

The Ghost Train	***El Tren de la Bruja***
It's very dark.	*Está muy oscuro*
I can't see.	*No puedo ver.*
I am frightened.	*Tengo miedo.*
Hold my hand.	*Sujeta mi mano.*
It will be over in a minute.	*Vuelvo en un minuto.*

The Dodgems	***Los Coches de Choque***
to wait for them to stop	*esperar a que se paren*
to climb in	*montarse*
to put your seat belt on	*ponerse el cinturón de seguridad*
to steer	*moverse / conducir / guiar*
to turn the wheel	*dar la vuelta al volante*
to the left / to the right	*a la izquierda / a la derecha*
to go round in circles	*dar vueltas en círculos*
to go the other way	*ir en la otra dirección*
to accelerate	*acelerar*
to chase	*perseguir*
to get stuck	*quedarse atrapado*
to hit / to bump	*golpear / chocar*
Let's try to bump them.	*Vamos a chocar contra ellos.*
Please don't bump us.	*Por favor no choqueis contra nosotros.*

The Waltzers	***Las Tazas Locas***
Where do you want to sit?	*¿Dónde te quieres sentar?*
Can I sit in the middle, please?	*¿Me puedo sentar en el medio, por favor?*
You're squashing me.	*¿Me estás apretando / estrujando?*
Please twirl us some more.	*Por favor, darnos más vueltas / gíranos un poco más.*
Please don't do that.	*Por favor, no hagas eso.*

FAIRGROUND RIDES cont. / *APARATOS DE FERIA cont.*

The Merry-go-Round	***Los Caballitos / El tiovivo***
Which horse / animal would you like to go on?	*¿En qué caballo / animal te quieres montar?*
Do you like to be on the inside or the outside?	*¿Quieres montarte en el interior o en el exterior?*

The Rollercoaster	***La montaña Rusa***
to scream	*gritar*
to feel sick	*sentir náuseas*
to hate it / to love it	*odiarla / encantarte*
to loop the loop	*rizar el rizo*
to be upside down	*estar boca abajo*

The Helter Skelter	***Los escurridores gigantes***
to take a mat	*coger una alfombrilla*
to climb to the top	*subir a la cumbre*
to slide down	*escurrirse*

A Centrifuge	***El Pulpo***
the centrifugal force	*la fuerza centrífuga*
to be pinned to the side	*ser empujado hacia un lateral*

A Simulator	***Un simulador***
realistic	*realista*
not very realistic	*no muy convincente*

THE FAIR cont. *LA FERIA cont.*

Darts and the rifle range	***Dardos y escopetillas de ferias***
a dart	*un dardo*
a dartboard	*una diana*
to throw	*tirar*
to aim	*atinar*
to score	*puntuar*
a gun / a rifle	*una pistola / un rifle*
to point	*apuntar*
to shoot	*disparar*
the target	*el objetivo*
to hit / to miss	*golpear / perder*
to hit the bull's eye	*dar en el blanco*
I need twenty more.	*Necesito veinte más.*
I have to score one hundred.	*Tener que marcar cien.*

Hoopla	***Los Aros / Las Anillas***
to throw the ring	*tirar una anilla*
to get the ring over	*poner la anilla por encima*
nearly	*casi*
to win	*ganar*

A Coconut Shy	***Un Tiro al Coco***
to throw a ball	*tirar la bola*
to try to hit	*intentar golpear*
to throw harder	*tirar más fuerte*
to make it wobble	*hacer que se tambalee / hacer tambalear*
to knock it down	*derribarlo*
to fall off	*caer*
to win a coconut	*ganar un coco*

THE FAIR cont. — *LA FERIA cont.*

WINNING PRIZES — *LOS PREMIOS PARA GANADORES*

Well done!	*¡Bien hecho!*
What prize would you like?	*¿Qué premio quieres?*
I would like a..	*Quisiera un...*
• goldfish	• *pez de colores*
• a teddybear	• *un osito de peluche*
• one of those	• *uno de esos*
Have you won anything yet?	*¿Has ganado algo ya?*
Yes, I've won this.	*Sí, he ganado esto.*
No, I never win anything.	*No, nunca gano nada.*

THE GAMES ARCADE — *LOS JUEGOS*

I haven't any change.	*No tengo cambio.*
Where do you get change from?	*¿Dónde se cambia dinero?*
There is a change machine over there.	*¿Hay una máquina para cambiar dinero allí?*
What coins does this game take?	*¿Qué monedas se necesitan para este juego?*
a fruit machine	*una fruit machine*
a pinball machine	*un flíper*
Where do you put the money in?	*¿Dónde se pone la moneda?*
How do you play?	*¿Cómo se juega?*
You have to…	*Tienes que...*
to roll a coin	*rodar la moneda*
to make it land on..	*hacer que caiga en...*
to pull this handle	*mover esta palanca*
to press this button	*apretar este botón*

THE FAIR cont. — *LA FERIA cont.*

FOOD — *LA COMIDA*

Candy Floss	***Algodón Azucarado***
on a stick	*en palo*
in a bag	*en una bolsa*
pink	*rosa*
yellow	*amarillo*

Hot Dogs	***Perritos Calientes (m)***
Do you want your hot dog with..?	*¿Quieres el perrito caliente con...*
• mustard	• *mostaza (f)*
• tomato ketchup	• *ketchup (f) / catsup (m)*
• fried onions	• *cebollas (f)*
• plain	• *solo*
• a lot of	• *muchos(as)*
• just a little	• *un poquito de*
• no onions, thanks.	• *sin cebollas, gracias.*

Popcorn	***Palomitas de Maíz (f.pl)***
a bag of	*una bolsa de*
a carton of	*un cucurucho de*
large / medium / small	*grande / mediano / pequeño(a)*
sweet	*dulce*
salted	*salado*
Would you like some of my popcorn?	*¿Quieres palomitas?*

THE FAIR cont. — *LA FERIA cont.*

PROBLEMS — *PROBLEMAS*

a pickpocket	*un ladrón*
My money has been stolen.	*Me han robado el dinero.*
Take care of your money.	*Ten cuidado con tu dinero.*
My purse / wallet has disappeared.	*Mi monedero / cartera ha desaparecido.*
I feel dizzy / a bit sick.	*Me estoy mareando / siento náuseas.*
It's rather noisy.	*Hay mucho ruido.*
Can we go home soon?	*¿Podemos volver a casa pronto?*

USEFUL ADJECTIVES — *ADJETIVOS UTILES*

amusing	*gracioso(a)*	fun	*diversión(noun)*
awful	*horrible*	funny	*divertido*
dizzy	*mareado(a)*	horrible	*horrible*
excellent	*excelente*	terrible	*terrible / malo*
fantastic	*fantástico(a)*	terrifying	*terrorífico(a)*
frightening	*que da miedo*		

THE CIRCUS — *EL CIRCO*

THE BIG TOP — *LA CARPA*

the ring	*el circo*
sawdust	*el serrín*
the seats	*los asientos*

THE PEOPLE — *LA GENTE*

The Ring Master	***El presentador***
a top hat	*un sombrero de copa*
a whip / to crack the whip	*un látigo / dar un latigazo*

THE CIRCUS - THE PEOPLE cont

EL CIRCO - LA GENTE cont.

The Clown	***El Payaso***
a big nose	*una nariz grande*
big feet	*unos pies grandes*
to walk on stilts	*andar sobre zancos*
to ride a monocycle	*montar una motocicleta*
to trip up	*tropezar*
to fall down	*caer*
to squirt water	*echar agua*
to make people laugh	*hacer reír a la gente*

The Acrobats	***Los Acróbatas***
a trapeze artist	*un trapecista*
the high wire	*un alambre*
a safety net	*la red de seguridad*
a ladder	*una escalera*
a swing / to swing	*un tobogán / balancearse*
to balance	*balancearse*
to wobble	*tambalearse / perder el equilibrio*
to fall	*caer*

Other Circus Performers	***Otros artistas de Circo***
a bareback rider	*un montador de caballos*
a lion tamer	*un domador de leones*

CIRCUS ANIMALS

LOS ANIMALES CIRCENSES

a horse	*un caballo*
a lion	*un león*
an elephant	*un elefante*

THE ZOO — *EL ZOO*

PARTS OF THE ZOO — *PARTES DEL ZOO*

the elephant house	*la casa de los elefantes*
the aquarium	*el acuario / el acuárium*
a tank	*el tanque*
the cages / the monkeys' cage	*las jaulas / la jaula de los monos*
the reptile house	*las jaulas de los reptiles*
the model train	*el trenecillo*
Would you like a ride on the model train?	*¿Te gustaría montar en el trenecillo?*
Do you want to go to the adventure playground?	*¿Quieres ir al parque de aventuras?*
a lake / an island	*un lago / una isla*
the cafeteria / the toilets	*la cafetería / los servicios*

THE ANIMALS (abc) — *LOS ANIMALES*

a bat	*un murciélago*	a monkey	*un mono*
a bear	*un oso*	an ostrich	*una avestruz*
a crocodile	*un cocodrilo*	a panda	*un oso Panda*
a dolphin	*un delfín*	a pelican	*un pelícano*
an elephant	*un elefante*	a penguin	*un pingüino*
an emu	*un emú*	a rhinoceros	*un rinoceronte*
a fish	*un pez*	a seal	*una foca*
a pink flamingo	*un flamenco rosa*	a snake	*una serpiente*
a giraffe	*una jirafa*	a tarantula	*una tarántula*
a hippopotamus	*un hipopótamo*	a tiger	*un tigre*
a kangaroo	*un kanguro*	a tortoise	*una tortuga*
a leopard	*un leopardo*	a turtle	*una galápago*
a lion	*un león*	a zebra	*una cebra*

SIGHTSEEING
VISITANDO / HACIENDO TURISMO

STATELY HOMES & CASTLES
CASERONES / CASAS SOLARIEGAS Y CASTILLOS

OPENING HOURS	*HORAS DE APERTURA AL PUBLICO*
What are your opening hours?	*¿Qué horas de apertura teneis?*
Are you open every day of the week?	*¿Abrís todos los días de la semana?*
How much is it to go round?	*¿Cuánto cuesta entrar?*
Is there a guided tour?	*¿Hay guías?*
What time is the tour?	*¿A qué hora empieza la visita con guía?*
Is there a commentary one can listen to?	*¿Hay comentarios en cinta para escuchar?*
Do you have the commentary in English / French / Spanish / German?	*¿Teneis cintas en inglés / francés / español / alemán?*
How do the headphones work?	*¿Cómo funcionan los auriculares?*
Could I have a guide book, please?	*¿Me puede dar una guía, por favor?*

COULD I HAVE A TICKET FOR...?	*¿ME DA UNA ENTRADA PARA?*
• the house only	• *la casa solo*
• the gardens only	• *los jardines solo*
• one adult	• *una para adulto*
• one student	• *una para estudiante*
Is there a reduction for students / groups?	*¿Hacen descuentos para estudiantes / grupos?*

STATELY HOMES & CASTLES cont. / *CASAS SOLARIEGAS Y CASTILLOS cont.*

ARCHITECTURAL STYLES / *ESTILOS ARQUITECTONICOS*

Who was the architect?	*¿Quién fue el arquitecto?*
What style was this built in?	*¿A qué estilo pertenece este edificio?*

English	Spanish	English	Spanish
Norman	*Normando*	Baroque	*Barroco*
medieval	*medieval*	Classical	*Clásico*
gothic	*gótico*	Georgian	*Georgiano*
Tudor	*Tudor*	Regency	*de Regencia*
Renaissance	*Renacentista*	Victorian	*Victoriano*

TYPES OF BUILDINGS / *TIPOS DE EDIFICACIONES*

(in approximately descending size)	*(en escala descendiente respecto al tamaño)*
a palace / a castle	*un palacio / un castillo*
a mansion / the manor house	*una mansión / un caserón*
the court	*???*
a priory / the chapel	*un priorato / una capilla*
the lodge	*la casa del guardia*
the gatehouse	*la caseta de entrada / la casa del vigilante / portero*
a folly	*???*
a conservatory	*un conservatorio*
a coach house	*una carrecería / una caballeriza*
(a coach)	*una carroza*
(a royal coach)	*una carroza real*
a thatched cottage	*una casa de campo con tejado de paja*
a stable	*un establo*
a greenhouse	*un invernadero*

STATELY HOMES & CASTLES cont. / *CASAS SOLARIEGAS Y CASTILLOS cont.*

EXTERNAL DETAILS	*DETALLES EXTERNOS*
(top downwards)	*(de arriba hacia abajo)*
a turret	*un torreón / una torre*
battlements / the parapet	*almenas / el parapeto*
a facade	*una fachada*
a balcony / the windows	*un balcón / las ventanas*
French windows	*puerta ventanas / contra ventanas*
the porch / the door	*el porche / la puerta*
a flight of steps	*un tramo de escalera*
a portcullis	*un rastrillo*
a drawbridge / a moat	*un puente elevadizo / un foso*
a rampart	*una muralla / una defensa / un terraplén*
the gateway / flood lighting	*el pasillo de entrada / focos*

THE PARK AND GARDENS		*EL PARQUE Y LOS JARDINES*	
the park	*el parque*	a path	*un camino*
the garden	*el jardín*	a terrace	*una terraza*
a formal garden	*un jardín francés*	an informal garden	*un jardín estilo inglés*
a rose garden	*un jardín de rosales*	a wild flower garden	*un jardín de flores salvajes*
a ha-ha	*un ha-ha*		

A MAZE	*UN LABERINTO*
to go in	*entrar*
to get lost	*perderse*
to turn back	*dar la vuelta*
to try to get out	*tratar de salir*
to find your way out	*encontrar la salida*
to be gone ages	*estar perdido por un largo rato*

STATELY HOMES & CASTLES cont.	*CASAS SOLARIEGAS Y CASTILLOS cont.*

GARDEN BUILDINGS AND ORNAMENTS	***EDIFICACIONES Y ADORNOS DE JARDIN***
a conservatory	*un conservatorio*
an orangery / a greenhouse	*un naranjal / un invernadero*
a dovecote / a dove	*un palomar / una paloma*
a statue	*una estatua*
an urn / a pedestal	*una urna / un pedestal*

WATER FEATURES	***RASGOS DISTINTIVOS DEL AGUA***
a lake / an island	*un lago / una isla*
a river	*un río*
a fountain	*una fuente*
a waterfall	*una cascada*
an ornamental pond	*un estanque ornamental*
water lilies	*nenúfares*
goldfish	*un pececillo de color*
a water garden	*un jardín de agua*
When are the fountains turned on?	*¿Cuándo se ponen las fuentes en marcha?*

HIRING BOATS	***ALQUILANDO BOTES***
a boat	*un bote / una barca*
a motorboat	*una lancha motora*
to go for a trip	*ir a dar una vuelta*
to start the engine	*arrancar*
a canoe / to go canoeing	*una canoa / montar en canoa*
a paddle / to paddle	*un patinete / montar en patinete*
on the right / left	*la derecha / a la izquierda*
to steer	*guiar / conducir*
to row	*remar*
to moor	*amarrar / echar las amarras*
to collide with someone	*chocar con alguien*
to try to avoid someone	*intentar evitar el choque*

STATELY HOMES & CASTLES cont.	***CASAS SOLARIEGAS Y CASTILLOS cont.***

THE TEA ROOM	***LA CAFETERIA / EL CAFE***
Where is the tea room?	*¿Dónde esta el café?*
Shall we have a cup of tea?	*¿Vamos a tomar una taza de té?*
Shall we take it into the garden?	*¿Salimos al jardín a tomarlo?*
Shall we stay inside?	*¿Nos quedamos dentro?*

THE GIFT SHOP	***LA TIENDA DE REGALOS***
Do you want to look round the gift shop?	*¿Quieres echar un vistazo en la tienda de regalos?*
Do you want to buy something for your family?	*¿Quieres comprar algo para tu familia?*
Would you like to buy some postcards?	*¿Quieres comprar postales?*

INTERNAL DETAILS	***DETALLES DE INTERIOR***
THE MAIN ROOMS	***LAS HABITACIONES PRINCIPALES***
(in descending importance)	*(en orden descendiente de importancia)*

THE MAIN HALL	***EL RECIBIDOR / HALL PRINCIPAL (m)***
a suit of armour	*una armadura*
chain mail	*cota de malla (f)*
heraldry	*heráldica (f)*
a coat of arms	*un escudo / un emblema nobiliario*
weapons	*armas (f)*
guns / pistols	*pistolas (f)*
swords / shields	*espadas (f) / escudos (m)*

STATELY HOMES & CASTLES cont. / *CASAS SOLARIEGAS Y CASTILLOS cont.*

THE STATEROOM		***EL CUARTO DE ESTAR***	
the mirrors	*los espejos*	the plasterwork	*la escayola*
the portraits	*los retratos*	a mural	*un mural*
the paintings	*los cuadros*	a fresco	*un fresco*
a bust	*un busto*	the carpet	*la alfombra*
the fireplace	*la chimenea*	the curtains	*las cortinas*
the ceiling	*el techo*	the furniture	*los muebles*

THE BALLROOM	***LA SALA DE BAILE***
the chandelier	*la araña / el chandelier*
the mirrors	*los espejos*

THE BANQUETING HALL		***LA SALA DE BANQUETES***	
the dining table	*el comedor*	the silver	*la plata*
the chairs	*las sillas*	the tureens	*las soperas*
a dinner service	*el servicio de cena*	a banquet	*un banquete*

THE DRAWING ROOM	***EL ESTUDIO***
the panelling	*los paneles de madera*
a grandfather clock	*el reloj de pie*
the sofas	*los sofas*
the armchairs	*los sillones*
a tapestry	*el tapiz (un tapiz)*
porcelain	*la porcelana*

THE LIBRARY	***LA BIBLIOTECA***
the bookcases	*las estanterías*
valuable books	*libros de valor*
antique books	*libros antiguos*
a family tree	*un árbol de familia / un árbol genealógico*

STATELY HOMES & CASTLES cont. — ***CASAS SOLARIEGAS Y CASTILLOS cont.***

THE MUSIC ROOM		*LA HABITACION PARA LA MUSICA*	
a harpsichord	*un clavecín*	a harp	*un arpa*

THE STAIRCASE & GALLERY	*LAS ESCALERAS Y LA GALERIA*
a spiral staircase	*una escalera de caracol*
a back staircase	*una escalera de servicio / de atrás*
a minstrels' gallery	*una elevación para músicos / una galería de músicos*
a servants' staircase	*una escalera de servicio*
a secret staircase	*un pasadizo secreto*
to look down on	*mirar hacia abajo*

THE NURSERY	*LA HABITACION DE LOS NINOS*
a cradle / a cot / a dolls' house	*una cuna / una casa de muñecas*
toys / a desk	*juguetes / un pupitre*
a rocking horse	*un caballito de juguete / un balancín de caballo*

THE KITCHEN	*LA COCINA*
a fireplace / an inglenook	*una chimenea / una rinconera*
a hook / a rotisserie	*un gancho / una rotisserie*
a spit	*un asador / un espetón*
to turn / to cook / the cook	*dar la vuelta/ cocinar/ el cocinero*
the range / to smoke	*el fogón / hacer homo / ahumar*
a kitchen table	*una mesa de cocina*
pots and pans / utensils	*sartenes y cazos / los utensilios*
copper / pewter	*de cobre / de zinc*
the sink / the cold store	*el fregadero / la alacena*
a dumb waiter	*un montaplatos*

STATELY HOMES & CASTLES cont. / *CASAS SOLARIEGAS Y CASTILLOS cont.*

OTHER ROOMS	*OTRAS HABITACIONES*
Servants' accommodation	***Las habitaciones para criados***
the servants' rooms	*las habitaciones de los criados*
the attic	*el ático / la buhardilla*
The cellar	***El Sótano***
a wine cellar	*una bodegilla*
The dungeons	***Las Mazmorras / Los Calabozos***
the torture chamber	*la cámara de torturas*
a chamber of horrors	*una cámara de los horrores*

THE ROYAL FAMILY		*LA FAMILIA REAL*	
a King	*un rey*	a Prince	*un príncipe*
a Queen	*una reina*	a Princess	*una princesa*
the Queen Mother	*la reina madre*	a Duke / Duchess	*un duque / una duquesa*

THE SERVANTS	*LOS SIRVIENTES / LOS CRIADOS*
the butler	*el mayordomo*
the chef / the cook	*el cocinero / chef*
the footmen	*los lacayos*
a maidservant	*un sirviente de la señora*
a manservant	*un sirviente del señor*

STATELY HOMES & CASTLES cont. / *CASAS SOLARIEGAS Y CASTILLOS cont.*

USEFUL DESCRIPTIVE WORDS (abc)		***PALABRAS UTILES PARA DESCRIBIR***	
added on	*añadido(a)*	dilapidated	*demolido(a)*
ancient	*viejo / antiguo(a)*	dusty	*polvoriento(a)*
attractive	*atractivo / llamativo*	elegant	*elegante*
austere	*austero(a)*	expensive	*caro(a)*
authentic	*auténtico(a)*	faded	*descolorido(a)*
baroque	*barroco(a)*	gold	*oro*
beautiful	*bonito(a)*	gothic	*gótico(a)*
built by	*construido(a) por*	imposing	*impresionante*
burnt down	*quemado(a)*	in ruins	*en ruinas*
century	*siglo*	luxurious	*lujoso(a)*
eleventh	*once*	modern	*moderno(a)*
twelfth	*doce*	modernised	*modernizado(a)*
thirteenth	*trece*	old	*viejo(a)*
fourteenth	*catorce*	ornate	*adornado(a)*
fifteenth	*quince*	over-restored	*demasiado restaurado(a)*
sixteenth	*dieciséis*	rare	*raro(a)*
seventeenth	*diecisiete*	rebuilt	*reconstruido(a)*
eighteenth	*dieciocho*	reclaimed	*reclamado(a)*
nineteenth	*diecinueve*	restored by	*restaurado por*
twentieth	*veinte*	ruined	*en ruinas / arruinado*
twenty first	*veintiuno*	splendid	*espléndido(a)*
charming	*encantador*	sumptuous	*suntuoso(a)*
commonplace	*normal / corriente*	valuable	*valioso(a)*
designed by	*diseñado por*	wonderful	*maravilloso(a)*

CHURCHES *IGLESIAS*

ARCHITECTURAL CLASSIFICATIONS		*CLASIFICACION ARQUITECTONICA*	
Romanesque	*Románica*	Flamboyant	*Extravagante / Flamboyant*
Saxon	*Periodo de los Saxons*	Jacobean	*Jacobea*
Norman	*Periodo Normando*	Renaissance	*Renacentista*
Gothic	*Gótica*	Baroque	*Barroca*
Early English	*Temprano estilo inglés*	Classical	*Clásica*
Decorated	*Decorado*	Georgian	*Georgiana*
Perpendicular	*Perpendicular*	Victorian	*Victoriana*
Tudor	*Tudor*		

EXTERNAL DETAILS		*DETALLES EXTERNOS*	
a buttress	*un contrafuerte*	the churchyard	*un cementerio*
a flying buttress	*un contrafuerte*	a grave	*una tumba*
a gargoyle	*un gárgola*	a tombstone	*una tumba de piedra*
a pinnacle	*un pináculo*	an inscription	*una inscripción*
a spire	*una aguja*	to read	*leer*
a tower	*una torre*	Roman	*números*
a weathercock	*una veleta*	numerals	*romanos*

CHURCHES cont. — *IGLESIAS cont.*

INTERNAL DETAILS (abc)	*DETALLES INTERNOS*
the Lady Chapel	*la capilla de la Virgen*
alabaster / marble	*alabastro / mármol*
an arcade / an arch / the aisle	*un claustro / an arco / el pasillo*
the altar / to kneel at	*el altar / ponerse de rodillas ante*
(to pray)	*(rezar)*
the bell tower	*la torre del campanario*
to ring the bells	*tocar las campanas*
a candle / to buy	*un candelabro / comprar*
(to light)	*(encender / prender)*
the chancel / the choir	*el coro y el presbiterio / el coro*
a choir stall	*un coro*
a column	*una columna*
The Cross	*la cruz*
the crypt	*la cripta*
the door	*la puerta*
the font	*el frontal*
(a Baptism)	*(una pila bautismal / un bautismo)*
(a Christening)	*(un bautismo)*
a fresco / a mural	*un fresco / un mural*
the lectern / the pulpit	*el atrio / el púlpito*
(to give a sermon) / (to preach)	*(dar un sermon) / (dar un servicio)*
the nave	*la nave*
a niche	*un nicho*
the organ / to play the organ	*el órgano / tocar el órgano*
the organist	*el organista*
a pew	*un banco de iglesia*
a pillar	*un pilar*
the porch	*el pórtico*
the roof / a vault / a beam	*el tejado / una cripta / una viga*
a statue	*una estatua*
a tomb	*una tumba*
the transept	*el crucero*
a window / stained glass	*una ventana / vidriera (f)*

CHURCHES cont. / *IGLESIAS cont.*

USEFUL DESCRIPTIVE WORDS (abc)	***PALABRAS UTILES PARA DESCRIBIR***
cold	*frío(a)*
dark	*oscuro(a)*
dilapidated	*ruinoso / desvencijado*
elegant	*elegante / majestuoso(a)*
humble	*humilde*
intricate	*complicado(a)*
locked-up	*cerrado(a)*
musty	*que huele a cerrado / antiguo(a)*
open	*abierto(a)*
ornate	*decorado(a)*
peaceful	*tranquilo(a)*
rich	*rico(a)*
rural	*rural*
sombre	*sombrío(a)*

ART GALLERIES & EXHIBITIONS
GALERIAS DE ARTE Y EXPOSICIONES

ART GALLERIES	*GALERIAS DE ARTE*
an art collection	*una colección de arte*
an artist	*un artista*
a work of art	*un trabajo de arte / una obra de arte*
a painting	*un cuadro*
a private view	*una exposición a puerta cerrada*
an invitation	*una invitación*

MUSEUMS	*MUSEOS*
an exhibition	*una exposición*
an exhibit	*una exhibición*

USEFUL EXPRESSIONS	*EXPRESIONES UTILES*
There is an interesting exhibition on at the moment.	*Hay una exposición interesante en este momento.*
Would you like to go to it?	*¿Te gustaría ir?*
Is there a catalogue?	*¿Hay catálogo? ¿Tienes un catálogo?*
How much is an entrance ticket?	*¿Cuánto vale la entrada?*
Is there a reduction for students?	*¿Hacen descuentos para estudiantes?*
Entrance is free.	*La entrada es gratuita.*
How much do guide books cost?	*¿Cuánto valen las guías?*
How much are these postcards?	*¿Cuánto son las postales?*
Do you have a guide book in English / French / German / French?	*¿Hay guías en inglés / francés / alemán / español?*
Shall we split up and meet here in half an hour?	*¿Quieres ir por tu cuenta y encontrarnos aquí en media hora?*

ART GALLERIES cont. / *GALERIAS DE ARTE cont.*

WHO / WHAT IS YOUR FAVOURITE..?		***¿QUIEN / CUAL TE GUSTA MAS?***	
artist	*artista*	painting	*cuadro*
sculptor	*escultor*	piece of sculpture	*escultura*

Which artist / sculptor do you like most?	*¿Qué artista / escultor te gusta más?*
Which is your favourite artist / sculptor?	*¿Cuál es tu artista / escultor favorito?*
Which painting / piece of sculpture do you like most?	*¿Qué cuadro / escultura te gusta más?*
What is your favourite painting / piece of sculpture?	*¿Cuál es tu cuadro / escultura favorito / favorita?*

WHAT TYPE OF ART DO YOU LIKE MOST? (abc)		***¿QUE TIPOS DE ARTE TE GUSTA MAS?***	
abstract art	*arte abstracto*	post-impressionism	*post impresionismo*
art deco	*art deco*	Pre-Raphaelite	*Los Pre-rafaelistas*
classical art	*arte clásico*	primitive art	*arte primitivo*
cubism	*cubismo*	prints	*impresiones*
engravings	*grabados*	realism	*realismo*
etchings	*aguafuerte*	religious art	*arte religioso*
expressionism	*expresionismo*	romantic art	*arte*
impressionism	*impresionismo*	seascapes	*paisajes marinos*
landscapes	*paisajes*	self portraits	*auto retratos*
life drawings	*dibujos de modelos*	sporting works	*pinturas sobre deportes*
miniatures	*miniaturas*	still life	*bodegones*
nudes	*desnudos*	surrealism	*surrealismo*
oil paintings	*óleos*	symbolism	*simbolismo*
pastels	*pasteles*	townscapes	*paisajes rurales*
pop art	*pop art / arte pop*	water colours	*acuarelas*
portraits	*retratos*	wood cuttings	*grabados en madera*

ART GALLERIES cont. / *GALERIAS DE ARTE cont.*

WHAT IS YOUR FAVOURITE PERIOD?	***¿CUAL ES TU PERIODO FAVORITO?***
My favourite period is..	*Mi periodo favorito es...*
medieval	*el medievo*
Renaissance	*el Renacimiento*
High Renaissance	*el Renacimiento Tardío*
Baroque	*el Barroco*
eighteenth century	*el siglo dieciocho*
nineteenth century	*el siglo diecinueve*
twentieth century	*el siglo veinte*

WHAT IS YOUR FAVOURITE MEDIUM?		***¿CUAL ES TU MATERIAL FAVORITO?***	
I particularly like..		*me gusta en particular...*	
acrylics	*la pintura acrílica*	oil	*el oleo*
chalk	*la tiza gris*	pastels	*los pasteles*
charcoal	*el carboncillo*	tempera	*la Tempera*
crayon	*el lápiz de tiza / de color*	water colours	*la acuarela*
gouache	*el gouache*		

POSSIBLE POINTS FOR DISCUSSION (abc)	***POSIBLES TEMAS DE CHARLA / DISCUSION***
the allegorical meaning	*el significado alegórico*
the background / the foreground	*el fondo / el primer plano*
the colour	*el color*
the delicacy	*la delicadeza*
the effect on the viewer	*el efecto en el visitante / espectador*
the emotion	*la emoción*
the focus	*el foco*
the grouping	*el conjunto*
the light and shade	*la luz y sombra*
the meaning	*el significado*
the obscurity	*la oscuridad*

ART GALLERIES cont. / *GALERIAS DE ARTE cont.*

POSSIBLE POINTS FOR DISCUSSION (abc)	*POSIBLES TEMAS DE CHARLA / DISCUSION*
the poses	*las poses*
the power	*el poder*
the structure	*la estructura*
the subtlety	*la sutileza*
the suffering	*el sufrimiento*
the symbolism	*el simbolismo*
the technique	*la técnica*
the use of perspective	*el uso de la perspectiva*
the vanishing point	*el punto de fuga*

BASIC ART EQUIPMENT		*EQUIPO BASICO ARTISTICO*	
an easel	*un caballete*	a palette knife	*una espátula*
paper	*papel*	a pencil	*un lápiz*
canvas	*un lienzo*	a rubber	*una goma*
paints	*pinturas*	a water pot	*un recipiente para el agua*
a paintbrush	*una brocha / un pincel*	white spirit	*aguarrás*

PAINTING METHODS		*METODOS PICTORICOS*	
to blend	*mezclar*	to mix	*mezclar*
to copy	*copiar*	to paint over	*repintar / pintar encima*
to dab	*dar unos toques*	to re-paint	*repintar*
to dip	*impregnar*	to sketch	*hacer un croquis*
to glaze	*vidriar / barnizar*	to varnish	*barnizar*
to imitate	*imitar*	to wash	*lavar / limpiar*

ART GALLERIES cont. / *GALERIAS DE ARTE cont.*

ART CLASSIFICATIONS	*CLASIFICACIONES EN ARTE*
Fine Art	*Bellas Artes*
Applied Art	*Arte Aplicado*
jewellery	*joyería*
silversmithing	*platería*
porcelain making	*porcelana*
metalwork	*metalistería*
pottery	*alfarería / cerámica*
Decorative Art	*Artes Decorativos*
embroidery	*bordados*
tapestry	*tapices*

VINEYARDS
VIÑEDOS / VIÑAS

THE VINEYARD	*EL VIÑEDO / LA VIÑA*
a château	*un chateau*

THE VINES	*LAS VIDES / LAS PARRAS*
a grapevine	*una parra / la vid*
a bunch of grapes	*un ramo de uvas*
a grape	*una uva*
green / purple	*verde / tinta*

VINEYARDS cont. / *VIÑEDOS / VIÑAS cont.*

PICKING THE GRAPES	*RECOLECCION DE UVA*
ripe	*maduro*
unripe	*inmaduro, verde*
to harvest	*cosechar*
to pick	*recoger*
to gather	*recolectar*
to press	*exprimir*
the juice	*el jugo / el zumo*

STORING THE WINE		*RECOGIENDO EL VINO*	
a barrel	*un barril*	to ferment	*para fermentar*
wooden	*de madera*	fermentation	*fermentación*
oak	*roble*	to bottle	*embotellar*
steel	*acero*	a bottle	*una botella*
a vat	*una tinaja*	to label	*calificar*
a vatful	*bodega*	a label	*una etiqueta*

CLASSIFYING WINE	*CLASIFICANDO EL VINO*
an officially classified wine	*vino clasificado*
alcoholic content	*alcohólico contenido*
vintage / a good year / a bad year	*cosecha / un buen /un mal año*
country of origin	*país de origen*
region	*región*
a table wine	*vino de mesa*
red wine / white wine / rosé	*vino tinto/ blanco / rosado*
sweet wine / dry wine	*vino dulce / vino seco*
sparkling wine	*vino espumoso*
Spanish / French champagne	*cava / champán*
fortified wine	*vino fortalecido / vino fortificado*
an aperitif	*un aperitivo*
sherry	*vino de jerez / un jerez*
vermouth	*vermut*

VINEYARDS cont. / *VINEDOS / VINAS cont.*

SERVING WINE	*SERVIENDO EL VINO*
to serve at the right temperature	*servir a la ideal temperatura*
to chill	*enfriar*
to keep at room temperature	*mantener a la temperatura de ambiente*
to open a bottle	*abrir una botella*
to uncork	*descorchar*
a corkscrew	*sacacorchos*
to decant	*decantar*
sediment	*poso (m)*
to allow to breathe	*dejar respirar*
to pour	*verter*

TASTING WINE	*CATANDO VINOS*
a wine tasting	*una cata de vinos*
to savour	*saborear / catar*
the bouquet	*el bouquet*
the colour	*el color*
to hold up to the light	*mirar al trasluz*
to hold in the mouth	*probar / catar en la boca*
to spit	*escupir*
a spittoon	*una escupidera*
to sample	*catar*
to identify	*identificar*
to appreciate	*apreciar*
to have a good palate	*tener un buen paladar*

WALKS — *PASEOS*

A WALK	***UN PASEO***
Would you like to go for a walk?	*¿Te gustaría dar un paseo?*
How far do you feel like going?	*¿Hasta dónde quieres ir?*
Where would you like to go to?	*¿Dónde quieres ir?*
Do you like walking?	*¿Te gusta andar?*

TAKING THE DOG	***SACANDO AL PERRO***
I'm taking the dog for a walk.	*Voy a sacar al perro de paseo.*
Would you like to come?	*¿Quieres venirte?*
Where is its lead?	*¿Dónde está la correa?*
How do you put on its lead?	*¿Cómo le pones la correa?*
May I hold the lead?	*¿Puedo llevar la correa?*
Don't let it off the lead here.	*No le sueltes aquí.*
You can let it off the lead now.	*Aquí le puedes soltar.*
Dogs must be kept on the lead.	*Se prohibe dejar perros sueltos.*

CLOTHES — *ROPAS*

Footwear	***Calzado (m)***
socks	*calcetines (m)*
shoes	*zapatos (m)*
boots	*botas (f)*
wellingtons	*batas de agua / botas de goma*
Have you any walking shoes / boots / wellingtons with you?	*Tienes zapatos para andar (ir de paseo) / botas de agua?*
Would you like to borrow a pair of wellingtons?	*¿Quieres que te preste un par de botas de agua?*
We may have some that fit you.	*Quizá tenemos un par para tí.*
Try these.	*Pruébete éstas.*
Are they comfortable?	*¿Son cómodas?*
Do they fit?	*¿Son tu talla?*
They are too small / too big.	*Son demasiado pequeños / demasiado grandes.*

WALKS cont. — *PASEOS cont.*

Clothes for bad weather	***Ropa para el mal tiempo***
Bring…	*trae...*
a coat	*un abrigo*
a jacket	*una chaqueta*
a mackintosh	*un impermeable*
a pullover / a sweater	*un jersey / un suéter*
trousers	*pantalones (m)*
a hat	*un sombrero*
a scarf	*una bufanda*
a pair of gloves	*un par de guantes*
an umbrella	*un paraguas*
spare clothes	*ropa para cambiarte*

PICNICS	***PICNICS***
Shall we take a picnic?	*¿Nos llevamos cosas para hacer un picnic?*
Help me pack the picnic.	*Ayúdame a preparar las cosas para el picnic.*
What would you like to eat and drink?	*¿Qué te gustaría comer y beber?*
Shall we stop for something to eat and drink now?	*¿Hacemos una parada para comer y beber algo?*
Shall we take a rug?	*¿No llevamos una alfombrilla / esterilla?*
to sit down for a while	*sentarse un rato*

PICNIC FOOD & DRINK	***COMIDA Y BEBIDA PARA PICNICS***
a flask	*un termo*
to fill	*llenar*
to pour	*echar*
a hot drink	*una bebida caliente*
a cold drink	*una bebida fría*
to be thirsty	*estar sediento / tener sed*
to be hungry	*estar hambriento / tener hambre*

WALKS cont. / *PASEOS cont.*

PICNIC FOOD & DRINK cont. / *COMIDA Y BEBIDA PARA PICNICS cont.*

sandwiches	*bocadillos (m)*
What do you want on your sandwiches?	*¿Qué quieres poner en tu bocadillo?*
ham / chicken / salami / cheese / fish / salad / tomato / egg / mayonnaise	*jamón / pollo / salami (salchichón) / queso / pescado / ensalada / tomate / huevo / mayonesa*
a packet of crisps	*una bolsa de patatas*
a piece of cake	*un pedazo de tarta*
some fruit	*fruta (f)*
an apple / a banana / an orange / some grapes	*una manzana / un plátano / una naranja / uvas*
a bar of chocolate	*una tableta de chocolate*
Would you like a piece of chocolate?	*¿Quieres una onza de chocolate?*

DISCUSSING THE ROUTE	*ACORDANDO LA RUTA*
a plan / a sketch / a map	*un plano / un croquis / un mapa*
directions	*direcciones (f)*
Where are we? How far is that?	*¿Dónde estamos? ¿Está lejos?*
Show me where we are going to go.	*¿Muéstrame dónde vamos a ir?*
Are we lost?	*¿Nos hemos perdido?*
Are we going in the right / wrong direction?	*¿Vamos en buena dirección / en una dirección equivocada?*
Shall we ask someone?	*¿Por qué no preguntamos a alguien?*
to use a compass	*usar una brújula*
the needle / to point	*la aguja / apuntar*
North / South / East / West	*Norte / Sur / Este / Oeste*
We need to go in this direction.	*Tenemos que ir en esta dirección*

WALKS cont. / *PASEOS cont.*

PROBLEMS	*PROBLEMAS*
Is there a telephone box?	*¿Hay una cabina telefónica?*
Could we possibly use your telephone, please?	*¿Podemos usar tu teléfono, por favor?*
We are lost.	*Estamos perdidos.*
We are trying to get to…	*Queremos ir a... / estamos intentando llegar a...*
Where is the pub?	*¿Dónde esta el bar?*
Is there a village shop?	*¿Hay una tienda en el pueblo?*
I am tired.	*Estoy cansado(a)*
My legs are aching.	*Me duelen las piernas.*
I have a blister.	*Tengo una ampolla.*
My shoes are rubbing.	*Los zapatos me hacen rozadura.*
I fell over.	*Me caí.*
It's just a graze.	*Es sólo un rasguño.*
Have you a sticking plaster / an Elastoplast? ®	*¿Tienes una tirita / un esparadrapo?*
I hurt my foot / leg / hand / arm / back.	*Me he hecho daño en el pie / la pierna / el brazo / la espalda.*
I have sprained my ankle.	*Me he torcido el tobillo.*
I have been stung.	*Me ha picado algo.*
I have been bitten by something.	*Me ha mordido algo.*
Have you anything to put on a sting?	*¿Tienes algo para ponerlo en cabestrillo?*
Have you any fly repellent?	*¿Tienes un repelente de insectos? / ¿Tienes un matamoscas?*

WALKS cont. — *PASEOS cont.*

LANDMARKS — *LUGARES CONOCIDOS*

BUILDINGS etc (abc)	*EDIFICIOS*
a chemist's shop	*una farmacia*
the church	*la iglesia*
a cottage	*una casa de campo*
the graveyard	*un viñedo / una viña*
a house	*una casa*
the manor house	*una casa solariega / una casona*
a newsagent's shop	*un kiosco*
the playground	*un patio de recreo*
the police station	*una comisaría*
a post box	*un buzón*
the post office	*una oficina de correos*
the railway station	*una estación de trenes*
the recreation ground	*un parque recreativo*
a shop	*una tienda*
the telephone box	*una cabina de teléfono*
the village green	*el parque del pueblo*
the village hall	*el ayuntamiento del pueblo*
the village school	*el colegio del pueblo*
the village shop	*la tienda del pueblo*

TYPES OF ROAD	*TIPOS DE CARRETERAS*
a signpost	*una señal*
to point the way to..	*señalar el camina a...*
a road	*una carretera*
a main road	*una carretera principal*
a "B" road / a minor road	*una carretera secundaria*
a lane	*un callejón*
a bridleway	*un camino de herradura*
a rough track	*un sendero*
a footpath	*un camino*

WALKS cont. / *PASEOS cont.*

OBSTACLES		***OBSTACULOS***	
a stile	*escalones para saltar una cerca*	a bog	*un pantano*
a gate	*una verja*	a cowpat	*una boñiga*
a wall	*un muro*	a railway	*un paso de trenes*
a cattle grid	*una verja de castillo*	a railway bridge	*un puente con vías*

FARMS		***GRANJAS***	
a farmhouse	*una granja*	an egg	*un huevo*
a farmyard	*un corral*	to collect the eggs	*recoger los huevos*
the farmer	*el granjero*	a basket	*un cesto*
the dairy	*la vaquería*	the barn	*el granero*
the cowshed	*los establos para vacas*	a hayloft	*un pajar*
		a stable	*un establo*
a hen coop	*el gallinero*	a trough	*un comedero de animales*
a hen	*una gallina*		

WATER	***AGUA***
a river // a stream	*un río // una corriente / un arroyo*
a ford	*un vado*
a canal / a barge	*un canal / una barcaza*
a lock	*una esclusa*
the lock keeper	*el vigilante de la esclusa*
the towpath	*el camino para remolques*
a lake / an island	*un lago / una isla / una isleta*
a pond // a waterfall	*un estanque // una caída / cascada*
a puddle	*un charco / una charca*
rapids / the current / strong	*rápidos / el caudal / fuerte*
fast / dangerous	*rápido(a) / peligroso(a)*

WALKS cont. — ***PASEOS cont.***

CROSSING WATER	*ATRAVESANDO CORRIENTES DE AGUA*
stepping stones	*piedras para atravesar / ir de piedra en piedra*
slippery / wobbly	*escurridizo(a) / inestable*
to tread on / to jump / to cross	*pisar / saltar / atravesar*
a bridge / a footbridge	*un puente / un puente de peatones*

PADDLING	*CHAPOTEAR*
Shall we paddle?	*¿Chapoteamos?*
Take off your socks and shoes.	*Quítate los calcetines y los zapatos.*
Have you got a towel?	*¿Tienes una toalla?*
Dry your feet here.	*Sécate los pies aquí.*
It's freezing / quite warm.	*Está helada / esta bastante caliente*
It's deep / shallow.	*es profundo(a) / no es profundo(a)*
It's pebbly / muddy.	*Tiene rocas / barro*

HIGH GROUND	*ELEVACIONES*
a mountain / to go to the top	*una montaña / subir a la cima*
to climb	*trepar / subir / escalar*
to see the view	*ver la vista*
panoramic / spectacular	*panorámica / espectacular*
Can you see over there..?	*¿Puedes ver allí...*
on the horizon / in the distance	*el horizontal / en la lejanía*
a steep slope	*una inclinación abrupta*
to be careful	*tener cuidado*
a hill / a valley	*una colina / un valle*
a gentle slope	*una pendiente poco elevada*
a tunnel	*un túnel*
a cave / dark / to hide	*una cueva / oscuro(a) / esconderse*
to echo	*hacer eco*

WALKS cont. / *PASEOS cont.*

FIELDS etc.		*CAMPOS etc.*	
a meadow	*un prado / una pradera*	unploughed	*sín arar*
a field	*un campo*	sown	*sembrado*
ploughed	*arado*	a valley	*un valle*

WALKING CONDITIONS		*CONDICIONES DEL TERRENO*	
muddy	*embarrado*	tiring	*fatigoso*
slippery	*escurridizo*	boring	*aburrido*
steep	*abrupto*	good	*bueno*
flooded	*inundado*	perfect	*perfecto*

WEATHER CONDITIONS / *CONDICIONES CLIMATICAS*

Hot	***Caliente***
It's very sunny.	*Hace sol.*
It's stuffy.	*Es agobiante*
It may thunder.	*Puede que truene.*
It is too hot for me.	*Hace demasiado calor para mí.*
Can we go into the shade for a bit?	*¿Vamos a la sombra un rato?*
I am boiling.	*Estoy asfixiado / acalorado.*

Cold	***Frío / Fría***
It's freezing.	*Hace mucho frío / Está helando.*
It's icy.	*Está helando.*
It's rather slippery.	*Es muy escurridizo.*
Shall we slide on the ice?	*¿Quieres patinar sobre el hielo?*
I am frozen.	*Estoy helado.*

WALKS cont. / *PASEOS cont.*

WEATHER CONDITIONS cont. / *CONDICIONES CLIMATICAS cont.*

Wet	***Húmedo / Húmeda***
It's beginning to rain.	*Está empezando a llover.*
It's drizzling.	*Está chispeando.*
It's pouring down.	*Está diluviando.*
Everywhere is very muddy.	*Todo está embarrado.*
I am soaked.	*Estoy empapado.*
My feet are wet.	*Tengo los pies mojados.*
It may stop raining soon.	*Quizá pare de llover pronto.*
Shall we shelter here until it stops raining?	*¿Por qué no nos resguardamos en este refugio hasta que pare de llover.*

Thunder	***Trueno***
Did you hear the thunder?	*¿Has oido el trueno?*
I think there's going to be a thunderstorm.	*Me parece que va a haber tormenta.*
It just lightened.	*Es sólo un relámpago.*
Count how long between the flash and the thunder.	*Cuenta cuánto tipo pasa entre el relámpago y el trueno.*
It's a long way away.	*Está muy lejos.*
It's very close.	*Está muy cerca.*
We had better get back.	*Lo mejor es que volvamos.*

TREES / *ARBOLES*

a forest	*un parque forestal*
a wood	*un bosque*
a tree	*un árbol*
a bush	*un arbusto*

WALKS cont. *PASEOS cont.*

Parts of Trees		***Partes del árbol***	
the trunk	*el tronco*	strong	*fuerte*
a hollow trunk	*un tronco hueco*	rotten	*podrido*
massive	*enorme*	a twig	*una ramita*
a branch	*una rama*	a leaf	*una hoja*

Climbing trees		***Trepando Arboles***	
to climb up	*subir / trepar*	to grasp	*agarrarse*
to swing from	*balancearse de / colgarse de*	to get a foothold	*perder el equilibrio*

TYPES OF TREES		***TIPOS DE ARBOLES***	
deciduous	*de hoja*	ivy	*hiedra (f)*
evergreen	*de hoja perenne*	mountain ash	*fresno (m) de montaña*
ash	*un fresno*	oak	*un roble*
beech	*una haya*	pine	*un pino*
birch	*un abedul*	silver birch	*abedul plateado (m)*
Christmas	*arboles típicos en la Navidad*	spruce	*pícea (f)*
fir	*un abeto*	sycamore	*un sicomoro*
hawthorn	*un espino*	weeping willow	*un sauce llorón*
holly	*un acebo*	yew	*tejo (m)*

WALKS cont. — *PASEOS cont.*

ANIMALS (abc)	*ANIMALES*
a badger	*un tejón*
a cow / a bull	*una vaca / un toro*
a bullock // a calf	*un buey // un becerro / un ternero*
(a herd of cows)	*un rebaño de vacas*
a dog	*un perro*
a fox	*un zorro / una zorra*
a goat	*una cabra*
a hare	*una liebre*
a rabbit	*un conejo*
a rabbit hole / a burrow	*una madriguera de conejo*
a rabbit warren	*una madriguera / laberinto de conejos*
a sheep / a ram / a ewe	*una oveja / un carnero / una oveja*
a lamb	*un cordero*
a flock	*un rebaño*

BIRDS	*AVES / PAJAROS*
a blackbird	*un mirlo*
a duck / a drake	*un pato / un pato (macho)*
a duckling	*un patito*
a goose	*un ganso*
a gosling	*un gansito / un pollo de ganso*
a hen / a cock	*una gallina / un gallo*
a chicken	*un pollo*
a kingfisher	*un martín pescador*
a peacock / a peahen	*un / una pavo real*
tail feathers	*las plumas de la cola*
to display	*abrir / enseñar*
a robin	*un petirrojo*
a swallow	*una golondrina*
a swan / a cygnet	*un cisne / un pollo de cisne*
a thrush	*un tordo / un zorzal*

WALKS cont. | ***PASEOS cont.***

BIRDS & THEIR ACTIONS	***LOS PAJAROS Y SUS ACTIVIDADES***
to fly	*volar*
to sing / to whistle	*cantar / trinar*
to chirp	*gorjear / piar*
to build a nest	*construir un nido*
to lay an egg	*poner un huevo*
to hatch out	*romper el huevo*
to learn to fly	*aprender a volar*

FEEDING BIRDS	***ALIMENTANDO PAJAROS***
Shall we take some bread for the birds?	*¿Llevamos pan para los pájaros?*
Did you bring some bread?	*¿Has traido pan?*
Would you like to give them some?	*¿Quieres darles un poco de pan?*
to throw	*tirar / arrojar / lanzar*

INSECTS		***LOS INSECTOS***	
an ant	*una hormiga*	a spider	*una araña*
a bee	*una abeja*	a spider's web	*una tela de araña*
to sting	*picar*	a fly	*una mosca*
to buzz	*zumbar*	a wasp	*una avispa*

FRUIT PICKING	***RECOGIENDO FRUTAS***
Would you like to go fruit picking?	*¿Quieres que vayamos a recoger frutas?*
I want to make jam.	*Quiero hacer mermelada.*
to pick	*recoger*
Pick one's that are ripe/ sweet / sour.	*Recoge las que están maduras / dulces/ agrias.*
I don't want them too ripe / unripe.	*No las quiero muy maduras / verdes.*

WALKS cont. — ***PASEOS cont.***

FRUIT PICKING cont. — ***RECOGIENDO FRUTAS cont.***

to put in a basket	*poner en un cesto*
How many have you got?	*¿Cuántas tienes?*
I think we need a few more.	*Creo que necesitamos unas pocas más.*
That is probably enough now.	*Ya tenemos suficientes.*
There are a lot over here.	*Hay más allí.*
Don't eat too many.	*No comas demasiadas.*

Kinds of Fruit		***Tipos de frutas***	
apples	*manzanas (f)*	gooseberries	*grosellas (f)*
blackberries	*zarzamoras (f)*	raspberries	*frambuesas (f)*
blackcurrants	*grosellas negras*	redcurrants	*grosellas rojas*
cherries	*cerezas (f)*	strawberries	*fresas (f)*

PHOTOGRAPHY
FOTOGRAFIA

TAKING PHOTOGRAPHS	*TOMANDO FOTOGRAFIAS*
May I take a picture of you, please?	*¿Puedo hacerte una foto, por favor?*
Could you take a picture of me, please?	*¿Puedes hacerme una foto. por favor?*
Can you wait for a second while I take a photograph?	*¿Puedes esperar un momento que te eche una foto?*
Can you stand / sit over there, please?	*¿Puedes posar de pie / sentado allí, por favor?*
Could you move a little closer together, please?	*¿Podeis juntaros un poco más, por favor?*
Could you try to smile?	*¿Puedes sonreír un poco?*
Can you try to keep still, please?	*No te muevas, por favor.*
Should I bring my camera with me?	*¿Me llevo la cámara?*
Could you look after my camera for me, please?	*¿Puedes cuidarme la cámara, por favor?*
Don't you like having your photo taken?	*¿No te gustan las fotos?*
I like / hate having my photo taken.	*Me gustan / odio las fotos.*
I am not photogenic.	*No soy fotogénico.*
I would like to take a photo of you all to show my family.	*Me gustaría echar una foto de todos juntos para mostrar la familia entera.*
May I take a photo of your house?	*¿Puedo hacer una foto de la casa?*

PHOTOGRAPHY cont. / *FOTOGRAFIA cont.*

LOOKING AT PHOTOS	***MIRANDO FOTOS***
Have you any photos of when you were young?	*¿Tienes fotos de cuando eras pequeño?*
Can I look at your photo album?	*¿Puedo mirar el álbum de fotos?*
That photo of you is very good.	*Esta foto tuya es muy buena.*
That one doesn't look at all like you.	*Esta no se te parece en nada.*
You have changed a lot.	*Has cambiado mucho.*
You haven't changed much.	*No has cambiado mucho.*
Have you got photos of your holiday?	*¿Tienes fotos de las vacaciones?*
Are you in the photo?	*¿Estás en la foto?*
It's a very good photo.	*Es una foto buena.*
in the foreground..	*en el frente / al frente...*
in the background..	*en el fondo...*
This photograph is of..	*Esta es una foto de...*
This photo was taken two years ago.	*Esta foto es de hace dos años.*
That's where we used to live.	*Esta es de donde solíamos vivir.*
That one is of me as a baby.	*Esta es de cuando era un bebé.*

CAMERAS / *CAMARAS*

TYPES OF CAMERA	***TIPOS DE CAMARA***
Polaroid	*Una Polaroid*
instant	*Una instantánea*
automatic	*Una automática*
manual	*una manual*
disposable	*una deshechable / de usar y tirar*

PHOTOGRAPHY cont. / *FOTOGRAFIA cont.*

USING A CAMERA	*USANDO LA CAMARA*
a button / to press	*un botón / presionar*
a lever / to pull	*una manilla / tirar*
a switch / to switch	*un enchufe / enchufar*
the lens cap / to remove / to replace	*el protector (la tapa de las lentes) / quitar / volver a poner*
the lens / normal / wide angle / zoom	*las lentes / normal / apertura máxima / zoom*
to clean	*limpiar*
the viewfinder	*el graduador / el objetivo / el visor de imagen*
to focus	*enfocar*
in focus / out of focus	*enfocado / desenfocado*
auto-focus	*objetivo automático*
clear / blurred	*nítido / turbio*
the aperture / the aperture setting	*el objetivo / el graduador*
the shutter // the shutter speed	*el diafragma / el obturador // la velocidad del diafragma*
the flash	*el flash*
Did you use a flash?	*¿Has utilizado el flash?*
I need a new flash bulb.	*Necesito una bombilla nueva para el flash.*

CAMERA ACCESSORIES	*ACCESORIOS DE CAMARA*
a camera case	*una funda de cámara*
a camera bag	*una bolsa para la cámara*
a strap	*una correa*
a camera stand	*un soporte para la cámara*
a tripod	*un trípode*
a photo album	*un álbum de fotos*

PHOTOGRAPHY cont. / *FOTOGRAFIA cont.*

BUYING FILMS	***COMPRANDO LA PELICULA / EL CARRETE***
Do you sell films here?	*¿Vendeis carretes aquí?*
Could I have a colour / black and white film, please?	*¿Me puede dar un carrete en color / blanco y negro, por favor?*
What sort would you like?	*¿De qué tipo?*
Two hundred / three hundred / four hundred?	*de doscientos / trescientos / cuatrocientos*
How many would you like?	*¿Cuántos quiere?*
Twelve / twenty four / thirty six, please.	*Doce / veinticuatro / treinta y seis, por favor.*
thirty five millimetre format	*formato de treinta y cinco milímetros*
to load	*cargar / poner*
How do you load the film?	*¿Cómo se pone el carrete?*
Could you help me to load the film, please?	*¿Podría ayudarme a poner el carrete por favor?*
to rewind / automatic rewind	*rebobinar /rebobinado automático*
to remove the film	*quitar / sacar el carrete*

GETTING FILMS DEVELOPED	***REVELANDO LAS PELICULAS***
Could you develop these for me, please?	*¿Puede revelar esta película, por favor?*
I would like to collect them in one hour if possible / four hours / tomorrow.	*Quisiera recogerlas en una hora si es posible / en cuatro horas / mañana..*
Can you develop black and white film here?	*¿Revelan películas en blanco y negro aquí?*
Do you want just one set of prints?	*¿Quiere sólo una copia de cada?*
I would like an extra set of prints.	*Quiero una foto extra de cada original.*
These are under-exposed / over-exposed.	*Estas están muy oscuras / muy veladas / quemadas.*

VIDEO CAMERA RECORDERS (CAMCORDERS)
CAMARA PORTATIL DE VIDEO (VIDEOCAMERAS)

THE VIDEO CAMERA	*LA VIDEOCAMARA*
a camcorder case	*una funda para la video cámara*
to get the video camera out	*sacar la video cámara*
a grip strap	*una correa para agarrarla*
to hold	*sostener / aguantar*

TAPES	*CINTAS*
a tape	*una cinta*
a cassette	*una cinta de caset(t)*
a blank tape	*una cinta virgen*
a used tape	*una cinta grabada*
to insert / to eject	*meter / sacar*
to record on / to label	*grabar / etiquetar*

BATTERIES	*PILAS / BATERIAS*
a battery pack	*un paquete de baterías*
a battery charger	*un cargador*
to charge up the battery	*cargar la batería*
Plug it into the mains.	*Enchufar en la electricidad*
The battery is fully charged.	*La batería está cargada*
It is getting weak.	*Se está acabando.*
The battery has run down.	*La batería se ha acabado.*
Do you have an adaptor for this?	*¿Tienes un adaptador para esto?*
to attach the battery to the camcorder	*poner la batería en la video cámara*
to slide / to push	*introducir / empujar*
to click into place	*acoplar en el lugar*

CAMCORDERS cont. — *VIDEOCAMERAS cont.*

THE LENS	*LOS FOCOS / LAS LENTES*
a lens hood	*un protector / una tapa*
to remove	*quitar*
to replace	*volver a poner*
to clean the lens	*limpiar las lentes*

TURNING THE CAMCORDER ON AND RECORDING	*ENCENDIENDO LA VIDEO CAMARA Y GRABANDO*
the power switch	*el botón "power" / de encendido*
to switch on / off	*encender / apagar*
a flashing light	*una luz intermitente*
a warning light	*una luz de aviso (chivato)*
ready to record	*preparada para grabar*
standby	*standby*
record mode	*grabar*
Are you ready?	*¿Estás listo(a)?*
I am about to record now.	*Voy a empezar a grabar ya.*
the viewfinder	*el visor / el objetivo*
to focus	*enfocar*
to adjust	*ajustar*
to zoom	*ajustar el zoom*

GETTING THE SOUND RIGHT	*GRABANDO EL SONIDO BIEN*
the microphone	*el micrófono*
Can you speak up a bit, please?	*¿Puedes hablar un poco?*
That wasn't loud enough.	*No, más alto.*
That was too loud.	*Demasiado alto.*

CAMCORDERS cont. *VIDEOCAMERAS cont.*

PLAYING BACK	*REBOBINANDO*
to switch between camera and player	*ver lo que se ha grabado*
to playback	*rebobinar*
the playback switch	*el botón para rebobinar*
to rewind	*rebobinar*
to fast forward	*pasar rápido*
to stop	*parar*
to pause	*parar con el botón para pausa*

EDITING	*EDITANDO*
to edit	*editar*
to cut	*cortar*
to record over	*grabar encima*
the counter reset button	*el botón del contador automático*
to zero the counter	*poner el contador a cero*
to insert a marker	*insertar una señal*

SPORT
DEPORTES

TENNIS *TENIS*

DO YOU PLAY TENNIS?	*¿JUEGAS AL TENIS?*
Would you like to play tennis?	*¿Quieres que jugamos al tenis?*
Shall we just knock up for a while?	*¿Hacemos calentamiento un rato?*
Is the net the right height?	*¿Está la red a la altura correcta?*
Shall we check the height of the net?	*¿Echamos un vistazo a la altura de la red?*
It's too low / too high.	*Está demasiado baja / alta.*
Up a bit / down a bit / O.K.	*Un poco más arriba / abajo / ahí está (vale)*

EQUIPMENT	*EQUIPO*
a tennis racket	*una raqueta de tenis*
Which racket would you prefer?	*¿Qué raqueta prefieres?*
What weight of racket would you like?	*¿Qué peso de raqueta prefieres?*
a tennis ball	*una pelota de tenis*
new balls	*pelotas nuevas*
a racket press	*un tensador*
a holdall	*un bolsa para raquetas y pelotas*
a sportsbag	*una bolsa de deportes*
a towel	*una toalla*

TENNIS cont. / *TENIS cont.*

CLOTHES	***ROPAS***
I haven't got any tennis clothes with me.	*No tengo ropa para jugar al tenis aquí.*
You can borrow some clothes.	*Yo te puedo prestar algo.*
You can wear anything.	*Puedes ponerte cualquier casa.*
shorts / a T shirt	*pantalones cortos / una camiseta*
a tennis skirt	*una falda de tenis*
a tennis dress	*una ropa de tenis / un vestido de tenis*
tennis shoes	*unas zapatillas de tenis*
socks	*unas calcetas*
a sweatband / a headband	*una cinta*
a sun visor	*una gorra / un visor para el sol*
a track suit	*un chandal*

THE TENNIS COURT	***LA PISTA DE TENIS***
the net	*la red*
the base line	*la línea de fondo*
the service line	*la línea de servicio*
the centre line	*la línea central*
the tramlines	*las líneas laterales*
the side netting	*la central vertical*
the service box	*el área de servicio / saque*
the changing room	*los vestuarios*
a locker	*una taquilla*

STARTING A GAME	***EMPEZANDO EL JUEGO***
Do you want to carry on knocking up?	*¿Quieres seguir calentando?*
Shall we start to play now?	*¿Empezamos a jugar?*
How many sets shall we play?	*¿Cuántos set quieres echar?*

TENNIS cont. / *TENIS cont.*

STARTING A GAME cont. / *EMPEZANDO EL JUEGO cont.*

to toss up	*echar una moneda al aire / echar a suerte*
Let's toss for it.	*Echémoslo a suerte.*
Toss a coin.	*Echa una moneda al aire.*
Heads or tails? It's heads / tails.	*¿Cara o cruz? cara / cruz.*
Spin your racket.	*Gira tu raqueta.*
Rough or smooth?	*¿Fuerte o suave?*
It's rough / it's smooth.	*Es fuerte / es suave.*
You serve first.	*Tu empiezas sacando / tienes el servicio*
Which end do you prefer?	*¿Qué lado prefieres?*
I prefer this / that end.	*Prefiero éste / aquél.*
The sun is in my / your eyes.	*Tengo el sol de frente / tienes el sol de frente*

SERVING	*SACANDO*
to serve	*sacar*
to hold one's serve	*mantener el servicio*
to break someone's serve	*romper el servicio*
to serve an ace	*hacer ace*
first / second service	*primer / segundo servicio*
It's your service.	*Es tu servicio / tu saque*

TENNIS cont. / *TENIS cont.*

IN OR OUT?	***DENTRO O FUERA***
Was that in / out?	*¿Dentro o fuera?*
Out! The ball was definitely out.	*¡Fuera! La pelota cayó fuera.*
In! The ball was just in.	*¡Dentro! La pelota entró.*
I'm not sure.	*No estoy seguro(a)*
I didn't see it land.	*No la vi caer.*
It touched the line.	*tocó la línea.*
Shall we play it again?	*¿Volvemos a jugar el punto?*

FAULTS	***FALTAS***
a fault	*una falta*
a double fault	*una doble falta*
a foot fault	*una falta con el pie*

LET BALLS	***PELOTAS DE SAQUE***
to play a let	*echar una pelota para el saque*
Should we play a let?	*¿Echamos una pelota para ver quién saca?*

KEEPING THE SCORE	***LLEVANDO LOS PUNTOS***
What's the score?	*¿Cuántos vamos?*
I've forgotten what the score is.	*Se me ha olvidado como vamos.*
The score is	*El marcador es*
• love all	• *iguales a cero / nada*
• love fifteen	• *cero / quince*
• fifteen love	• *quince / nada*
• fifteen all	• *iguales a quince*

TENNIS cont. | ***TENIS cont.***

KEEPING THE SCORE cont. | ***LLEVANDO LOS PUNTOS cont.***

• thirty forty	• *treinta / cuarenta*
• deuce	• *deuce / iguales*
• That's deuce.	• *es deuce / iguales / iguales a cuarenta*
• Advantage.	• *Ventaja*
• My / our / your advantage.	• *Mi / nuestra / tu / vuestra ventaja*
• Game / Game to you.	• *Juego / Juego a tu favor*
• That's game.	• *Juego*
• Change ends	• *Cambio de campo*

SCORING cont.	***PUNTUANDO***
Three games to two, first set.	*Tres juegos a dos en el primer set*
Match point?	*¿Punto de partido?*
Game, set and match.	*Juego, set y partido.*
a tie-breaker	*un tie-break*
a sudden-death-tie-breaker	*la muerte súbita*
Shall we play another game?	*¿Echamos otro juego?*

STROKES	***GOLPES***
forehand	*de derechas*
a forehand drive / volley	*un golpe / una volea de derechas*
backhand	*de revés*
a backhand drive / volley	*un golpe / una volea de revés*
to lob / a high lob / a top spin lob	*hacer un globo / un globo / globo al fondo*
a smash / an overhead smash	*un mate / un mate profundo*
a service / an ace	*un servicio / un ace*
first / second service	*primer / segundo servicio*
a drop shot / a slice	*una dejada / una vaselina*
a volley / a half volley	*una volea / una semi-volea*
a slam	*un mate a través / un Slam*

TENNIS cont. / *TENIS cont.*

LOSING THE BALL	*PERDIENDO LA PELOTA*
Did you see where the ball went?	*¿Has visto dónde cayó la pelota?*
We've lost the ball.	*Hemos perdido la pelota.*
It went somewhere here.	*Cayó por allí.*
I can't find it.	*No la encuentro.*
I've found it.	*La encontré.*
Let's look for it later.	*¿Por qué no la buscamos luego?*
Have you any more balls?	*¿Tenemos más pelotas?*

THE OFFICIALS	*LOS ARBITROS*
an umpire	*un árbitro*
Will you be umpire?	*¿Quieres ser árbitro?*
the referee	*el arbitro / el juez de silla*
the net judge	*el juez de red*
the foot-fault judge	*el linier de fondo / el juez de línea de fondo*
the line judge	*el linier*
a ball boy / a ball girl	*el recogepelotas / una recogepelotas*

DIFFERENT GAMES	*TIPOS / MODALIDADES DE TENIS*
singles	*individual*
ladies' singles / men's singles	*individuales femeninos / masculinos*
doubles // mixed doubles	*dobles / parejas // dobles mixtos*
ladies' doubles / men's doubles	*dobles femeninos / masculinos*
lawn tennis	*tenis sobre hierba (artificial)*
tennis on a hard surface	*tenis sobre tierra batida / pista rápida*
to play tennis on grass	*tenis sobre hierba*

TENNIS cont. — *TENIS cont.*

TENNIS TOURNAMENTS	*TORNEOS DE TENIS*
the first round	*la primera ronda*
the second round	*la segunda ronda*
the quarter final	*los cuartos de final*
a semi final	*la semi final*
the final	*la final*
the championship	*el campeonato*
the grand slam	*el gran Slam*
a seeded player	*un jugador clasificado*
first seed	*primer clasificado*
He was seeded third.	*Sea clasificado el tercero*

HOW WELL YOU PLAYED	*COMO DE BIEN JUGASTE*
You play well.	*Jugaste bien.*
Well played! / Good shot!	*¡Bien jugado! ¡Buen golpe!*
Bad luck!	*¡Mala suerte!*
I haven't played for ages.	*No he jugado desde hace mucho.*

RIDING — *MONTAR A CABALLO*

CAN YOU RIDE?	*¿PUEDES MONTAR A CABALLO? / ¿SABES MONTAR A CABALLO?*
How long have you ridden?	*¿Cuándo empezaste a montar?*
I have ridden for five years.	*Llevo montando cinco años.*
Would you like to have a riding lesson with me?	*¿Te gustaría tomar lecciones de equitación conmigo?*
Shall we go for a ride?	*¿Vamos a montar a caballo?*
You ride well.	*Montas bien.*
Who are you riding?	*¿Quién vas a montar?*
What is your horse's name?	*¿Cómo se llama tu caballo?*

CLOTHES AND EQUIPMENT	*ROPA Y EQUIPO DE MONTA*
a riding hat	*una gorra de montar*
a riding jacket	*una chaqueta de montar*
jodhpurs	*pantalones de montar (m.pl)*
riding boots	*botas de montar (f.pl)*
a whip	*una fusta*
gloves	*guantes (m.pl)*

THE STABLE	*LOS ESTABLOS*
the stable yard	*los establos*
the tackroom	*la sala para los útiles de las caballerizas*
a gate	*una puerta*
a mounting block	*un edificio para la monta*
the school	*la escuela*
a barn	*un granero*
a horse box	*un establo*

RIDING TERMS	*TERMINOS DE MONTA*
to hold the reins	*sujetar las riendas*
to give someone a leg up	*poner apoyo para subir a alguien*

RIDING TERMS cont. ***TERMINOS DE MONTA cont.***

to mount / to dismount	*montarse / desmontar*
to ride	*montar*
to walk / to trot	*andar / trotar*
to canter / to gallop	*ir a medio galope / ir al galope*
to jump	*saltar*
to kick	*dar una patada*
to rein back	*tirar de las riendas*
to fall off	*caerse*
to rear	*dar coces / encabritarse / desbandarse*
to buck / to shy	*corcovear / espantarse*
to walk a horse	*pasear al caballo*
to neigh	*relinchar*

HACKING	***MONTAR A CABALLO***
a hack / to go for a hack	*una monta / ir de monta*
a road	*una carretera*
a lane	*un callejón / un carril*
a bridleway	*un sendero*
a footpath	*un camino*
a ditch	*un dique*
a field	*un campo*
a gate / to jump	*una cancela (puerta) saltar*
to open / to shut	*abrir / cerrar*
private land	*un coto privado*

RIDING cont. — *MONTAR A CABALLO cont.*

TACK	*UTILES DE MONTAR*
to saddle up / the saddle	*ensillar / la silla de montar*
the flaps / the girth	*las sacudidas / la cincha*
to tighten / to loosen	*apretar / dejar sueltas*
a buckle / a hole	*una hebilla / un agujero*
the fasten	*el cierre*
the seat	*el asiento*
the pommel / the cantle	*el pomo / el galopeo*
the stirrups	*los estribos*
to lengthen / to shorten	*alargar / acortar*
even / uneven	*a nivel / desnivelado*
the bridle // the bit	*la brida // el bocado / el freno*
the reins / a leading rein	*las riendas / la rienda de guía*
a head collar	*un collar / un collarín*
a blanket	*una manta*

GROOMING A HORSE	*CEPILLANDO AL CABALLO*
to groom / to brush / to rub down	*cepillar / almohazar*
a currycomb	*un cepillo de cerdas finas*
a dandybrush	*un cepillo de cerdas*
soft / hard	*suave / fuerte*
a bucket / water / a tap	*un cubo / agua / un grifo*
a sponge / to sponge	*una esponja / pasar la esponja*

HOOF PROBLEMS	*PROBLEMAS CON LA PEZUNA*
a hoof pick	*una astilla en la pezuña*
to lose a horseshoe	*perder una herradura*
a stone / lame	*una piedra / cojo(a)*
the blacksmith	*el herrero*
to shoe	*poner una herradura / calzar*

RIDING cont. — *MONTAR A CABALLO cont.*

TYPES OF HORSE	*TIPOS DE CABALLO*
a thoroughbred	*un pura sangre*
a mare / a stallion	*una yegua / un semental*
a foal / a colt	*un potrillo / un potro*
a pony	*un jaca / un caballito*
a Shetland pony	*un pony de Shetland*
a carthorse	*un caballo de tira*
a shirehorse	*un percherón*
a racehorse	*un caballo de raza*

DESCRIBING HORSES	*DESCRIBIENDO CABALLOS*
How old is your horse?	*¿Cuántos años tiene tu caballo?*
He / she is three years old.	*Tiene tres años.*
How tall is he / she?	*¿Qué altura tiene?*
She is … hands.	*Es... centímetros de altura.*
What colour is your horse?	*¿De qué color es?*

grey	*gris*	the tail	*el rabo / la cola*
bay	*bayo(a)*	the hindquarters	*los cuartos traseros*
chestnut	*avellano(a)*	the temperament	*el temperamento*
palomino	*Palomino*	frisky	*brioso(a)*
dappled	*moteado(a)*	gentle	*gentil*
broken	*domado*	lazy	*perezoso(a)*
unbroken	*salvaje*	fast	*rápido(a)*
the coat	*el pelaje*	nervous	*nervioso(a)*
the mane	*las crines*	temperamental	*temperamental*

RIDING cont. — *MONTAR A CABALLO cont.*

COMPETITIONS	*COMPETICIONES*
hunter trials	*cacerías con caballos*
equitation	*equitación*
a three day event	*una jornadas de tres días (de duración)*
dressage	*el atuendo*
collected / extended trot	*trote colectivo (m) / trote rápido*
cross country	*campo a través*
show jumping	*competición de saltos de exhibición*
to jump / a jump / height	*saltar / un salto / altura*
three feet high	*tres pies de altura*
a water jump / a ditch	*un lago / un dique*
a fence // a pole	*una barrera/ una valla // los palos*
a gate	*una puerta*
a double	*un obstáculo doble*
a fault	*una penalización / una falta*
a double fault	*una doble penalización*
a time fault	*una penalización por exceder el tiempo*
a penalty	*una penalización*
a time limit	*un límite de tiempo*
a race against time	*una carrera a contra reloj*
to start the clock	*empezar a cronometrar*
a refusal / three refusals	*un amago / tres amagos*
to disqualify	*descalificar*
to have a clear round	*no derribar ningún obstáculo en una ronda*
a jump-off	*una subida / o bajada / a algo de un salto*

RIDING cont. / *MONTAR A CABALLO cont.*

USEFUL EXPRESSIONS	***EXPRESIONES UTILES***
You can borrow a hat at the riding school.	*Puedes pedir prestada una gorra en la escuela de equitación.*
Does that hat fit you properly?	*¿Te sienta / está bien?*
Put your feet in the stirrups.	*Pon los pies en los estribos.*
Use your whip.	*Usa la justa.*
Kick harder.	*Hinca el talón más fuerte.*
Can you trot / canter / gallop?	*¿Puedes ir al trote / a medio galope / al galope*
Would you like to try a jump?	*¿Te gustaría saltar?*
What height can you jump?	*¿A qué altura puedes saltar?* *¿Qué altura puedes saltar?*

SKIING
ESQUIAR

CLOTHES	*ROPA*
a ski suit / a salopette	*un equipo de esquí / un salopete*
a ski jacket	*una chaqueta para la nieve*
a hood	*una caperuza*
gloves / mittens	*guantes / manoplas*
thermal	*termal*
sunglasses	*gafas de sol*

EQUIPMENT	*EQUIPO*
skis	*esquíes (m.pl)*
ski bindings	*ataduras (f.pl)*
ski boots	*botas de esquiar (f.pl)*
fastens / clasps	*cierres (m.pl)*
to tighten / to loosen	*apretar / dejar suelto*
ski poles / handgrips	*guías / correas para las manos*
straps	*correas*
a ski pass	*un pase para esquiar*
a photo	*una foto*
suntan cream	*la crema protectora para el sol*

USEFUL EXPRESSIONS	*EXPRESIONES UTILES*
Don't forget your…	*No te olvides de traer...*
Have you got your…?	*¿Tienes tus...?*
May I borrow..?	*¿Puedes prestarme...?*
I can't find my..	*No puedo encontrar mi / mis...*
I've forgotten where I left my…	*He olvidado dónde deje mi / mis...*

SKIING cont. / *ESQUIAR cont.*

SKI HIRE	***ALQUILER DE ESQUIES***
I would like to hire boots / skis / poles, please?	*Quiero alquilar botas de esquiar / esquíes / guías por favor.*
What size boots are you?	*¿Qué talla de pie tienes?*
Try these.	*Pruébate éstas.*
Are those comfortable?	*¿Te están bien?*
Where do they feel tight / loose?	*¿Dónde te aprietan / te están grandes?*
How do you adjust them?	*¿Cómo se ajustan?*
You can adjust the fastens like this..	*Se ajustan así.*
What length skis do you normally wear?	*¿Qué tamaño de esquíes usas normalmente?*
How tall are you?	*¿Cuánto mides?*
What do you weigh? I weigh..	*¿Cuánto pesas? Peso...*
How experienced are you?	*¿Tienes experiencia?*
I'm a beginner.	*Soy principiante.*
I'm intermediate.	*Tengo algo de experiencia.*
I'm experienced.	*Tengo experiencia.*
Try these poles.	*Prueba estas guías.*
Choose poles with yellow handles.	*Elige guías con mangos amarillos.*
These poles are too short / too long.	*Estas guías son demasiado cortas / largas.*
Bring the boots back if the are uncomfortable.	*Tráeme las botas sí no son cómodas.*
Can I change my boots, please?	*¿Puedo cambiar estas botas?*
They are too narrow.	*son demasiado pequeñas (estrechas).*
They squash my toes.	*Me están apretando mucho.*
They hurt here.	*Me hacen daño.*
Can you sharpen my skis, please?	*¿Podría afilar los esquíes, por favor?*

SKI HIRE cont.	*ALQUILER DE ESQUIES cont.*
Can you wax my skis, please?	*¿Puede poner cera a mis esquíes?*
Can I hire..?	*Quisiera alquilar...*
• a monoski	*• un mono esquí*
• a toboggan	*• un trineo*
• skating boots	*• un par de botas para esquiar*
• a crash helmet	*• un casco protector*
• a ski board	*• una tabla de esquiar*

WEATHER CONDITIONS	*LAS CONDICIONES METEOROLOGICAS*
Have you heard the weather forecast?	*¿Qué sabes del tiempo?*
It's raining.	*Está lloviendo.*
It's cloudy.	*Está nublado / hay nubes*

SNOW	*NIEVE*
It's snowing. / There's no snow.	*Está nevando. / No hay nieve.*
It's snowing heavily.	*Está nevando mucho.*
The snow is a metre deep.	*Hay un metro de nieve.*
fresh snow / powder	*nieve suelta / polvo*
The snow is powdery.	*La nieve es muy fina.*
It's very icy.	*La nieve es muy dura.*
The snow is slushy.	*La nieve está medio derretida.*
a blizzard	*una ventisca*
danger of avalanche	*peligro de avalancha*

TEMPERATURE	*TEMPERATURAS*
It's below freezing point.	*Hace una temperatura de bajo cero.*
It's six degrees below zero.	*Hace seis grados bajo cero.*
It's freezing.	*Está helado.*
It's thawing.	*Se está descongelando.*
The snow is melting.	*La nieve se está derritiendo.*

SKIING cont. — *ESQUIAR cont.*

VISIBILITY	*VISIBILIDAD*
The visibility is poor.	*La visibilidad es mala.*
It's foggy.	*Hace niebla / hay niebla.*
It's misty.	*Hay neblina.*
It's difficult to see far.	*Es dificil ver de lejos.*
freezing fog	*niebla fría.*

THE SKI RUNS	*LAS PISTAS DE ESQUI*
a map of the ski area	*un mapa del arrea de esquí*
the level of difficulty	*el nivel de dificultad / peligrosidad*
nursery slopes	*rampas para entrenamiento y principiantes*
easiest runs	*pistas para principiantes*
easy runs / average runs	*pistas fáciles / pistas corrientes*
most difficult runs	*pistas de alto nivel de dificultad*
off-piste / dangerous	*fuera de pista / peligroso(a)*
narrow / wide	*estrecho(a) / ancho(a)*
gentle	*suave*

SKI LIFTS	*TELESQUÍ / TELESILLA*
What time do the lifts open / close?	*¿A que hora abren / cierran las telesillas?*
Where do I buy a ski pass?	*¿Donde compro un pase?*
You will need a photograph.	*Necesitaras una fotografía.*
Where is there a photo booth?	*¿Donde está la fotocabina?*
What coins does it take?	*¿Que monedas toma?*
It takes…	*Toma...*
a tow bar / a button lift	*un remolque / un elevador / un ascensor*
a drag lift / a chair lift	*un dragador / una telesilla*
a cable car / a gondola	*un teleférico / una góndola*
a safety bar / a foot rest	*una barrera protectora / posapiés*
a ski rack	*una rejilla*

SKIING cont. — *ESQUIAR cont.*

QUEUEING	*HACIENDO COLA*
to form a queue	*hacer cola*
to queue up	*estar en la cola*
crowded	*lleno / muy concurrido*
a short / long queue	*una corta / larga cola*
a queue jumper	*un salto de cola*
Wait your turn.	*Espera tu / su turno.*
He pushed in front of me.	*El pasó delante de mi de un empujón.*

SKI SCHOOL	*ESCUELA DE SKI*
Where is the ski school meeting place?	*¿Donde será la reunión de la escuela de ski?*
a ski instructor	*el entrenador / el profesor*
a ski class	*la clase de ski*
Which class are you in?	*¿En qué clase estás?*
Which class should I join?	*¿A qué grupo piensas debería ir?*
How much skiing have you done?	*¿Cuántos veces has esquiado antes?*
I have been skiing three times.	*He esquiado tres veces.*
I have only been skiing on a dry ski slope.	*Sólo he esquiado en pistas artificiales.*
I am a beginner / intermediate / experienced.	*Soy un principiante / tengo un poco de experiencia / tengo experiencia*
I only began skiing last year.	*Empecé el año pasado a esquiar.*
You have to do a ski test.	*Tienes que hacer un test de esquí.*
Show me how you ski.	*Muéstrame como esquías.*
Go and join that group over there.	*Ve a aquel grupo de allí.*
Join that class.	*Ve a aquel grupo.*

LEARNING TO SKI	*APRENDIENDO A ESQUIAR*
Put on your skis.	*Ponte los esquíes.*
The bindings need to be open.	*Tienes que abrir las correas.*
Sidestep up the hill.	*Sube la colina andando de lado.*
Have you ever used a drag lift?	*¿Has subido a un telesférico antes?*
to ski	*esquiar*
to fall down	*dejar caer / caerse*
to get up	*levantarse*
to turn round	*darse la vuelta*
to traverse	*atravesar*
to snow plough	*deslizarse en línea sobre la nieve*
a snowplough turn	*un giro*
a stem turn	*un giro en firme*
a parallel turn	*un giro en paralelo*
to mono-ski	*montar en un monoesquí*
to ski board	*montar en una tabla de esquiar*
slalom racing	*carrera de obstáculos / slalom*
the course	*el recorrido*
the poles / the flags	*los palos / las banderillas*
the gates	*las puertas de entrada*

FALLING DOWN	*CAYÉNDOSE*
Can you do an emergency stop?	*¿Puedes hacer una parada de emergencia?*
to fall down	*caerse*
Are you hurt?	*¿Te has hecho daño?*
I'm fine.	*Estoy bien.*
I hurt here..	*Me duele aquí.*
I can't get up.	*No puedo levantarme.*

LEARNING TO SKI cont.	***APRENDIENDO A ESQUIAR cont.***
FALLING DOWN cont.	***CAYÉNDOSE cont.***
How do you get up from a fall?	*¿Cómo te debes levantar cuando te caes?*
Sort out your skis.	*Pon los esquíes en posición.*
Edge your skis.	*Pon los esquíes de lado.*
Plant your poles and push.	*Clava las guías y empuja.*
Stand up.	*Levántate.*
Take your skis off.	*Quítate los esquíes.*
Put the lower ski on first.	*Ponte el esquí trasero primero.*
Push the inside edge into the snow.	*Empuja con el borde interno en la nieve.*

APRES SKI	***DESPUES DE ESQUIAR***
a bar / a restaurant	*un bar / un restaurante*
a disco / a nightclub (See 201-203)	*una discoteca / una disco / un club*
expensive / cheap	*caro(-a) / barato (-a)*
a skating rink (See 282-283)	*una pista de hielo*
to ice skate	*patinar sobre hielo*
to toboggan	*tirarse por un tobogán*
to go for a sleigh ride	*montar en trineo*
a sleigh	*un trineo*

ACCIDENTS	***ACCIDENTES***
There has been an accident.	*Ha habido un accidente.*
Someone is hurt.	*Alguien está herido.*
Where do you hurt? (See 237, 411, 420)	*¿Dónde te duele?*
Don't move him / her.	*No le / la muevas.*
Can you stand up?	*¿Te puedes levantar?*
Fetch the rescue service.	*Ve a buscar al equipo de rescate.*
Help / Get help.	*Socorro / Busca ayuda.*
Warn other people.	*Avisa a la gente.*

SKIING cont. — *ESQUIAR cont.*

RESCUE SERVICES	***SERVICIOS DE SALVAMENTO***
a helicopter / an air lift	*un helicóptero / un servicio aéreo*
a doctor	*un medico / un doctor*
a stretcher / a blood wagon	*una camilla / un vagón de sangre*
a broken arm / leg	*un brazo roto / una pierna rota*
What is your name?	*¿Cual es tu nombre? / Como te llamas?*
Where are you staying?	*¿Donde té / sé aloja?*
Are you insured?	*¿Tienes un seguro? / ¿Estás asegurado?*

HOW ARE YOU FEELING?	***¿COMO TE / SE ENCUENTA? / ¿COMO TE / SE SIENTE?***
I am cold / hot.	*Tengo frío / calor.*
I am tired / feel fine.	*Estoy cansado / estoy bien.*
I am thirsty // hungry.	*Estoy sediento / tengo sed // Estoy hambriento.*
I want to stop now.	*Quiero parar ahora.*
I want to carry on.	*Quiero seguir.*
I can't do this. / I am scared.	*No puedo hacer esto./Tengo miedo.*
This is good fun.	*Esto es muy divertido.*
Can we do it again?	*¿Podemos hacerlo otra vez?*
My legs hurt.	*Me duelen las piernas.*
My boots are rubbing.	*Las botas me hacen daño.*
Can we stop for lunch soon?	*¿Podemos parar para el almuerzo?*
I would like a drink.	*Me gustaría una bebida / un refresco.*
I need the toilet.	*Necesito el servicio / el baño.*
Let's go to that mountain café.	*Vamos a la cafetería de esa montaña.*
Shall we stop for a few minutes?	*¿Hacemos un alto por unos minutos?*
I'd like to go back to the hotel / chalet now.	*Me gustaría volver al hotel / chalet ahora.*
I have to be back at four o'clock.	*Necesito volver a las cuatro en punto.*
Shall we meet again after lunch?	*Nos vemos de nuevo después del almuerzo?*
Where / when shall we meet?	*¿Donde / cuando nos vemos?*

FOOTBALL
FUTBOL

THE PITCH	*EL TERRENO*
the goal / the goal posts	*la portería / los postes*
the cross bar	*el larguero*
the netting	*la red*
the goal area / the goal line	*el área de gol / la línea de gol*
the penalty area	*el área de penalty*
the touch line	*el punto de penalty*
the corner	*la esquina*
offside / mid-field	*las bandas / el medio campo*
the terrace / a stand	*los palcos / una tribuna*
the bench	*un banquillo*
floodlighting	*los focos*
muddy	*embarrado(a)*

THE PLAYERS (abc)	*LOS JUGADORES*
an amateur	*un amateur*
to award a free kick	*pitar un penalty*
the away team	*el equipo de fuera*
to be on the bench	*estar en el banquillo*
to blow the whistle	*tocar el pito / pitar*
a coach	*un entrenador*
a defender	*un defensa*
the favourites	*los favoritos*
a footballer	*un futbolista*
a forward	*un delantero*
a goal keeper	*un portero / guardameta*
the home team	*el equipo de casa*
a manager	*un directivo*
a mid-fielder	*un centro campista*

FOOTBALL cont. — *FUTBOL cont.*

THE PLAYERS cont. (abc) — *LOS JUGADORES cont.*

an opponent	*un oponente / rival*
a penalty	*un penalty*
a professional	*un profesional*
a referee	*un árbitro*
a striker	*un puntero*
the strong side	*el punto fuerte*
a substitute	*un sustituto / suplente*
to be substituted on / off	*ser sustituido*
a sweeper	*un líbero*
the teams	*los equipos*
to transfer	*cambiar / transferir*
a transfer fee	*una cantidad*
the weak side	*el punto flaco*

THE SPECTATORS	*LOS ESPECTADORES / SEGUIDORES*
a spectator	*un espectador*
a fan	*un fan*
a supporter	*un seguidor*
the crowd	*la multitud*
a ticket holder	*el espectador*
a tout	*un revendedor*
to cheer	*animar*
to shout	*gritar*
to chant	*canturrear*
to sing	*cantar*
the national anthem	*el himnonacional*
a football hooligan	*un hooligan / un gamberro*

FOOTBALL cont. — *FUTBOL cont.*

PLAY	***JUEGO***
a kick / to kick off	*una patada / dar una patada*
a free kick / a corner kick	*una falta directa / un saque de esquina*
a goal kick	*un saque de portería*
an indirect free kick	*una falta indirecta*
to pass // to dribble	*pasar // regatear / driblar*
to head	*pasar / dar de cabeza*
a header	*un cabeceador*
to throw in	*lanzar a*
to tackle / a tackle	*tacklear / un tackle*
to intercept // to challenge	*interceptar / roztar// desafiar*
a good / bad challenge	*un buen / mal desafío*
to take a corner	*rechazar de saque de esquina / lanzar un saque de esquina*
to be offside	*estar fuera de juego*
to be sent off	*expulsar*
to be shown the red / yellow card	*mostrar la tarjeta amarilla / roja*
tactics	*tácticas (f.pl)*
the rules	*las reglas*
the rule book	*el libro de reglas / el reglamento*
against the rules	*en contra de las reglas*
foul play / a foul	*juego sucio / una falta*
a penalty	*un penalty*
the penalty spot	*el punto de penalty*
a penalty goal	*un gol de penalty*
a penalty shoot out	*un tiro de penalty*

THE SCORE	***EL MARCADOR***
an aggregate score	*un marcador conjunto*
What is the score?	*¿Cuántos van?*
to score an own goal	*marcar un gol en propia meta*
to equalize	*igualar*
to win	*ganar*

FOOTBALL cont. — *FUTBOL cont.*

THE RESULT	*EL RESULTADO*
a win / to win	*una victoria / ganar*
a victory	*una victoria*
a walk over	*una victoria aplastante*
a draw / to draw	*empate (m) / empatar*
a defeat / to be defeated	*una derrota / ser derrotado*
to lose	*perder*
a tie / to tie	*un desempate / desempatar*
a replay	*una prorroga*
a match	*un partido*
a friendly	*un partido amistoso*
no score	*empates a cero*

STAGE OF THE GAME	*PERIODOS DEL JUEGO*
first half	*primera mitad / parte*
second half	*segunda mitad / parte*
half time	*la mitad del tiempo*
full time	*el final del tiempo*
extra time	*tiempo añadido*
injury time	*tiempo por lesión*

GENERAL TERMS	*TERMINOS GENERALES*
soccer	*futbolista*
the football season	*la temporada futbolística*
the football league	*la liga de fútbol*
divisions	*las divisiones*
first / second / third division	*primera / segunda y tercera división*
League Division One	*La Primera División de Liga*
the Premier League	*La Liga Profesional*
a cup / a trophy	*una copa / un trofeo*

FOOTBALL cont. *FUTBOL cont.*

EQUIPMENT	***EQUIPO***
a football	*un balón de fútbol*
kit	*el conjunto / los colores*
home kit	*colores / conjunto de casa*
away kit	*conjunto / colores para jugar fuera de casa*
team strip	*banda de capitán de equipo*
shorts	*pantalones cortos de fútbol*
a shirt	*una camiseta*
socks	*calcetas*
football boots	*botas de fútbol*
a sweatband	*una cinta*

USEFUL EXPRESSIONS	***EXPRESIONES UTILES***
Who's playing?	*¿Quienes juegan?*
What's the score?	*¿Cómo van?*
There's no score yet.	*No se han marcado goles todavía?*
to play injury time	*Están en una suspensión de tiempo por lesión.*
They won by five goals to nil.	*Ganaron por cinco goles a cero.*
They failed to score.	*No marcaron.*
It was a draw.	*Empataron.*
They took the lead in the second half.	*Se pusieron en cabeza en la segunda parte.*

RUGBY
RUGBY

THE PLAYERS	***LOS JUGADORES***
the forwards	*los delanteros*
the back row / the front row	*la línea trasera / el frontal*
the second row	*la segunda fila*
a hooker / a flanker	*un escolta / un atacante*
the half backs	*medios traseros*
scrum half / fly half	*medio de melée / medio libre*
three quarter backs / fullback	*cuartos traseros / traseros*
wing three quarter	*cuarto lateral*

THE FIELD	***EL CAMPO***
the goal	*la portería / los palos*
the uprights	*los postes / montantes*
the cross bar	*el larguero*
halfway line	*la línea de centro de campo*
goal line	*la línea de gol*
the twenty two line	*la línea de veintidós*

THE PLAY (abc)	***EL JUEGO***
to bounce	*botar / rebotar*
converted	*convertido*
a drop kick	*una patada botada*
to drop kick	*dar una patada botada*
a free kick	*una patada en reposo*
to hook	*placar*
a line out	*un desmarque*
mark	*señal*
a penalty	*un penalty / un saque de castizo*
a penalty try	*un intento*
a scrummage / scrum	*una melée*
to touch down	*hacer touch down*

ICE SKATING
EL PATINAJE SOBRE HIELO

WOULD YOU LIKE TO GO ICE SKATING?	***¿TE GUSTARIA PATINAR SOBRE HIELO?***
Can you skate?	*¿Sabes patinar?*
How long have you skated?	*¿Cuándo aprendiste a patinar?*
Would you like to have a go at it?	*¿Te gustaría intentarlo?*

THE ICE RINK	***LA PISTA DE PATINAJE***
the ticket office	*La taquilla para la venta de entradas*
Could we have four tickets, please?	*¿Queremos cuatro entradas?*
Have you got your own boots?	*¿Tienes vuestras propias botas?*
Do you want to hire boots?	*¿Quereis alquilar patines?*
Could I have two tickets for the ice rink and we would like to hire boots, please.	*Quiero dos entradas para la pista de patinaje, y nos gustaría alquilar botas de patinar.*

BOOT HIRE	***ALQUILER DE PATINES***
What size of shoe do you take?	*¿Qué talla de pies tienes?*
I am size six.	*Tengo la talla seis*
I am a continental size forty.	*Tengo la talla cuarenta continental.*
You take your shoes off and hand them in at the boot hire shop.	*Tienes que quitarte los zapatos y dejarlos en la tienda de alquiler.*
Try your skates on.	*Pruebate los patines.*
How do you fasten them?	*¿Cómo se abrochan?*
You fasten them like this.	*Se abrochan así.*
Are they comfortable?	*¿Te están bien?*
These boots hurt.	*Estas botas me hacen daño.*
Can I change my boots, please?	*¿Puedo probarme otras?*

ICE SKATING cont. / *EL PATINAJE SOBRE HIELO cont.*

ON THE ICE	*SOBRE EL HIELO*
Hold on to the handrail at first.	*Sujétate a la barra al principio.*
Should we skate round the edge until you're used to it?	*¿Quieres patinar cerca del borde hasta que te acostumbres?*
to fall over	*caerse*
to get knocked down	*ser derribado*
Someone pushed me over.	*Alguien me empujó.*
Can you help me to get up, please?	*¿Puedes ayudarme a levantarme?*
Are you O.K.?	*¿Estás bien?*
You're doing really well.	*Lo estás haciendo muy bien.*
I think I'll just watch for a bit.	*Creo que voy a mirar por un ratito solamente.*

TYPES OF SKATING	*TIPOS DE PATINAJE*
speed skating	*patinaje de velocidad*
figure skating	*patinaje de exhibición*
ice dancing	*baile sobre hielo*
solo skating	*patinaje sobre hielo individual*
pair skating	*patinaje sobre hielo en odalidad de parejas / en doble*
a leap	*un salto / un brinco*
a spiral	*una espiral / un tirabuzón*
a jump	*un salto*
a spin	*un giro*

TABLE TENNIS
PING-PONG / TENIS DE MESA

CAN YOU PLAY TABLE TENNIS?	***¿JUEGAS AL PING-PONG?***
Would you like to play table tennis / ping pong?	*¿Quieres jugar al ping-pong?*
Do you have a table tennis table?	*¿Tienes mesa de ping-pong?*
Do you play much?	*¿Juegas mucho?*
I haven't played for ages.	*¿No he jugado desde hace mucho tiempo?*
I've forgotten how to play.	*Se me ha olvidado como jugar*
Shall I teach you how to play?	*¿Quieres que te enseñe a jugar?*

EQUIPMENT	***EQUIPO***
a table tennis table	*una mesa de ping-pong*
the white line	*una línea blanca*
the net	*la red*
the edge of the table	*el borde de la mesa*
a bat	*una pala / una raqueta*
Which bat do you prefer?	*¿Qué pala / raqueta prefieres?*
I'll take this one.	*Me quedo con ésta.*
a table tennis ball	*Una pelota de ping-pong*
Have you got any more balls?	*¿Tienes más pelotas?*
This ball isn't bouncing properly.	*¿Está pelota bota raro?*

PLAYING	***JUGANDO***
Let's choose ends.	*Vamos a elegir el campo.*
Spin the racket.	*Lanza la raqueta.*
Toss for it.	*Échalo a suerte.*
We change ends every game.	*Se cambia de campo cada juego.*

TABLE TENNIS cont. / *PING-PONG / TENIS DE MESA cont.*

DOUBLES	***DOBLES / EN PAREJAS***
In doubles the players take alternate shots.	*En parejas los jugadores golpean alternativamente.*
You have to serve from the right to the right.	*Tienes que sacar desde la derecha hacia la derecha.*
Each player receives service for five points.	*Cada jugador tiene cinco saques.*

SINGLES	***INDIVIDUALES***
You serve first.	*Sacas primero.*
You change service every five points.	*Se cambia el saque cada cinco puntos.*
Whose service is it?	*¿Quién saca?*
It's mine / yours.	*Yo / tú*
It's your service now because five points have been scored.	*Te toca sacar porque se han marcado cinco puntos.*

SHOTS	***GOLPES***
to hit forehand	*golpear de derechas*
to hit backhand	*golpear de revés*
to serve	*servir / sacar*
You hit the net.	*Has dado en la red.*
Where did the ball land?	*¿Dónde golpeó la pelota?*
Was it in or out?	*¿Está dentro o fuera?*
It was in / out.	*Cayó dentro / fuera.*
It didn't land on the table.	*No cayó en la mesa.*
It was a let.	*Ha sido media.*
Play it again.	*Saca otra vez.*
Can you find the ball?	*¿Puedes encontrar la pelota?*
Did you see exactly where it went?	*¿Viste dónde cayó exactamente?*

TABLE TENNIS cont. / *PING-PONG / TENIS DE MESA cont.*

SCORING	***PUNTUANDO***
What's the score?	*¿Cómo vamos?*
Love all.	*iguales a cero.*
One love.	*Uno a cero.*
Three, two.	*Tres, dos.*
Twenty, twenty.	*Iguales a veinte.*
The service changes every point now.	*El saque cambia en cada punto ahora.*
The winner is the first person to score twenty one points.	*El ganador es el primero en llegar a veintiuno.*
You have to get two points ahead of me to win.	*Tienes que sacarme dos puntos de diferencia para ganar.*
You won easily.	*Me ganaste con facilidad.*
Well played! / Bad luck!	*¡Bien jugado! / ¡Mala Suerte!*
It was a close game.	*Ha estado muy empatado / reñido.*
Shall we play the best of three games?	*¿Jugamos a ver quién gana tres juegos?*

GOLF
EL GOLF

THE GOLF COURSE		*EL TRAYECTO DE GOLF*	
the links	*la cancha de golf*	thirteenth	*trece*
a hole	*un hoyo*	fourteenth	*catorce*
first	*el primero*	fifteenth	*quince*
second	*el segundo*	sixteenth	*dieciséis*
third	*el tercero*	seventeenth	*diecisiete*
fourth	*el cuarto*	eighteenth	*dieciocho*
fifth	*el quinto*	the fairway	*la calle*
sixth	*el sexto*	the rough	*la hierba*
seventh	*el séptimo*	the green	*el green*
eighth	*el octavo*	the putting green	*el área del hoyo*
ninth	*el noveno*	a flag	*la banderilla*
tenth	*el décimo*	the hole	*el hoyo*
eleventh	*el once*	a tee	*un primer golpe / la salida / tee*
twelfth	*el doce*		

OBSTACLES		*OBSTACULOS*	
a hazard	*un obstáculo*	sand	*arena*
long grass	*la hierba*	a ditch	*un dique*
bushes	*arbustos*	a pond	*un estanque*
trees	*árboles*	a lake	*un lago*
a bunker	*un bunker*		

OTHER PARTS OF THE GOLF CLUB	*OTRAS PARTES DEL CLUB DE GOLF*
the club house / the bar	*la caseta del Club / el bar*
the practice ground / green	*el campo / "green" de ensayo*
miniature golf	*el Mini-Golf*
crazy golf	*el golf "loco"*

GOLF cont. / *EL GOLF cont.*

THE EQUIPMENT	*EL MATERIAL*
a golf bag	*una bolsa de golf*
a caddie	*un cadi*
a set of golf clubs	*un juego de palos*
the woods	*los palos de madera*
a driver	*un palo de golf para golpear*
one / two / three / four / five	*uno / dos / tres / cuatro/ cinco*
the irons	*los palos de golf de hierro*
six / seven / eight / nine	*seis / siete / ocho / nueve*
the putter	*un putter*
a golf ball	*una pelota de golf*
a tee	*un primer golpe*

THE STROKES	*LOS GOLPES*
You must shout "Fore!".	*Tienes que gritar por todas partes*
to tee up / to strike	*dar el primer golpe / golpear*
to drive	*hacer un drive*
a beautiful drive	*un drive bueno*
to hook	*dejar colgada*
to slice	*dar efecto*
to make an approach shot	*dar un toque de acercamiento*
to putt	*hacer un putt*
a putt	*un putt*
to tap	*un golpecito / un toque*
to hole	*embocar / meter en el hoyo*
a shot	*un golpe*
a long shot	*un golpe largo*
a chip shot	*un empuje / un toque ligero*
a low / high shot	*un golpe bajo / alto*
to swing	*un swing*
a short / long swing	*un swing corto / largo*

GOLF cont. / *EL GOLF cont.*

THE SCORING	***LA PUNTUACION***
par / under par / over par	*par / bajo par / sobre par*
a birdie	*un Birdie*
an eagle / a double eagle	*un Eagle / un doble Eagle*
a hole in one	*un hoyo de una*
a bogey / a double bogey	*un Bogey / un doble Bogey*
a handicap	*un handicap*
What is your handicap?	*¿Cuál es tu handicap?*

MOTOR RACING
CARRERAS DE COCHES

THE COURSE	*EL TRAYECTO*
the starting line	*la línea de salida*
the finishing line	*la línea de meta*
the chequered flag	*la bandera de cuadros*
the track	*la pista*
a lane	*un carril*
the inside / outside lane	*el carril de dentro / de fuera*
a lap / to do a lap	*una vuelta / dar una vuelta*
to lap someone	*sacar una vuelta de ventaja a alguien*
to do a lap of honour	*dar una vuelta de honor*
a five lap course	*una carrera de cinco vueltas al circuito*
a circuit	*un circuito*
a bend	*una curva*
a double bend	*una doble curva*
a hairpin bend	*una curva peligrosa*
He took the bend too fast.	*tomó la curva demasiado deprisa*
a chicane	*una chicana*
the pits	*las boxes*
a crash barrier	*una barrera protectora*

THE PEOPLE	*LA GENTE*
a racing driver	*un corredor de carreras*
a champion	*un campeón / una campeona*
an ex-champion	*un ex-campeón / una ex-campeona*
a winner	*un ganador / una ganadora*
a runner-up	*un subganador / una subganadora*
a loser	*un perdedor / una perdedora*
a spectator	*un espectador*
a mechanic	*un mecánico*
a co-driver	*un copiloto*

MOTOR RACING cont. — *CARRERAS DE COCHES cont.*

THE RACING CAR	***UN COCHE DE CARRERAS***
the steering wheel	*el volante*
the accelerator	*el acelerador*
the brakes	*los frenos*
the tyres / new tyres	*las neumáticos / los neumáticos de recambio (nuevos)*
a puncture	*un pinchazo*
to change the tyres	*cambiar los neumáticos*
the bumper	*el parachoques*
the chassis	*el chasis*
the body	*la carrocería*
the make of car	*la marca del coche*
the engine size	*el tamaño del motor*
the horse power	*el cilindraje*
the speed	*la velocidad*

THE VERBS (abc)	***VERBOS***
to accelerate	*acelerar*
to be out of control	*perder el control*
to brake / to slow down	*frenar / reducir la velocidad*
to collide / to crash	*chocar / chocar*
to correct a skid	*corregir un derrape*
to drive / to race	*conducir / echar una carrera*
to finish	*finalizar*
to lap / to overtake	*dar una vuelta / adelantar*
to lose	*perder*
to show the chequered flag	*enseñar la bandera de llegada*
to skid / leave skid marks	*derrapar / dejar marcas de derrape*
to start	*arrancar*
to steer	*girar*
to take on the inside	*tomar el carril interior / de dentro*
to win	*ganar*

ATHLETICS
ATLETISMO

THE KIT	***EL CONJUNTO***
a track suit / a sweat shirt	*un chandal / una sudadera*
shorts / a shirt	*unos pantalones / una camisa*
a skirt	*una falda*
a leotard	*un leotardo*
trainers	*unas zapatillas de deporte*
spikes	*zapatillas con clavos*
a towel	*una toalla*
a sports bag	*una bolsa de deporte*

THE ATHLETES	***LOS ATLETAS***
a jogger / to jog	*un corredor / hacer jogging*
I go jogging.	*Hago jogging.*
to keep fit	*Mantenerse en forma*
a sprinter / to sprint	*Un corredor de distancias cortas / un sprinter / hacer un sprint*
to run / to race against	*correr / correr contra*
a middle distance runner	*un corredor de distancias medias*
a marathon runner	*un corredor de maratón*

JUMPERS	***SALTADORES***
to jump	*saltar*
a hurdler	*un saltador de vallas*
to hurdle / a hurdle	*saltar una valla / una valla*
a high jumper / a long jumper	*un saltador de altura / de longitud*
a pole vaulter	*un saltador de pértiga*
to vault	*saltar con la pértiga*

THROWERS	***LANZADORES DE DISCOS***
a discus thrower / to throw	*un lanzador de disco / lanzar*
a javelin thrower	*un lanzador de jabalina*
a shot putter	*un lanzador de pesos*

ATHLETICS cont. / *ATLETISMO cont.*

OTHER SPORTSMEN AND WOMEN	*OTROS DEPORTISTAS*
a gymnast	*un(a) gimnasta*
a decathlete / a heptathlete	*un(a) decatleta / un(a) hepatleta*
an amateur / a professional	*un amateur / un profesional*
a coach	*un entrenador / una entrenadora*

RECORD HOLDERS	*POSEEDORES DE RéCORDOS*
to break the record	*romper un record / marca*
a record breaker / a champion	*una persona / atleta que rompe un record / un campeón*
Well inside the record time.	*Lejos del tiempo record*
Just inside the record time.	*Cerca del tiempo record*
a world record holder	*un plusmarquista mundial*
to run one's personal best	*conseguir una mejor marca personal*

EVENTS	*EVENTOS*
a meeting	*una reunión*
warm-up exercises	*ejercicios de calentamiento*
to warm up	*calentarse / hacer calentamiento*
track events	*las modalidades de pista*
runs / walks	*carreras / marcha*
field events	*las actividades de campo*
jumps / throws	*saltos / lanzamientos*
short races / sprints	*carreras cortas / carreras de corta distancia*
one hundred metres	*los cien metros*
middle distance races	*carreras de distancias medias*
one thousand five hundred metres	*los mil quinientos metros*
long distance races	*carreras de largas distancias*
the half marathon / the marathon	*el medio-maratón / el maratón*
a steady pace	*una marcha regular*
a final spurt	*una remontada final*

ATHLETICS cont. — *ATLETISMO cont.*

RELAY RACES	***CARRERA DE RELEVOS***
the baton	*el testigo*
a leg	*una pierna*
the first / last leg	*la primer / la segunda pierna*
a hand over	*un relevo*

HURDLING	***SALTANDO VALLAS***
hurdles / to hurdle	*vallas / saltar vallas*
to clear	*pasar*

LONG JUMP	***SALTO DE LONGITUD***
distance	*distancia*
the take off	*la salida / el despegue*
the landing	*la caída*

HIGH JUMP	***SALTO DE ALTURA***
the cross bar	*la barra*
the height	*la altura*
to raise	*subir*
to attempt	*hacer un intento*
to clear	*pasar*
three attempts	*tres intentos*
the first / second / third attempt	*el primer / segundo / tercer intento*
the final attempt	*el último intento*
to be disqualified	*ser descalificado*

TRIPLE JUMP	***EL TRIPLE SALTO***
a hop / a skip / a jump	*un bote / un brinco / un salto*

ATHLETICS cont. — *ATLETISMO cont.*

POLE VAULTING	*SALTO DE PERTIGA*
the pole	*la pértiga*
the cross bar	*la barra*
a height increase	*un aumento de altura*
to dislodge the bar	*derribar la barra*
three misses	*tres intentos fallados*
to disqualify	*ser descalificado*

SHOT PUT	*EL LANZAMIENTO DE PESOS*
the longest throw	*el lanzamiento más largo*
the discus throw	*el lanzamiento de disco*
the javelin throw	*el lanzamiento de jabalina*

GYMNASTICS — *GIMNASIA*

Qualities needed (abc)		*La cualidades requeridas*	
agility	*agilidad*	grace	*gracia*
balance	*equilibrio*	rhythm	*ritmo*
flexibility	*flexibilidad*	strength	*fuerza*

The moves (abc)	*Los Movimientos*
a balance / a cartwheel	*un equilibrio / un giro completo*
a drop	*caída*
(a back drop / a front drop)	*una caída de espaldas / de frente*
the floor exercises	*los ejercicios de suelo*
the grip changes	*los cambios de muñecas*
a handstand	*un pino*
a jump / a landing	*un salto / un aterrizaje*
a leap / a skip / a turn	*un brinco / un brinco / una vuelta*
(a half / fullturn)	*una media-vuelta / un giro*
a vault	*un puente*

ATHLETICS cont. / *ATLETISMO cont.*

THE APPARATUS	***LOS APARATOS***
a horizontal bar	*la barra horizontal*
a horse vault	*un caballo de anillas*
the parallel bars	*la paralelas*
the rings	*las anillas*
the side horse	*el caballo de salto*
a springboard	*un trampolín*
a trampoline	*un trampolín*
the uneven bars	*las barras*

THE STADIUM	***EL ESTADIO***
the arena / the track	*la arena / la pista*
the lanes	*los callejones*
the inside / outside lane	*el callejón de dentro / exterior*
the middle lane	*el callejón del medio*
the starting line / block	*la línea / la casilla de salida*
the starting pistol	*la pistola de salida*
a false start	*la falsa salida*
On your marks, get ready, go!	*En sus puestos / marcas ¡preparados, listos, ya!*

MEDALS	***MEDALLAS***
a Gold / Silver / Bronze medal	*una medalla de oro/ plata/ bronce*
to be awarded / to win	*ser galardonado / ganar*
to be presented	*ser presentado*

THE OLYMPICS	***LOS JUEGOS OLIMPICOS / LAS OLIMPIADAS***
an Olympic medal	*una medalla olímpica*
the Olympic games	*los juegos olímpicos*
the Olympic torch	*la antorcha olímpica*
to light / to carry / to burn	*encender / llevar / quemar*
an Olympic Champion	*un campeón olímpico*
the next / last Olympics	*las próximas / últimas olimpiadas*

CRICKET
EL CRÍCKET / EL CRÍQUET

Although cricket is not generally played on the Continent, this section may be useful to help your foreign exchange to understand the game when he/she visits England.

Aunque el cricket no es muy jugado en el continente, este apartado te será útil en tu intercambio para comprender el juego cuando él o ella visiten Inglaterra.

CLOTHES	***ROPAS***
cricket whites	*el conjunto blanco*
leg pads	*las rodilleras*
a pullover	*un jersey*
trousers	*los pantalones*
a shirt	*una camisa*
gloves	*guantes*

EQUIPMENT	***EQUIPO***
a cricket bat	*un bate de cricket*
a cricket ball	*una pelota de cricket*
the wickets	*tres palos*
the grooves	*las ranuras*
thc bails	*dos palillos horizontales*

THE CRICKET FIELD	***EL CAMPO DE CRICKET***
the pitch	*el campo*
the wickets	*los palos*
the boundary	*la línea de fuera*
the bowling crease	*la línea de lanzamiento*

CRICKET cont. — *EL CRÍCKET / EL CRÍQUET cont.*

THE FIELDERS' POSITIONS	*LA POSICION DE LOS CAMPISTAS*
slip	*slip*
second slip	*segundo slip*
gully	*gully*
point	*point*
cover point	*cover point*
mid off	*medio derecha*
long off	*largo derecha*
long on	*largo izquierda*
mid on	*medio izquierda*
mid wicket	*media distancia desde los palos a la izquierda*
legside	*izquierda*
offside	*derecha*

THE PLAYERS	*LOS JUGADORES*
the captain	*el capitán*
the umpires	*los árbitros*
the teams	*los equipos*
the batsman	*el bateador*
the bowler	*el boleador / el lanzadór*
the wicket keeper	*el guardia de los palos*
the fielders	*los jugadores de campo / las campista*

PLAYING CRICKET	*JUGANDO A CRICKET*
to toss a coin	*echar una moneda al aire*
to win / lose the toss	*ganar / perder en la suerte*
to bat first	*batear primero*
to position the fielders	*colocar a los jugadores de campo*

CRICKET cont. / *EL CRÍCKET / EL CRÍQUET*

BOWLING	***LANZANDO LA BOLA***
to bowl	*bolear / lanzar la bola*
to bowl overarm / underarm	*bolear alta / baja*
to bowl out	*eliminar*
to be bowled out	*ser eliminado*
to throw	*lanzar*
a bye / a leg bye	*un bye / un leg bye*
a wide	*un wide*
no ball	*no ball*
a full-pitch ball	*una boleada larga*
a shooter	*una shooter*
a yorker	*una yorker*
to spin the ball	*dar efecto a la pelota*
an over (= six balls)	*un over (= seis pelotas)*
a maiden over (= an over with no score)	*un over sín puntuación*
a fast bowler	*un lanzador rápido*
a spin bowler	*un lanzador de efectos*

BATTING	***BATEANDO***
to bat / to hit / to cut	*batear / golpear / cortar*
He is batting now.	*El batéa ahora / le toca batear ahora*
She is a good batter.	*Batea muy bien / Es una buena bateadora*
to be out / to be bowled out	*ser eliminado*
leg before wicket (L.B.W.)	*pierna delante de los palos*
to hit the wicket	*golpear los palos*
to be stumped out	*ser eliminado por el boleador al derribar los palos*
to be run out	*golpear los palos cuando el jugador esta corriendo de base en base*
to be caught out	*coger la pelota al vuelo*

CRICKET cont. — ***EL CRÍCKET / EL CRÍQUET cont.***

BATTING cont.	*BATEANDO cont.*
to be out for a duck (= to score no runs)	= *no marcar ninguna vuelta*
to score	*marcar*
a run	*una vuelta / una carrera*
a four (= hit the ball to the boundary)	*golpe directo en bote o rodando (golpear la pelota y mandarla fuera del campo)*
a six (= as a four but without the ball bouncing)	*golpe directo al vuelo (sin que bote)*
a century (=one hundred runs)	= *cien carreras*

FIELDING	*ESPERANDO EN PIE PARA RECOGER LA PELOTA*
to field	*estar a la espera de una recogida*
to catch	*coger al vuelo*
to drop a catch	*dejar caer un catch*
a good catch	*una buena recogida al vuelo*

AN INNINGS	*UN TURNO DE BATEO*
the first innings	*el primer bateo / la primera ronda*
the second innings	*el segundo bateo / la segunda ronda*

TYPE OF GAME	*TIPOS DE JUEGOS*
a test match	*un partido internacional*
one day cricket	*una jornada de cricket*
a friendly match	*un partido amistoso*

SWIMMING
NATACION

DO YOU LIKE SWIMMING?	*¿TE GUSTA NADAR?*
Yes, I love swimming.	*Sí, me encanta nadar.*
No, I'm sorry, but I can't swim.	*No, lo siento, pero no sé nadar.*
Would you like to go swimming?	*¿Te gustaría ir a nadar?*
I don't really like swimming.	*No me gusta nadar.*

TYPES OF POOL	*TIPOS DE PISCINAS*
a public / private swimming pool	*una piscina pública / privada*
an indoor / outdoor pool	*una piscina cubierta / al aire libre*
a heated / unheated pool	*una piscina con sistema de calefacción / una piscina sín sistema de calefacción*
an aquatic park	*un aquapark*

CLOTHES AND EQUIPMENT	*ROPA Y EQUIPO*
a swimming costume	*un bañador*
a bikini	*un bikini*
trunks	*unos pantalones cortos / un bañador boxer*
shorts	*unos pantalones cortos*
a swimming hat	*un gorro para el agua*
a towel	*una toalla*
goggles	*una gafas de nadar*
a snorkel	*un snorkel*
flippers	*una aletas*
a rubber ring	*un flotador*
armbands	*unos brazaletes*
a lilo	*una tumbona para el agua*
a float	*un flotador*

SWIMMING cont. — *NATACIÓN cont.*

BUYING TICKETS	*COMPRANDO LA ENTRADA*
an adult's ticket	*una entrada para adulto*
a child's ticket	*una entrada para niño*
a swimmer's ticket	*una entrada para nadar*
a spectator's ticket	*una entrada para el palco de espectadores*
Could I have tickets for two children, please?	*¿Me da dos entradas para menores?*
Could I have two adult spectator tickets, please?	*¿Me da dos entradas para adulto?*
Are there tubes at this swimming pool?	*¿Hay toboganes en la piscina?*
Could we have tickets to go down the tubes, please?	*¿Me da entradas para montar en los toboganes?*

TIMES OF SESSIONS	*TIPOS DE SESIONES / TURNOS*
When does this session start?	*¿A qué hora empieza este turno?*
When does this session end?	*¿A qué hora termina este turno?*
When does our session end?	*¿Cuando termina nuestro turno?*
They blow a whistle at the end of the session.	*Hacen una señal con el silbato cuando se acaba.*
When does the next session start?	*¿A qué hora es el próximo turno?*
What time does the pool open on Saturday?	*¿A qué hora abre la piscina los sábados?*
What time does the pool close?	*¿A qué hora cierra la piscina?*

SWIMMING cont. — *NATACIÓN cont.*

THE PARTS OF THE POOL — *LAS PARTES DE LA PISCINA*

NON-SWIMMING AREAS	*AREAS FUERA DE LA PISCINA*
The Spectator Area	***El Palco de Espectadores***
I think I will sit and watch, if you don't mind.	*Creo que sí no te importa prefiero sentarme y mirar.*
The Café	***El Café / La Cafetería***
I shall go and get something to eat and drink.	*Voy a comprar algo de beber y comer*
The Drinks Machine	***La Máquina de bebidas***
What change does the drinks machine take?	*¿Qué moneda necesito para la máquina de bebidas?*

THE CHANGING ROOMS	*LOS VESTUARIOS*
Where are the changing rooms?	*¿Dónde están los vestuarios?*
Is there a family changing room?	*¿Hay vestuarios familiares?*
They are all individual cubicles.	*Todos son cambiadores individuales.*
There are separate changing rooms for men and women.	*Hay vestuarios de caballeros y señoras.*
The changing rooms are for both sexes.	*Los vestuarios son unisex.*

SWIMMING cont. — ***NATACIÓN cont.***

GETTING CHANGED	*CAMBIÁNDOSE*
Shall we get changed together?	*¿Nos cambiamos a la vez?*
I'll use this cubicle.	*Voy a meterme en este cambiador.*
to get undressed / to get dressed	*desvestirse / vestirse*
to dry oneself / one's hair	*secarse / secarse el pelo*
to use talcum powder	*poner polvos de talco*
a coin operated hair dryer	*un secador por monedas*
a hair brush / to brush	*un cepillo / cepillarse*
a comb / to comb	*un peine / peinarse*
a mirror / to look in	*un espejo / mirarse en*

THE LOCKERS	*LAS TAQUILLAS*
What coins do you need for the lockers?	*¿Qué moneda necesito para las taquillas?*
How do the lockers work?	*¿Cómo funcionan las taquillas?*
Don't forget the number of your locker.	*No olvides el número de tu taquilla.*
Can you remember our locker number?	*¿Te acuerdas del número de nuestra taquilla?*
I have forgotten the number of my locker.	*Me he olvidado del número de nuestra taquilla.*
My locker was somewhere here.	*Mí taquilla es una de éstas.*
to lock / unlock the door	*cerrar / quitar la llave para abrir.*
Don't lose your key.	*No pierdas la llave.*
Put your clothes in here.	*Pon tu ropa aquí dentro.*

THE FOOTBATH AND SHOWERS	*EL TERRPLEN DE AGUA PARA LOS PIES Y LAS DUCHAS*
You have to walk through the footbath.	*Tienes que mojarte los pies aquí.*
You are supposed to shower before getting into the pool.	*Tienes que ducharte antes de entrar en la piscina.*

SWIMMING cont. / *NATACIÓN cont.*

THE POOLS	*LAS PISCINAS*
the paddling pool	*la piscina para niños pequeños*
the children's pool	*la piscina para menores*
the main pool	*la piscina principal*

PARTS OF THE POOL	*LAS PARTES DE LA PISCINA*
the deep end	*la parte profunda*
the shallow end	*la parte baja*
a length / a width	*un largo / un ancho*
How long is the pool?	*¿Qué longitud tiene la piscina?*
How wide is it?	*¿Qué anchura tiene?*
the depth	*la profundidad*
How deep is it at the deep / shallow end?	*¿Cómo es de profunda en la parte profunda / en la parte baja?*
the diving board	*el trampolín de saltos*
the slide	*el tobogán*

WAVE MACHINES	*LA MAQUINA DE OLEAJE*
Does this pool have a wave machine?	*¿Tiene esta piscina máquina de oleaje?*
They put the wave machine on at intervals.	*Ponen la máquina a intervalos.*
The waves are just starting.	*Las olas van a empezar.*
They usually have the waves on for five minutes.	*Normalmente ponen las olas unos cinco minutos.*
There's also a water spout.	*También hay un tobogán con corriente de agua / bocas de agua.*

SWIMMING cont. / *NATACIÓN cont.*

TUBES	*TUBOS / TOBOGANES*
Pick up a mat.	*Cógete una alfombrilla.*
This session is using blue / red / yellow mats.	*En este turno se usan las alfombrillas azules / rojas / amarillas.*
You sit on a mat.	*Sientate en una alfrombrilla.*
Wait till the tube is clear.	*Espera hasta que el tobogán este desocupado.*
You can go down now.	*Baja / tírate ahora.*
What is this tube like?	*¿Qué tal te los pasas en el tobogán?*
It's steep.	*Está muy inclinado.*
It has a gentle slope.	*Está ligeramente inclinado.*
It bends a lot.	*Tiene muchas curvas.*
There's a corkscrew.	*Tiene un rizo.*
That one is really fast.	*Ese es muy rápido.*
It's like a water chute.	*Es como un chorro de agua.*
Which tube do you like best?	*¿Qué tobogán te gusta más?*
I like this one / that one best.	*Me gusta éste / ese mucho más.*
Have you been down all the tubes?	*¿Has probado todos los toboganes?*
I didn't like that one.	*No me gustó ese.*
That one was brilliant.	*Ese está fenomenal.*

SWIMMING STROKES	*ESTILOS DE NATACION*
to swim / to go for a swim	*nadar / ir a nadar*
to float on your back / front	*flotar boca arriba / abajo*
to swim breast stroke	*nadar a braza*
back stroke / side stroke	*estilo de espalda / estilo de lado*
crawl / butterfly stroke	*crawl / estilo mariposa*
Can you swim back stroke?	*¿Sabes nadar de espalda?*
I can't do butterfly.	*No se nadar a mariposa.*

SWIMMING cont. / *NATACIÓN cont.*

UNDERWATER SWIMMING	***BUCEO***
Can you swim under water?	*¿Sabes bucear?*
I only like swimming under water with goggles on.	*¿Sólo buceo con gafas de bucear?*
How far can you swim under water?	*¿Cuánto aguantes bajo el agua?*
to swim between someone's legs	*nadar por debajo de las piernas de álguien*

RACING	***ECHAR CARRERAS***
to race	*echar una carrera*
Let's have a race.	*Vamos a echar una carrera.*
I'll race you to the far end.	*Te echo una carrera a ver quien llega al otro lado primero.*
I won / you won.	*Gané / has ganado.*
It was a draw.	*Empates.*
Let's see who can swim furthest?	*¿Vamos a ver quien nada más lejos?*
How many lengths can you swim?	*¿Cuántos largo puedes hacerte nadando?*

DIVING	***TIRARSE DE CABEZA***
to dive	*tirarse de cabeza*
Is it deep enough for diving?	*¿Tiene profundidad suficiente para tirarse de cabeza?*
I can dive but I'm not very good.	*Sé tirarme pero no se me da bien.*
Did I splash a lot then?	*¿He salpicado mucho?*
What did that dive look like.	*¿Qué tal me he tirado?*

SWIMMING cont. / *NATACIÓN cont.*

DIVING FOR COINS	*TIRÁNDOSE A LA BUSCA DE MONEDAS*
Should we dive for coins?	*¿Nos tiramos a buscar monedas?*
Have you any coins?	*¿Tienes monedas?*
Will you throw some coins in for us to find?	*¿Quieres lanzar monedas para que las busquemos?*

SAFETY	*SEGURIDAD*
a lifeguard	*el salvavidas / el socorrista*
the First Aid post	*la enfermería de primeros auxilios*
Can you life save?	*¿Has hecho socorrismo alguna vez?*
Don't go out of your depth.	*No vayas donde te cubre.*
Stay in the children's pool.	*Quédate en la piscina para menores.*
Don't run in case you slip.	*No corras, no vaya a ser que patines.*
You shouldn't swim just after eating.	*No creo que debieras nadar inmediatamente después de comer.*
I sometimes get cramp.	*A veces me dan calambres (m).*
I have got cramp in my right / left leg.	*Me ha dado un calambre en la pierna derecha / izquierda*

GETTING OUT OF THE POOL	*SALIENDO DE LA PISCINA*
They just blew the whistle to get out.	*Han tocado ya el silbato para indicar que tenemos que salir.*
It's the end of our session now.	*Se ha acabado nuestro turno.*
Shall we get out just before the end of our session so the changing rooms won't be so busy?	*¿Qué tal sí salimos de la piscina antes que se termine el turno para que nos encontremos los vestuarios sin demasiada gente.*
My mother said we have to get out now.	*Mí madre dice que tenemos que salir ya.*
You're looking cold / shivering.	*Tienes frío / Estás temblando.*
I think we should get out now.	*Creo que debieramos salir ahora.*
Can't we have five more minutes?	*¿Nos podemos quedar cinco minutos más?*

THE BEACH
LA PLAYA

THE SEA		*EL MAR*	
the tide	*la marea*	to go out	*retirarse*
high tide	*la marea alta*	a wave	*una ola*
low tide	*la marea baja*	to break	*romper*
to come in	*entrar*	spray	*salpicar*

THE BEACH	*LA PLAYA*
the sand / a pebble	*la arena / una piedrecita rodada*
a rock / a rock pool	*una roca / una charca entre rocas*
a starfish	*una estrella de mar*
shingle	*trozos de almejas y otras conchas*
the cliffs / a sand dune	*los acantilados/una duna de arena*
a jellyfish / seaweed	*una medusa / algas*

CLOTHES AND EQUIPMENT	*ROPA Y EQUIPO DE PLAYA*
a swimming costume	*un bañador*
a bikini / trunks	*un bikini / unos boxers*
to get changed / to get dressed	*cambiarse / vestirse*
to dry oneself / a towel	*secarse / una toalla*
a rubber ring	*un flotador*
armbands	*unos brazaletes / unos manguitos*
a surfboard / an inflatable	*una tabla de surf / un inflable*
a lilo / to float	*una cama de agua / flotar*
to have a turn on / with	*ser el turno tuyo / tocarme*
a deckchair	*una amaca*
a beach mat	*una alfombrilla de playa*
a wind break / a parasol	*una pantalla para el aire / un quitasol*

SWIMMING AND SNORKELLING	***NADANDO Y BUCEANDO CON SNORKEL***
Swimming - see pages 301-308	***Nadar***
to float	*flotar*
to ride on the waves	*tomar las olas*
Snorkelling	***Haciendo buceo con un snorkel / tubo***
to snorkel / a snorkel	*hacer buceo con tubo / un snorkel*
a mask	*una máscara*
a mouthpiece	*una boquilla*
a tube	*un tubo*
flippers	*aletas*
goggles	*gafas de bucear*

BUILDING SANDCASTLES	***HACIENDO CASTILLOS DE ARENA***
a bucket / a spade	*un cubo / una paleta*
a sandcastle	*un castillo de arena*
battlements / a drawbridge	*almenas / un puente elevadizo*
a tower / a flag	*una torreta / una bandera*
a moat / a mound / a tunnel	*un foso / un montón / un túnel*
to build	*construir*
to collect shells	*amontonar conchas*
to decorate with pebbles	*decorar con piedras rodadas*
to dig / to fill	*excavar / llenar*
to jump on // to knock down	*saltar / apretar// derribar*
to make / to pat	*hacer / aplastar*
to smooth	*suavizar / limar / rebajar*
to tunnel	*hacer un túnel*
to turn out	*sacar*
to wait for the tide to come in	*esperar a / que la marea entre*

THE BEACH cont. / *LA PLAYA cont.*

WALKING ON THE BEACH	*PASEANDO EN LA PLAYA*
to go for a walk	*ir de paseo*
along the beach	*a lo largo de la orilla*
on the cliffs / over the rocks	*en los acantilados / por las rocas*
at the edge of the sea	*a la orilla del mar*

COLLECTING SHELLS	*RECOGIENDO CONCHAS*
an unusual one / a pretty one	*una rara / una bonita*
a different type	*un tipo diferente*
broken	*rota*
to wash the sand off	*quitarle la arena*
to put in a bucket	*poner en un cubo*

SHRIMPING	*COGIENDO CAMARONES*
a fishing net	*una redecilla / un retal*
to catch	*coger*
to look at the rock pools	*mirar en las charcas de las rocas*
a crab / a shrimp	*un cangrejo / un camarón*

CRICKET AND FRENCH CRICKET	*CRIQUET Y CRIQUET FRANCES*
Cricket - see pages 297-300	***Criquet***
French Cricket	***Criquet Francés***
a bat / a ball	*un palo / una pelota*
to bat / to bowl / to field	*batear / bolear / recoger*
to throw / to catch / to drop	*lanzar / coger / dejar caer (derribar)*
to get hit by the ball below the knee	*ser golpeado por la pelota por debajo de la rodilla*
to swivel round	*darse la vuelta*

THE BEACH cont. / *LA PLAYA cont.*

FRENCH CRICKET / *CRIQUET FRANCÉS*

FRENCH CRICKET	*CRIQUET FRANCÉS*
to stand still	*estar de pie*
You're not allowed to move your feet.	*No puedes mover los pies.*
to hit the ball into the sea	*golpear la pelota hacía el mar.*
to hit the ball a long way	*golpear la pelota muy lejos*
to be out	*ser eliminado*
It's your turn to bat now.	*Es tu turno de batear.*
Well caught!	*¡Bien cogida!*
Out!	*¡out! / !Fuera!*

DONKEY RIDES	*PASEOS EN BORRICO / BURRO*
to have a ride on a donkey	*ir de paseo en un burro*
to put your feet in the stirrups	*poner los pies en los estribes / pedales*
to hold on to the reins	*sujetar las riendas*
to sit in the saddle	*sentarse en la silla de montar*
to pat	*patear*
to walk / to trot	*ir a paseo / ir al trote*

OTHER ACTIVITIES	*OTRAS ACTIVIDADES*
to paddle	*chapotear*
to get wet	*mojarse*
to play boules	*jugar a la petanca / a los bolos*
to play catch	*jugar a lanzar la pelota*
to play pig in the middle	*jugar al balón prisionero*
to play with a beach ball	*jugar a la pelota con una pelota de playa*
to ride	*montar a caballo*
to run into the water	*correr dentro del agua*
to stay at the edge	*quedarse en la orilla*
to swim a long way out / to surf	*nadar mas adentro / hacer surfin*

THE BEACH cont. — *LA PLAYA cont.*

EATING ON THE BEACH	*COMIENDO EN LA PLAYA*
to have something to eat	*tomar algo de comer*
a stick of rock	*un palo de caramelo*
an ice cream	*un helado*
an iced lolly	*un polo*
a cold drink	*una bebida fría*
a picnic (See page 235-236)	*un picnic*
a sandwich	*un bocadillo*
a barbecue (See page 184-185)	*una barbacoa*
a disposable barbecue	*una barbacoa desmontable*
to gather firewood	*amontonar leña*
driftwood	*maderas rotas / trozos de madera*
to build a wind shield	*poner una protección para el viento*

WATER SKIING	*ESQUI ACUATICO*
to have a water skiing lesson	*tomar clases de esquí acuático*
a motorboat	*un fueraborda*
to tow / to be towed	*remolcar / ser remolcado*
a towrope	*una cuerda o soga para remolcar*
a handle	*un gancho*
skis / bindings	*esquíes / correas*
a life-jacket	*un chaleco salvavidas*
to crouch	*agacharse*
to hold the towrope	*agarrarse a la soga de remolque*
to accelerate	*acelerar*
to stand upright	*ponerse de pie*
the surface of the water	*la superficie del agua*
to skim	*deslizarse sobre la superficie*
to zigzag	*hacer zig zag*
to fall	*caerse*
to get back up again	*levantarse de nuevo*

WINDSURFING	HACER SURFING CON VELA
to windsurf	*hacer surfing con vela*
to surfboard / a surfboard	*hacer surfing / una tabla de surfing*
the crest of a wave	*la cima de la ola*
a big / small wave	*una ola grande / pequeña*
a breaking wave	*un rompeolas*
There's a huge wave coming.	*Viene una ola muy grande.*

PROBLEMS	PROBLEMAS
Take care, there is…	*Cuidado, hay...*
• broken glass / a jellyfish	• *cristales / una medusa*
• sewage	• *porquería*
• a steeply shelving beach	• *una playa con promontorio*
• a strong current	• *una corriente fuerte*

WARNING AND SAFETY SIGNS	SENALES DE SEGURIDAD Y PELIGRO
Bathing Forbidden	*Prohibido bañarse*
Unsupervised Bathing	*Ausencia de Socorrista*
First Aid Post	*Puesto de primeros auxilios*
Lifeguard / Lifebuoy	*Socorrista / boya de socorrista*

BOATS	BOTES
a speed boat / to have a ride on	*una lancha / montarse en*
a rowing boat / an oar / to row	*un bote de remos / un remo/ remar*
a yacht / to sail	*un yate / navegar*
a sail	*una vuelta en bote*
the crew / to go yachting	*la tripulación / ir de viaje en yate*
to race / to win / to lose	*echar una carrera / ganar / perder*
a canoe / a paddle / to paddle	*una canoa / un patín / chapotear*
a pedal-boat / to pedal	*un bote de pedales / pedalear*
to hire	*alquilar*

CRUISES	*CRUCEROS*
to go for a cruise	*ir de crucero*
to pay the fare	*pagar el coste*
a short / long cruise	*un crucero corto / largo*
a two hour cruise	*un crucero de dos horas*
the captain / the crew	*el capitán / la tripulación*
a sailor	*un marinero*
to go aboard	*embarcar*
to go on deck	*salir a la cubierta*
to get soaked by the spray	*mojarse con el oleaje*
to go back inside	*meterse dentro otra vez*
to get out of the wind	*cobijarse del viento / reguardarse del viento*
to have a drink in the bar	*tomar una bebida en el bar*
to feel seasick	*sentirse mal*

THE HARBOUR	*EL PUERTO*
the quay	*el dique*
the lighthouse	*el faro*
a flashing light	*una luz intermitente*
a warning siren	*una sirena de aviso*
the fishing boats	*los botes pesqueros*
the nets	*las redes*
the catch	*la pesca*
the fishes	*los peces*
to anchor	*echar el ancla*
an anchor	*un ancla*

SUNBATHING
TOMANDO EL SOL

SUNBATHING EQUIPMENT	*EQUIPO PARA TOMANDO EL SOL*
a sunbed / a deckchair / a rug	*una tumbona / una alfombrilla*
a cushion / a sunshade	*un cojín / una sombrilla*
suntan cream / lotion	*crema / loción bronceadora*
suntan oil / coconut	*aceite bronceador / aceite de coco*
water resistant	*a prueba de agua*
after sun lotion	*loción para después del sol*
a sun bed	*una cama de rayos solares*
a sun lamp	*lámpara de rayos uva*

USEFUL EXPRESSIONS	*EXPRESIONES UTILES*
Can you put some cream on my back, please?	*Por favor ¿Me pones crema en la espalda?*
May I borrow some suntan cream, please?	*Por favor ¿Me das un poco de crema bronceadora?*
What factor is your cream?	*¿Qué factor tiene tu crema?*
It's too hot for me.	*Es demasiado caliente para mí.*
I am going to move into the shade for a bit.	*Me voy a la sombra un rato.*
I am going to cool off in the swimming pool / sea.	*Me voy a pegar un baño en la piscina / el mar.*
I don't like to sunbathe in the middle of the day.	*No me gusta tomar el sol en pleno día.*

SUNBATHING cont. / *TOMANDO EL SOL cont.*

USEFUL EXPRESSIONS cont. / *EXPRESIONES UTILES cont.*

Can you see the mark where my strap was?	*¿Ves la marca de mi bañador?*
Is my back looking brown?	*¿Tengo la espalda morena?*
I have got sunburnt.	*Me he quemado.*
My skin is peeling.	*Me estoy pelando.*
I am sore.	*Me duele el cuerpo.*
Have you any calamine lotion?	*¿Tienes loción para sobre exposición?*
Insects keep biting me.	*Los insectos no paran de picarme.*
I don't want skin cancer.	*No quiero tener cáncer de piel.*
You are looking rather red.	*Estás muy rojo(a)*

THE WEATHER	***EL TIEMPO***
The sun has gone in.	*El sol se ha ocultado.*
I wish the sun would come out again.	*Espero que el sol salga de nuevo.*
The sun is about to go behind that cloud.	*El sol se va a ocultar detrás de esas nubes.*
There's not a cloud in the sky.	*No hay nubes en el cielo. / Está despejado por completo.*

FAMILY AND FRIENDS
FAMILIA Y AMIGOS

IMMEDIATE FAMILY	*FAMILIARES CERCANOS*
mother / Mum / Mummy	*madre / mamá / mami*
father / Dad / Daddy	*padre / papá / papi*
a sister	*una hermana*
an older sister	*una hermana mayor*
the oldest sister	*la hermana mayor*
a younger sister	*una hermana más pequeña*
the youngest sister	*la hermana pequeña*
brother	*un hermano*
an older brother	*un hermano mayor*
the oldest brother	*el hermano mayor*
a younger brother	*un hermano más pequeño*
the youngest brother	*el hermano pequeño*
a twin	*un gemelo*
identical twins	*mellizos*
non-identical twins	*gemelos*
a daughter	*una hija*
a son	*un hijo*

COMMON QUESTIONS	*CUESTIONES COMUNES*
How many brothers and sisters have you?	*¿Cuántos hermanos y hermanas tienes?*
I have one of each.	*Tengo uno de cada.*
I have two sisters and one brother.	*Tengo dos hermanas y un hermano.*
Are you the eldest / the youngest?	*¿Eres el mayor o el más pequeño?*

FAMILY AND FRIENDS cont. / *FAMILIA Y AMIGOS cont.*

COMMON QUESTIONS / *CUESTIONES COMUNES*

How old is your sister / brother?	*¿Qué edad tiene tu hermano(a)?*
What are your brothers and sisters called?	*¿Cómo se llaman tus hermanos?*
The oldest / youngest is called..	*La / el mayor se llama / el/la pequeña se llama...*
The next one is thirteen and is called..	*La / el siguiente tiene trece años y se llama...*

THE GENERATIONS	*LAS GENERACIONES*
the older generation	*la generación mayor*
the younger generation	*la generación más joven*
my / our / your generation	*mí / nuestra / tu generación*
the generation gap	*el salto generacional*

CLOSE RELATIVES	*FAMILIARES CERCANOS*
a grandmother / granny / grandma	*una abuela / abuelita / tata*
a great-grandmother	*una tatarabuela*
a grandfather / granddad /grandpa	*un abuelo / abuelito / tato*
a great-grandfather	*un tatarabuelo*
a granddaughter	*una nieta*
a great-granddaughter	*una hija de la nieta*
a grandson	*un nieto*
a great-grandson	*un hijo del nieto*
an aunt / aunty	*una tía*
a great-aunt	*una tía segunda*
uncle	*un tío*
a great-uncle	*un tío segundo*
a niece	*una sobrina*
a nephew	*un sobrino*
a cousin	*un primo*
a first / second cousin	*un primo hermano / primo segundo*
a cousin once / twice removed	*un primo lejano*

FAMILY AND FRIENDS cont. — *FAMILIA Y AMIGOS cont.*

RELATIVES BY MARRIAGE	*FAMILIARES INDIRECTOS*
a wife	*una esposa*
a husband	*un marido*
a mother-in-law	*una suegra*
a father-in-law	*un suegro*
a daughter-in-law	*una cuñada*
a son-in-law	*un cuñado*
a sister-in-law	*una hermana de un(a) cuñado(a)*
a brother-in-law	*un hermano de un(a) cuñado(a)*

SEPARATION AND DIVORCE	*SEPARACION Y DIVORCIO*
to decide to separate	*decidir separarse*
to have a trial separation	*tener un juicio para separarse*
My parents are separated.	*Mis padres se han separado.*
to divorce	*divorciarse*
a divorce	*un divorcio*
My parents are divorced.	*Mis padres son divorciados.*
to decide where the children will live	*decidir con quien van a vivir los hijos.*
I live with my father in the holidays.	*Vivo con mi padre durante el periodo de vacaciones.*
I live with my mother in term time.	*Vivo con mi madre durante el periodo de colegio.*
I spend alternate weekends with each parent.	*Paso los fines de semana alternativamente con mi padre y mi madre.*
a one parent family	*una familia de un solo padre.*
to have access to the children	*tener derecho a ver a los hijos*
to pay maintenance	*pagar la manutención*
to spend the holidays with	*pasar las vacaciones con...*

FAMILY AND FRIENDS cont. / *FAMILIA Y AMIGOS cont.*

SEPARATION AND DIVORCE cont. / *SEPARACION Y DIVORCIO cont.*

My father / mother has re-married.	*Mi padre / madre se ha vuelto a casar.*
My father and mother have both re-married.	*Mi padre y mi madre se han vuelto casar con distintas personas.*
a stepmother / a stepfather	*una madrastra / un padrastro*
a stepdaughter / a stepson	*una hijastra / un hijastro*
a stepsister / a stepbrother	*una hermanastra / un hermanastro*

FRIENDS	***AMIGOS***
an acquaintance	*un conocido*
a friend of the family	*un amigo de la familia*
a god parent	*un padrino*
to become friends	*dar la bienvenida a los amigos*
a good friend / a best friend	*un buen amigo / un mejor amigo (masc.) / una buena amiga / una mejor amiga (fem)*
a friend of mine	*un amigo mio / una amiga mia*
a boyfriend / a girlfriend	*un novio / una novia*
a group of friends	*un grupo de amigos*
I go around with a group of people.	*Salgo con una pandilla de gente.*
I don't have one particular boyfriend / girlfriend.	*No tengo un novio / novia.*
I have a boyfriend. His name is..	*Tengo un novio. Se llama...*
My girlfriend is called..	*Tengo una novia. Se llama...*
a fiancée	*una novia formal*
a lover	*un(a) amante*
to live with	*vivir con*

FAMILY AND FRIENDS cont. — *FAMILIA Y AMIGOS cont.*

LIKING / NOT LIKING PEOPLE — *CAER BIEN O MAL*

LIKING	***CAER BIEN***
to like	*caer bien*
to get on well with	*llevarse bien con*
to make friends with	*hacerse amigos*
to fancy	*gustar*
to chat up	*ligarse*
to get off with	*llevarse bien con*
to have a date with	*tener una cita con*
to go out with	*salir con*
to flirt with	*tirar los tejos a*
to fall for	*estar enamorado de / morirse por*
to fall in love	*estar enamorado*
to love	*amar*
to adore	*adorar*

NOT LIKING	***NO CAER BIEN / NO GUSTAR***
not to get on well together	*no llevarse bien juntos*
to fall out	*reñir*
to have a row	*tener una pelea*
to dislike / to get fed up with	*no gustar / hartarse de*
to hate	*odiar*
to break up with	*romper con*
to finish a relationship	*terminar una relación*

FAMILY AND FRIENDS cont. *FAMILIA Y AMIGOS cont.*

PHYSICAL RELATIONSHIPS	*CONTACTO CORPORAL*
to hold hands	*cogerse de las manos*
to put your arm round someone	*poner el brazo alrededor de álguien*
to cuddle	*abrazar*
to kiss / to snog	*besar / morrear*
to go to bed together	*ir a la cama*
to make love	*hacer el amor*
to have sex	*tener sexo / tener relaciones sexuales*
to be faithful / unfaithful	*ser fiel / no ser fiel*
to live with	*vivir con*
to use contraception	*usar contraceptivos*
to have safe sex	*tener sexo seguro*
to use a condom	*usar condones*
to be on the pill	*tomar la píldora*
to sleep around	*tener varias relaciones*
the morning after pill	*tomar la píldora de la mañana siguiente*
AIDS	*SIDA*
VD	*Enfermedades venéreas*
a late period	*un retraso en el periodo*
a missed period	*una falta*
to do a pregnancy test	*hacer un test de embarazo*
to be pregnant	*estar embarazada*
a urine sample	*una prueba de orina*
to see the doctor	*ver al doctor*
to go to the family planning clinic	*ir a una clínica de planificación familiar*
to get advice	*pedir consejo*
to decide on a termination	*decir parar / interrumpir el embarazo*
to have a baby	*tener un bebé*

FAMILY AND FRIENDS cont. — *FAMILIA Y AMIGOS cont.*

BABIES	***BEBES***
birth	*nacimiento*
to be born	*nacer*
What time were you born?	*¿A qué hora naciste?*
Where were you born?	*¿Dónde naciste?*
a baby / twins / triplets / quads	*un bebé / gemelos / trillizos / cuatrillizos*
When is your birthday?	*¿Cuándo es tu cumpleaños?*
My birthday is..	*Mi cumpleaños es el...*
I am adopted.	*Soy adoptado(a)*

BABIES' PROBLEMS	***PROBLEMAS CON LOS BEBES***
to cry	*llorar*
to need the nappy changed	*cambiar de pañal*
disposable nappies	*pañales desechables / usar y tirar*
towelling nappies	*toallitas*
a safety pin	*una tira adhesiva*
plastic pants	*pantis de plástico*
to be tired	*estar cansado(a)*
to sleep	*dormir*
to be hungry	*tener hambre*
to have wind	*tener gases*

FEEDING BABIES	***ALIMENTANDO AL BEBE***
to need a feed	*dar una toma*
to have a feed / to feed	*tomar una comida / alimentar*
breast fed / bottle fed	*dar el pecho / biberón*
to sterilize the bottles	*esterilizar los biberones*
to warm a bottle	*un biberón tíbio*
demand feeding	*demanda de alimento*
to be fed four hourly	*ser alimentado cada cuatro horas*
milk / solid food	*leche / comida sólida (papillas)*

FAMILY AND FRIENDS cont. — *FAMILIA Y AMIGOS cont.*

BABY EQUIPMENT	***LOS UTENSILIOS DEL BEBE***
a carry cot / a cot	*un carricoche / una cuna*
a pram	*un carricoche*
a baby sling	*unas correas para llevar al bebe / correas indias*
a baby seat for the car	*un asiento de bebé para el coche*
a high chair	*una silla alta para el bebé*
a play pen	*un tacataca*
a changing mat	*una alfombrilla para cambiar al bebé*
a bib	*un chupete*
toys / a musical box	*muñecos / caja musical*
a mobile	*un juguete desmontable*

YOUNG CHILDREN	***NINOS***
to learn to roll over / to crawl	*aprender a gatear / gatear*
to stand up / to walk	*levantarse / andar*
for the first time	*por primera vez*
to say his / her first words	*decir las primeras palabras*
to go to nursery school	*ir a la guardería*
to play	*jugar*
to draw / to colour / to paint	*dibujar / colorear / pintar*
to do jigsaws	*hacer rompecabezas (m)*
to learn the alphabet	*aprender el alfabeto*
to learn to count	*aprender a contar*
to learn to read and write	*aprender a leer y escribir*

ADOLESCENCE	***ADOLESCENCIA***
to be a teenager	*ser un adolescente*
to be independent	*ser independiente*
to grow up	*crecer*
a social life	*una vida social*
to go out with friends	*salir con amigos*

FAMILY AND FRIENDS cont. — *FAMILIA Y AMIGOS cont.*

ADOLESCENCE cont.	***ADOLESCENCIA cont.***
to go to parties	*ir a fiestas*
to go to bed late	*ir a la cama tarde*
to lie in	*quedarse dormido hasta tarde*
to come of age	*ser mayor de edad*
to have the right to vote	*tener derecho a votar*
to be old enough to drink	*tener edad para beber*
to learn to drive (See 397-398)	*aprender a conducir*
to be adult	*ser un adulto*

MARITAL STATUS	***ESTADO CIVIL***
unmarried	*soltero(a)*
a spinster	*una mujer joven soltera*
a bachelor	*un licenciado*
to get engaged	*estar comprometido*
a fiancé / fiancée	*una novia / novio formal*
an engagement ring	*una alianza*
to announce the engagement	*anunciar el compromiso*

WEDDINGS	***BODAS***
to decide on a wedding day	*decidir el día de la boda*
to send out invitations	*enviar las invitaciones*
to look at a wedding present list	*mirar a la lista de regalos de boda*
to get married in church / in a registry office	*casarse por la iglesia / por el juzgado*
the bride / bridegroom	*la novia / el novio*
the best man	*el padrino de boda*
a bridesmaid / a pageboy	*la dama de honor / un paje*
the vicar / the registrar	*el cura / el registro oficial*
the organist / the choir	*el organista / el coro*

FAMILY AND FRIENDS cont. — *FAMILIA Y AMIGOS cont.*

WEDDINGS cont. — *BODAS cont.*

the photographer	*el fotógrafo*
to pose for photos / to have photos taken	*posar para las fotos / tomar fotos*
the guests	*los invitados*
the wedding dress / the veil / the train / the wedding ring	*el vestido de bodas / el velo / la cola / el anillo de bodas*
a bouquet / to carry	*un ramo / llevar*
to throw / to catch	*lanzar / coger al vuelo*
a buttonhole	*un ojal*
the wedding service	*el servicio de bodas*
to walk down the aisle	*andar a lo largo del pasillo*
the father of the bride	*el padre de la novia*
to kneel	*ponerse de rodillas / arrodillarse*
to sing hymns / to pray	*cantar himnos / rezar*
to throw confetti / rice	*lanzar confeti / arroz*

THE WEDDING RECEPTION	*LA RECEPCION DE BODAS*
to shake hands	*darse la mano*
to welcome guests	*dar la bienvenida a los invitados*
to make a speech	*dar un discurso*
the best man's speech	*el discurso del padrino*
to make a joke	*gastar bromas*
to make a toast	*hacer un brindis*
to raise your glasses	*levantar las copas para brindar*

THE HONEYMOON	*LA LUNA DE MIEL*
to leave the reception	*salir de la celebración*
to get changed	*cambiarse de ropa*
to go on honeymoon	*ir de luna de miel*
to decorate the car	*decorar el coche*
newly married	*recien casados*
to throw confetti	*lanzar confeti*
to wave goodbye	*decir adiós*

FAMILY AND FRIENDS cont. — *FAMILIA Y AMIGOS cont.*

WEDDING ANNIVERSARIES	*ANIVERSARIOS DE BODAS*
a silver wedding	*bodas de plata*
a golden wedding	*bodas de oro*
a diamond wedding	*bodas de diamantes*
to celebrate a wedding anniversary	*celebrar un aniversario de bodas*

MIDDLE AGE	*EDAD MEDIA*
to be middle aged	*tener / ser de edad media*
to have grown up children	*criar niños*
to become a grandparent	*convertirse en abuelos*
to go through the menopause	*atravesar la menopausia*
middle age spread	*la curva de la felicidad*
hormone replacement therapy	*terapia de hormonas*
to feel depressed	*sentirse deprimido*
to start getting wrinkles	*aparecer las primeras arrugas*
to have more free time	*tener más tiempo libre*
to take up new interests	*tener nuevos hobbies*

OLD AGE	*SENECTUD*
to retire	*retirarse*
to take partial / early retirement	*retirarse parcialmente / retirarse antes de tiempo*
to enjoy retirement	*disfrutar la jubilación*
a pension / a senior citizen	*una pensión / una ayuda por tercera edad*
to get discounts	*tener derecho a descuentos*
to live on one's own	*vivir solo*
to live with one's family	*vivir con la familia*
to go into sheltered housing	*ir a una casa albergue*
a retirement home	*un retiro de ancianos*
to be looked after / to be nursed	*ser cuidado / ser atendido por una enfermera*

FAMILY AND FRIENDS cont. / *FAMILIA Y AMIGOS cont.*

DEATH	***LA MUERTE***
to die	*morir*
to have a heart attack	*sufrir un ataque al corazón*
to have a stroke	*tener un ataque al corazón*
to have cancer	*tener cáncer*
to be unconscious	*estar inconsciente*
to be unable to talk properly	*ser incapaz de hablar bien*
to forget things	*olvidar cosas*
to be in pain	*tener dolores*
to take painkillers	*tomar tranquilizantes*
to die in one's sleep	*morir mientras se está durmiendo*
to die peacefully	*morir en paz*
to call the doctor	*llamar al doctor*
to sign the death certificate	*firmar el certificado de defunción*
to call the mortuary	*llamar a la funeraria*
the funeral	*el funeral*
a church / a crematorium	*una iglesia / un crematorio*
the coffin / a grave	*un ataúd / una tumba*
a wreath / flowers	*una corona / flores*
to mourn / to weep	*lamentar / llorar*
to pray	*rezar*
to comfort	*confortar*
a widow / a widower	*una viuda / un viudo*

CONTACTING PEOPLE BY POST & BY TELEPHONE

PONIÉNDOSE EN CONTACTO CON GENTE POR CARTA Y POR TELEFONO

BY POST — *POR CORREO*

STATIONERY — *ARTICULOS DE ESCRITORIO Y OFICINA*

Notepaper	***Papel para notas***
headed	*con cabecera*
lined / unlined	*con rayas / sin rayas*
white / cream /	*blanco / color crema*
azure	*azul celeste*
blue	*azul*
a line guide	*una línea de margen*

Postcards	***Postales***
a picture postcard	*una postal de un cuadro*
a funny postcard	*una postal graciosa*
a scenic postcard	*una postal paisjística / una tarjeta postal*
a photograph	*una foto*
an art reproduction	*una reproducción de obra de arte*

CONTACTING PEOPLE BY POST cont.

PONIÉNDOSE EN CONTACTO CON GENTE POR CARTA cont.

Envelopes	***Sobres***
an envelope	*un sobre*
to seal	*cerrar*
to lick	*chupar*
to slit open	*abrir, rajar para abrir*
to address	*dirigir*
a padded envelope	*un sobre para objetos o papeles delicados*
to enclose a stamped addressed envelope (an SAE)	*adjuntar un sobre con la dirección y sello*

Stamps	***Sellos***
a stamp	*un sello*
to lick	*chupar*
to stick on	*pegar / poner*
to buy	*comprar*
a book of stamps	*un libro de sellos*
a first class stamp	*un sello de primera clase*
a second class stamp	*un sello de segunda clase*

USEFUL EXPRESSIONS	***EXPRESIONES UTILES***
What stamp do I need for ..?	*¿Qué sello le pongo a...?*
How much does it cost to send a letter to America?	*¿Cuánto cuesta enviar una carta a América?*
by the cheapest means possible	*de la forma más barata posible*
as fast as possible	*tan rápido como sea posible*
How long will it take to get there?	*¿Cuánto va a tardar en llegar allí?*
How much does it weigh?	*¿Cuánto pesa?*
Put it on the scales.	*Ponla en la báscula.*

CONTACTING PEOPLE BY POST cont. / *PONIÉNDOSE EN CONTACTO CON GENTE POR CARTA cont.*

USEFUL EXPRESSIONS cont. / *EXPRESIONES UTILES cont.*

USEFUL EXPRESSIONS cont.	*EXPRESIONES UTILES cont.*
Guaranteed next day delivery	*reparto garantizado en el día siguiente.*
to send by recorded delivery	*enviar por correo grabado*
by air mail	*por avión / por vía aérea*
an international reply coupon	*un cupón internacional de respuesta*
to fill in details on a form	*rellenar los detalles en la ficha*
the sender	*el remitente*
the recipient	*el destino*
Surname	*apellido*
Christian names	*nombre*
address and postcode	*dirección y código postal (C.P)*
date	*fecha*
contents	*contenidos*
value	*valor*

PARCELS	***PAQUETES***
to wrap up a parcel	*envolver un paquete*
wrapping paper / gift wrap	*papel para envolver / papel de regalo*
brown paper / tissue paper	*papel marrón / papel de seda*
corrugated paper / bubble wrap	*papel ondulado / burbujas*
sellotape / to sellotape	*celofán / pegar con celofán*
string / to tie a knot	*cuerda / hacer un nudo (atar)*
to put your finger on the knot	*poner el dedo sobre el nudo*
scissors / a knife / to cut	*tijeras / un cuchillo / cortar*
tape / to stick	*cinta / pegar*
to undo	*deshacer*
Fragile! Handle with Care!	*¡Frágil! ¡Material delicado!*
This way up!	*¡Hacia arriba!*

POST cont. / *CORREO cont.*

POST BOXES	***BUZON DE CORREOS***
Is there a post box near here?	*¿Hay un buzón cerca de aquí?*
to take a letter to the post	*llevar una carta a correos*
What are the collection times?	*¿Cuales son las horas de recogida?*
the first post / the next post	*la primer recogida / la próxima recogida*
to catch the last post	*llegar a punto a la última recogida*
to miss the post	*llegar tarde para la recogida*
Local Mail Only	*Nacionales y Correo Local / Cuidad y Capital*
Other Desinations	*Internacionales*
Working Days	*Días laborales*
Public Holidays	*Días vacacionales / días puente / días festivos / fiestas*

THE POST OFFICE	***LA OFICINA DE CORREOS***
to queue up	*hacer cola*
to wait to be served	*esperar a ser atendido*
to go to the counter	*ir al mostrador*

POSTAL DELIVERIES	***ENTREGAS / REPARTOS POSTALES***
a postman / a post van	*un cartero (una cartera) / una furgoneta de entregar postales*
a postal round	*un recorrido postal*
What time does the post usually arrive?	*¿A qué hora llega el correo normalmente?*
Has the post been delivered yet?	*¿Ha llegado el cartero?*
Is there a letter for me?	*¿Hay alguna carta para mí?*

CONTACTING PEOPLE BY POST cont.

PONIÉNDOSE EN CONTACTO CON GENTE POR CARTA cont.

WRITING LETTERS

ESCRIBIENDO CARTAS

Formal letters	***Cartas formales***
Dear Sir.......Yours faithfully,..	*Estimado Señor... Atentamente*
Dear Mr. / Mrs./ Miss....	*Querido Señor / Señora / Señorita...*
.....Yours sincerely	*...Atentamente*
Informal letters	***Cartas informales***
Dear James, ...	*Querido Jaime,...*
With best wishes / Affectionately / Love / Lots of love / All my love..	*un abrazo / con cariño / un beso / con mucho cariño / con todo mi cariño*

BY TELEPHONE

PAR TELEFONO

To telephone England from Spain dial 07, followed by 44 (the U.K. code), followed by your area code minus the first zero and finally the rest of the telephone number.	*Para llamar a Inglaterra desde España marca 07, seguido de 44 (código para el Reino Unido), seguido del prefijo de tu área quitando el primer cero y finalmente el resto del número de teléfono.*

To telephone to Spain from England dial 00, followed by 34, followed by the area code minus the first 9 followed by the person's telephone number.	*Para llamar a España desde Inglaterra marca 00, seguido de 34, seguido del prefijo menos el nueve inicial, seguido del número de teléfono de la persona.*

CONTACTING PEOPLE BY TELEPHONE cont.

PONIÉNDOSE EN CONTACTO CON GENTE PAR TELEFONO cont.

British Directory Enquiries = 192	*Información Nacional = 192*
International Directory Enquiries in the U.K. = 153	*Información Internacional en el Reino Unido = 153*
Spanish Directory Enquiries = 003	*Información Nacional (Española) = 003*
Spanish International Directory Enquiries = 025	*Información Internacional (Española) = 025*

Spain's ringing tone consists of long equal on/off tones (slower than the U.K.'s engaged tone). Spain's engaged tone is similar to the U.K.'s engaged tone.	*El tono de línea en España consiste en largos tonos separados por más largos pausas. El tono de "ocupado" en España es similar al de el Reino Unido pero más rápido.*

THE TELEPHONE	***EL TELEFONO***
the receiver	*el auricular*
to pick up / to listen	*coger / escuchar*
The telephone is ringing.	*el teléfono está sonando*
Shall I answer it? I'll get it.	*¿Lo cojo yo? Yo lo cojo.*
I'll take it in the kitchen.	*Lo cojo en la cocina*
the dial / to dial a number	*el marcador (el dial) / marcar un número*

TELEPHONE cont.	*TELEFONO cont.*
THE TONES	***LOS TONOS***
the dialling tone	*el tono de marcado.*
to get the engaged tone	*obtener un tono de "ocupado."*
It's engaged. // It's ringing.	*Está ocupado / la línea está ocupada // Está sonando / da línea.*
It's ringing.	*Está sonando / da línea.*
It's out of order.	*Está roto (averiado).*
It's unobtainable.	*No se puede llamar.*
There isn't any dialling tone.	*No da señal.*
Can you help me, please?	*¿Puedes ayudarme, por favor?*
I was cut off.	*Se me cortó la línea.*

ANSWERING THE PHONE	*RESPONDIENDO EL TELEFONO*
Hello, is that Peter?	*!Hola! ¿es Pedro?*
Could I speak to your mother?	*¿Puedo hablar con tu madre?*
Is Julia there please?	*¿Está Julia, por favor?*
Who is that speaking?	*¿Quién es?*
Who do you want to talk to?	*¿Con quién quieres hablar? ¿A quién llamas?*
To whom do you want to speak?	*¿Con quién quieres hablar?*
Hang on.	*Espera, un momento.*
I'll just get him / her for you.	*Voy a llamarle / llamarla.*
He / she won't be a minute.	*Tarda un minuto.*
I am sorry he / she isn't in at the moment.	*Lo siento pero no está en este momento.*
When will he / she be back?	*¿Cuándo va a volver?*
Can you say I rang?	*¿Puede decirle que he llamado?*
Could you give him / her a message, please?	*¿Puedo dejar un mensaje para él/ella, por favor?*
I will ring again another time.	*Llamare más tarde.*
We are just about to eat. Can we ring you later?	*Estamos a punto de comer. ¿Puedes llamarnos más tarde?*
What is your number?	*¿Cuál es tu número de teléfono?*
Can I take a message?	*¿Quieres dejar un mensaje?*
Whom shall I say called?	*Quién digo que le/la llamó.*

CONTACTING PEOPLE BY TELEPHONE cont.

PONIÉNDOSE EN CONTACTO CON GENTE PAR TELEFONO cont.

FINDING TELEPHONE NUMBERS	***BUSCANDO NUMEROS DE TELEFONO***
a telephone directory	*una guía de teléfonos*
an address book	*un diario / una agenda*
to look up a number	*mirar un número*
What is their name?	*¿Cuál es su nombre?*
How do you spell it?	*¿Cómo se escribe / se deletrea?*
What is their initial?	*¿Cuál es la inicial del nombre?*
What is their address?	*¿Cuál es su dirección?*
Yellow Pages	*Las Páginas amarillas*
Directory Enquiries	*Información*

USING A PUBLIC CALL BOX	***USANDO UNA CABINA PUBLICA DE TELEFONO***
I need some change.	*Necesito cambio.*
What coins does it take?	*¿Qué monedas se necesita?*
a telephone token	*una ficha telefónica*
Does it take a 'phone card?	*¿Funciona con tarjetas telefónicas?*
a twenty five unit card	*una tarjeta de veinticinco unidades*
Could I reverse the charge, please?	*¿Puedo llamar a cobro revertido, por favor?*
out of order	*averiado(a)*
How do you use this telephone?	*¿Cómo se utiliza este teléfono?*
Can you use a chargecard?	*¿Funciona con tarjeta de crédito telefónico?*

CONTACTING PEOPLE BY TELEPHONE cont. / *PONIÉNDOSE EN CONTACTO CON GENTE PAR TELEFONO cont.*

ANSWERPHONES	*EL CONTESTADOR AUTOMATICO*
to switch on / off	*encender / apagar*
Is the answerphone on?	*¿Está puesto el contestador?*
There is a message on the answerphone for you.	*Hay un mensaje en el contestador para tí.*
The answerphone is flashing / beeping.	*El contestador tiene el intermitente encendido / está dando la señal para dejar el mensaje*
to play back the tape	*rebobinar la cinta*
to listen to the messages	*escuchar los mensajes*
to record a message	*grabar un mensaje*
to rewind	*rebobinar*
to reset	*volver a poner*

SCHOOL AND COLLEGE
ESCUELA Y COLEGIO

TYPES OF SCHOOL	***TIPOS DE ESCUELAS***
I go to..	*Yo voy a...*
• a nursery school	• *una guardería*
• a primary school	• *un colegio de enseñanza primaria*
• a secondary school	• *un instituto de enseñanza secundaría*
• a private school	• *un colegio privado*
• a state school	• *un colegio estatal*
• a coeducational school	• *un colegio de educación mixta*
• a sixth form college	• *un colegio para preparación para la selectividad*

SCHOOL BUILDINGS AND ROOMS	***EDIFICIOS Y HABITACIONES EN EL COLEGIO***
the school office	*la oficina del colegio*
the staff room	*la oficina del personal / del profesorado*

The assembly hall	***La Sala de Reuniones***
the platform / a microphone	*el escenario / un micrófono*
chairs / to stack	*sillas / apilar*
to put out in rows	*poner las sillas en hileras*

The classroom	***Las Clases / Las Aulas***
a desk / a desk lid	*un pupitre / un cajón de pupitre*
to open / to close	*abrir / cerrar*
a chair / to sit down	*una silla / sentarse*
the blackboard / to write on	*la pizarra / escribir*
chalk / a blackboard duster	*tiza / un borrador*
to wipe the blackboard	*borrar la pizarra*
the notice board	*el tablón de anuncios*
to pin up a notice	*clavar un mensaje*

SCHOOL BUILDINGS AND ROOMS cont. — *EDIFICIOS Y HABITACIONES EN EL COLEGIO cont.*

The dining room	***El Comedor***
the canteen	*la cafetería*
to queue up	*hacer cola*
to take a tray	*tomar una bandeja*
to ask for	*pedir*
to help yourself	*servirse uno mismo*
self-service	*autoservicio*
Could I have a little…, please?	*¿Me pones un poco de...? Por favor.*
Could I have a lot of…,please?	*¿Me pones mucho (de) ...? Por favor.*
to clear the table	*limpiar la mesa / recoger la mesa*
to wipe the table	*limpiar la mesa*

The gymnasium	***El gimnasio***
the wall bars	*las espalderas*
a vault	*un potro sin anillas*
to vault	*saltar un obstáculo*
a horse / a box	*un potro de anillas / una caja*
a monkey bar / to balance	*una barra / hacer equilibrio*
a rope / to climb	*una soga / trepar*
to swing	*balancearse / columpiarse*
a rope ladder	*una soga con nudos*
a spring board / a trampoline	*un trampolín*
a mat	*una alfombrilla*
the showers	*las duchas*
a changing room	*los vestuarios*

SCHOOL BUILDINGS AND ROOMS cont. / *EDIFICIOS Y HABITACIONES EN EL COLEGIO cont.*

The music rooms	***La clase de música***
a practice room	*un auditorio*
a piano	*un piano*
a music stand	*un atril*
lockers	*taquillas*
soundproofed	*aislado de ruidos*

(See pages 157-158 for music lessons and practice.)

The art room	***La clase de arte***
an easel	*un punzón*
paints	*pinturas*
paintbrushes	*pinceles*
paper	*papel*
to have a painting on the wall	*tener un fresco / una pintura al fresco*
to be on display	*tener expuesto*
an exhibition of work	*una exposición de obras*

(See page 230 for details of art equipment)

The science block	***La sección de ciencias***
a laboratory	*un laboratorio de experimentos*
an overall	*un mono / un mandril*
safety glasses	*gafas de seguridad*
a work bench	*un banco*
a sink	*un fregadero*
acid / alkali / litmus paper	*ácido / alcalino / papel universal para medir el PH*
the Periodic Table	*la Tabla Periódica*

SCHOOL BUILDINGS AND ROOMS cont. — *EDIFICIOS Y HABITACIONES EN EL COLEGIO cont.*

THE SCIENCE BLOCK cont. — *LA SECCIÓN DE CIENCIAS cont.*

Apparatus		***Aparatos***	
a beaker	*un vaso de precipitación*	a funnel	*un embudo*
a Bunsen burner	*un quemador Bunsen*	a gas jar	*una jarra de cristal*
a tripod	*un trípode*	a measuring cylinder	*una probeta graduada*
gauze	*gasa*	a pair of tongs	*unas tenacillas*
a condenser	*un condensador*	a pipette	*una pipeta*
a crucible	*un crisol*	scales	*una báscula*
a delivery tube	*una pipeta*	a spatula	*una espátula*
an evaporating basin	*una desvanezedora*	a stand	*un soporte*
filter paper	*un filtro de papel*	a clamp	*una nuez*
a flask	*un termo / un matraz*	a syringe	*una jeringuilla*
conical	*cónico*	a test tube	*un tubo de ensayo*
round bottomed	*aforado / con el fondo esférico*	a test tube holder	*un soporte para el tubo de ensayo*
flat bottomed	*con el fondo plano*	a test tube rack	*una base para tubos de ensayo*
a fractionating column	*una probeta métrica*	a thermometer	*un termómetro*

SCHOOL BUILDINGS & ROOMS cont. / *LOS EDIFICIOS Y HABITACIONES DEL COLEGIO cont.*

The library	***La biblioteca***
the librarian	*el bibliotecario*
to take a book out	*sacar un libro*
to return a book	*devolver un libro*
to be overdue	*sobrepasar el plazo*
to reserve	*reservar*
to read	*leer*
a reference book	*un libro de referencias*
a catalogue	*un catálogo*
a list of authors	*una lista de autores*
a list of titles	*una lista de títulos*
alphabetical	*alfabética*
to look up	*mirar / consultar*

The cloakroom	***El ropero***
a peg / to hang up	*una pinza / colgar*
a locker / to lock / to unlock	*una taquilla / cerrar / abrir con llave*
to put away / to get out	*quitar del medio / sacar*
the toilets / engaged / vacant	*los servicios / ocupado / vacante*
the washbasin	*el lavabo*
to wash one's hands	*lavarse las manos*
to dry one's hands	*secarse las manos*
a towel	*una toalla*
a mirror / to look in	*un espejo / mirarse en*
to brush one's hair	*cepillarse el pelo*

SCHOOL BUILDINGS & ROOMS cont. / *LOS EDIFICIOS Y HABITACIONES DEL COLEGIO cont.*

(For details of illnesses see pages 406-417)

The medical room	***La enfermería***
the nurse	*la enfermera*
to feel ill / to lie down	*sentirse mal / tumbarse*
to have a headache / to feel sick	*tener dolor de cabeza / estar enfermo*
to take your temperature	*tomar la temperatura*
to have an accident	*tener un accidente*
to go to hospital / to go home	*ir al hospital / ir a casa*
to ring your family	*llamar a tu familia*

THE SCHOOL GROUNDS	*LOS PATIOS DE RECREO EN EL COLEGIO*
the playground	*el patio de recreo*
the netball courts	*las pistas de juegos / de deportes*
the tennis courts (See pages 255-261for vocabulary for playing tennis)	*las pistas de tenis*
the sportsfield	*los campos de deportes*
the hockey / lacrosse pitch	*el campo de hockey / de lacrosse*
the swimming pool (See pages 301-308 for vocabulary for swimming)	*la piscina*

THE STAFF	*LA PLANTILLA / EL PROFESORADO*
the headmaster / headmistress	*el director / la directora*
the deputy headmaster/mistress	*el subdirector / la subdirectora*
the head of year	*el responsable del año / curso*
a head of department	*el jefe de departamento*
the form teacher	*el profesor de curso*
a subject teacher	*el profesor / maestro de una asignatura*
the cooks	*los cocineros / as*
the cleaners	*los empleados de mantenimiento*
the caretaker	*el bedel*

SCHOOL AND COLLEGE cont.

ESCUELA Y COLEGIO cont.

THE PUPILS	*EL ALUMINADO*
head boy / head girl	*delegado / delegada*
a prefect / a monitor	*un prefecto / un monitor*
a pupil	*un alumno*
a day pupil / a boarding pupil	*un estudiante de día / interno*
a weekly boarder	*un interno durante la semana*
a new girl / a new boy	*una chica nueva / un chico nuevo*
a first year	*un novato / un recién llegado*
a sixth former	*un alumno de COU*

(For detailed stationery vocabulary see pages 359-362)

CLOTHES AND EQUIPMENT	*ROPA Y EQUIPO*
school uniform	*el uniforme del colegio*
an overall	*un mono*
Do you have to wear school uniform?	*¿Tienes que llevar uniforme?*
What colour is your school uniform?	*¿De qué color es tu uniforme?*
Do you like your uniform?	*¿Te gusta llevar uniforme?*

SCHOOL AND COLLEGE cont. — *ESCUELA Y COLEGIO cont.*

A briefcase	***Un maletín***
a holdall / a satchel	*una bolsa de deporte / una cartera*
a school bag / a duffle bag	*una bolsa para el colegio / un saco*
a text book	*un libro de texto*
an exercise book	*un libro de ejercicios*
a notebook	*un libro de notas*
a file / a folder	*un archivo / un clasificador*
filepaper	*papel de archivo / para archivar*
a pencil case / a pen / a pencil	*un estuche / un boli / un lápiz*
a rubber / a pencil sharpener	*una goma / un sacapuntas*
a calculator	*una calculadora*

A sports bag	***Una bolsa de deportes***
sports kit	*una maleta para las cosas necesarias para el deporte*
sports shoes	*zapatillas de deportes / deportivas*
a towel	*una toalla*

THE SCHOOL DAY — *LA JORNADA EN EL COLEGIO*

Registration	***Pasando lista***
to take the register	*pasar lista*
to be present / absent	*estar presente / faltar*
to give out notices	*dar notas*

SCHOOL ASSEMBLY	***LA SALA DE REUNIONES***
to sing a hymn	*cantar un himno*
to pray	*rezar*
to march in / out	*hacer cola / deshacer la cola*
to walk in single file	*marchar en fila*

SCHOOL AND COLLEGE cont.

ESCUELA Y COLEGIO cont.

THE LESSONS (abc)		*LAS CLASES*	
Art	*Arte*	(English)	*(Inglés)*
Biology	*Biología*	(French)	*(Francés)*
Business Studies	*Comercio*	(German)	*(Alemán)*
Chemistry	*Química*	(Italian)	*(Italiano)*
Design	*Diseño*	(Russian)	*(Ruso)*
Domestic Science	*Hogar*	(French)	*(Español)*
General Studies	*Estudios Generales*	(Literature)	*(Literatura)*
Geography	*Geografía*	(Language)	*(Lengua)*
Greek	*Griego*	(Vocabulary)	*(Vocabulario)*
Gymnastics	*Gimnasia*	(Grammar)	*(Gramática)*
History	*Historia*	(to translate)	*(traducir)*
Information Technology	*Información Hogar / trabajos manuales*	Music	*Música*
Latin	*Latín*	Needlework	*Hogar*
Mathematics	*Matemáticas*	Physical Education	*Educación Física*
(Algebra)	*(Algebra)*	Physics	*Física*
(Geometry)	*(Geometría)*	Religious Studies	*Religión*
Metalwork	*Trabajo de metal*	Technical Drawing	*Dibujo*
Modern Languages	*Idiomas*	Woodwork	*Trabajos en madera*

THE TIMETABLE	*EL HORARIO*
a free period	*un periodo libre*
the mid-morning break / playtime	*el recreo de la mañana / el recreo*
lunchtime	*la comida*
afternoon break	*el recreo de la tarde*
a bell / to ring	*la campana / tocar*
the end of the school day	*el final del colegio*
homework	*deberes*

SCHOOL AND COLLEGE cont. — *ESCUELA Y COLEGIO cont.*

STUDYING	***ESTUDIANDO***
to study	*estudiar*
to work	*trabajar*
to concentrate	*concentrarse*
to do homework	*hacer los deberes*
to read	*leer*
to write	*escribir*
to take notes	*tomar notas*
headings	*títulos*
a synopsis	*un resumen*
an abbreviation	*una abreviación*
shorthand	*taquigrafía*

WRITING AN ESSAY	***ESCRIBIENDO UN ENSAYO***
the title	*el título*
to plan an essay	*hacer un esquema para el ensayo*
an introduction	*una introducción*
a new paragraph	*un párrafo nuevo*
a conclusion / to sum up	*una conclusión / resumir*
a quotation	*una cita*
a bibliography	*una bibliografía / una referencia bibliográfica*
to argue / an argument	*argumentar / un argumento*
to discuss / a discussion	*discutir / una discusión*
to describe / a description	*describir / una descripción*
to look at both sides	*mirar a ambos lados*
to examine	*examinar*
to include facts / dates	*incluir hechos / fechas*

SCHOOL AND COLLEGE cont. / *ESCUELA Y COLEGIO cont.*

LEARNING	***APRENDIENDO***
to learn	*aprender*
to memorize	*memorizar*
facts	*hechos / datos*
dates	*fechas*
a poem	*un poema*
to revise	*revisar*
to be tested on	*tener en examen en*
to test yourself	*examinarse uno mismo*

EXAMS	***EXAMENES***
to take an exam	*hacer un examen*
to pass exams	*pasar un examen*
to fail exams	*suspender un examen*
to re-take exams	*hacer un examen por segunda vez / repetir*
to take a course in	*hacer un curso sobre...*
to wait for the results	*esperar los resultados*
When do you hear your results?	*¿Cuándo te dan las notas?*
The results come on Wednesday.	*La notas salen el miércoles.*
How do you get your results?	*¿Cómo anuncian las notas?*
We have to go into school for them.	*¿Tenemos que ir al colegio a recogerlas?*
The results come by post.	*Las notas las envían por correos.*

SCHOOL AND COLLEGE cont. — *ESCUELA Y COLEGIO cont.*

ASSESSMENTS	***EVALUACION***
a school report	*un informe del colegio*
a mark / a percentage / a grade	*una nota / un porcentaje / una nota de letras*
an A grade / a B grade etc.	*una A (un sobresaliente) / una B (un notable)*
to be graded	*ser puntuado*
a distinction	*una matrícula de honor*
to come top	*ser el primero de la clase*
to be about average	*estar dentro de la media*
to be near the bottom	*sacar un nota muy baja*
to do one's corrections	*hacer correcciones / corregir*
to do better / worse than one had thought	*hacer mejor / peor que lo que te esperabas*
to be upset / disappointed	*estar triste / desilusionado(a)*
to be relieved	*estar aliviado(a)*
to be delighted	*estar encantado(a)*

THE SCHOOL YEAR	***EL ANO ESCOLAR***
the terms	*el trimestre*
the Autumn Term	*el trimestre de otoño*
the Spring Term	*el trimestre de primavera*
the Summer Term	*el trimestre de verano*
the holidays	*las vacaciones*
a half-term holiday	*las vacaciones de mediados de trimestre*
the Christmas holidays	*las vacaciones de Navidad*
the Easter holidays	*las vacaciones de Semana Santa*
the Summer holidays	*Las vacaciones de Verano*
Speech Day	*Día de la graduación*
Founder's Day	*Día del Fundador / patrón*
a Bank Holiday	*una fiesta / un día de fiesta*
a public holiday	*una fiesta pública*

SCHOOL AND COLLEGE cont. / *ESCUELA Y COLEGIO cont.*

USEFUL EXPRESSIONS	***EXPRESIONES UTILES***
My school is:-	*Mi colegio es:-*
• co-educational	• *un colegio mixto*
• a girls' school	• *un colegio de chicas*
• a boys' school	• *un colegio de chicos*
• selective	• *un colegio selectivo por examen*
• mixed ability	• *un colegio de educación selectiva en función de la habilidad intelectual*
• streamed	• *un colegio público*
• large / small	• *grande / pequeño*
• boarding / day	• *un colegio con residencia / un colegio medio-pensionista*
My school starts at nine o'clock.	*Mi colegio empieza a las nueve en punto.*
My lessons last forty minutes.	*Mis clases duran cuarenta minutos.*
We have / don't have school on Saturdays.	*Tenemos clase / No tenemos clase los sábados.*
We have four French lessons a week.	*Tenemos cuatro clases de Francés a la semana.*
What's your favourite subject?	*¿Cuál es tu asignatura favorita?*
I like Maths. best.	*Me gustan las matemáticas sobre todo*
I hate Latin.	*Odio el Latín.*
I think History is really interesting.	*Pienso que la historia es muy interesante.*

SCHOOL AND COLLEGE cont. / *ESCUELA Y COLEGIO cont.*

WHAT IS YOUR TEACHER LIKE?	*¿COMO ES TU PROFESOR(A)?*
I think my teacher is..	*Creo que mi profesor(a) es..*
• boring	• *aburrido(a)*
• excellent	• *excelente*
• quite good	• *muy bueno(a)*
• strict	• *estricto(a)*
• can't keep order	• *no puede manejar la clase*
• funny	• *divertido(a)*
• eccentric	• *excéntrico(a)*
My teacher is..	*Mi profesor(a) es..*
• old / young	• *viejo(a) / joven*
• male / female	• *un hombre / una mujer*

WHAT ARE YOU GOING TO DO WHEN YOU LEAVE SCHOOL?	*QUE QUIERES SER CUANDO SALGAS DEL COLEGIO*
I am planning to..	*Me gustaría...*
I have a place at…	*Tengo una plaza en...*
I don't know yet.	*No lo sé todavía*

HIGHER EDUCATION	*ESTUDIOS UNIVERSITARIOS*
to apply for a place at..	*pedir una plaza en...*
an interview	*una entrevista*
to be called for an interview	*ser llamado para hacer una entrevista*
to do an exam	*hacer un examen*
to get the examination results	*obtener los resultados*
the grade	*las notas*
A levels	*las notas de selectividad*

SCHOOL AND COLLEGE cont. — *ESCUELA Y COLEGIO cont.*

HIGHER EDUCATION cont. — *ESTUDIOS UNIVERSITARIOS cont.*

university entrance	*la admisión en la universidad*
to go to college	*ir a un instituto de educación avanzada*
to go to secretarial college	*ir a un instituto de educación avanzada para hacer secretariado*
technical college	*FP2*
a former polytechnic / a new university	*una de las nuevas universidades*
to get a place at	*ser admitido*
to read for a degree in	*estudiar la carrera de...*

LIVING AT COLLEGE	*VIVIENDO EN EL COLEGIO MAYOR*
to be in your first / second year	*estar en tu primer / segundo año*
to be a fresher	*ser un novato*
to be in your third / last year	*estar en tu tercer / cuarto año / último año*
to be an undergraduate / a student	*ser un licenciado / un estudiante*
to have a place in the hall of residence	*tener una vacante en la residencia de estudiantes*
self-catering	*autónomo*
to live in digs	*vivir en un piso en la ciudad*
to rent a flat	*alquilar un piso*
to live with some friends	*vivir con amigos*
the student union	*la fraternidad de estudiantes*
a faculty building	*una facultad*
the library	*la biblioteca*

HIGHER EDUCATION — *ESTUDIOS UNIVERSITARIOS*

UNIVERSITY DEGREES	***CARRERA UNIVERSITARIA***
a first degree	*una licenciatura*
a further degree	*una post-licenciatura*
a doctorate	*un doctorado*
a degree in	*una carrera de*
a graduate	*un licenciado / una licenciada*
What class of degree did you get?	*¿Qué nota de licenciatura sacaste?*
What class are you hoping for?	*¿Qué nota esperas sacar?*
a first class degree	*Matrícula de Honor (4)*
an upper second	*sobresaliente (3)*
a lower second	*sobresaliente (3)*
a third	*Notable (2)*
a pass degree	*Apto (1)*
an honours degree	*Licenciatura con honores = titulo de licenciado de categoría superior*

HIGHER EDUCATION — *ESTUDIOS UNIVERSITARIOS*

DEGREE COURSES		*CARRERAS*	
accountancy	*contabilidad*	librarianship	*bibliotecario / dirección de bibliotecas*
architecture	*arquitectura*	literature	*literatura*
the Arts	*bellas artes*	mathematics	*matemáticas*
biochemistry	*bioquímica*	mechanical engineering	*ingeniero mecánico*
botany	*botánica*	media studies	*periodismo*
business studies	*empresariales*	medicine	*medicina*
classics	*clásicas*	modern languages	*idiomas / filología*
computer sciences	*informática*	philosophy	*filosofía*
dentistry	*dentista*	politics	*política*
Divinity	*religión*	psychology	*psicología*
economics	*economía*	sociology	*sociología*
electrical engineering	*ingeniería electrónica*	social sciences	*ciencias sociales*
engineering	*ingeniería*	statistics	*estadística*
film production	*cinematografía*	theatre production	*dirección dramática*
geography	*geografía*	theology	*teología*
geology	*geología*	veterinary science	*veterinaria*
history	*historia*	zoology	*zoología*
law	*derecho*		

STATIONERY
ARTICULOS DE ESCRITORIO Y OFICINA

PAPER	***PAPEL***
coloured paper	*papel de color*
file paper / ring reinforcers	*papel archivado / anillas*
graph paper	*papel para gráficas*
headed notepaper	*papel de notas con cabecera*
lined / unlined paper	*papel con rayas / sin rayas*
squared paper	*papel cuadriculado*
tracing paper	*papel de calco*
writing paper	*papel de escribir*

BOOKS	***LIBROS***
an exercise book / a rough book	*un libro de ejercicios / de apuntes*
a note book	*un libro de notas*
a text book	*un libro de texto*

FILES	***FICHEROS***
to file	*fichar / archivar*
a ringbinder file	*una carpeta de anillas / clasificador*
an envelope file	*un archivador de cartas*
a folder	*un archivo / un archivador*
a file divider	*un divisor / un partidor / un separador*

WRITING EQUIPMENT — ***EQUIPO DE ESCRIBIR***

A pencil case	***Un estuche de lápices***
to open / to close	*abrir / cerrar*
to zip up / to unzip / a zip	*abrir / cerrar la cremallera / cremallera*

STATIONERY cont. / *ARTICULOS DE ESCRITORIO Y OFICINA cont.*

Pens	***Bolis***
a ball point pen	*un bolígrafo (bic)*
a biro	*un bolígrafo / birome*
a felt-tip pen	*un rotulador*
a fine tip	*un boli de punta fina*
a thicker tip	*un boli de punta gorda*
a fountain pen	*una estilogáfica*
a fine nib	*una punta fina*
a medium nib	*una punta mediana*
a thick nib	*una punta gorda*
a cartridge pen	*una pluma de cartuchos*

Ink	***Tinta***
a bottle of ink	*un bote de tinta*
to fill the pen	*llenar el boli / la estilográfica*
to run out of ink	*quedarse sín tinta*
a cartridge	*un cartucho*
to need a new cartridge	*necesitar un cartucho nuevo*
to put a cartridge in	*poner un cartucho*
a full / half-full / empty cartridge	*un cartucho lleno / medio / vacío*
What type of cartridge does it take?	*¿Qué tipo de cartucho necesita / usa?*
an ink eradicator	*un quitador / estripador de tinta*
a mistake	*un error / una falta*
blotting paper / to blot	*papel secante / secar*
an ink blot	*una mancha de tinta*
to spill the ink	*derramar la tinta*

STATIONERY cont. — *ARTICULOS DE ESCRITORIO Y OFICINA cont.*

Pencils	***Lápices***
a lead pencil	*un lápiz de carbón / de minas*
a colouring pencil	*un lápiz de color*
hard / soft	*duro / blando*
the point / blunt / sharp	*la punta / rota / afilada*
to break the lead	*romper la mina*
a pencil sharpener	*una sacapuntas*
to sharpen	*sacar punta*
to throw away the shavings	*tirar las virutas*

Rubbers	***Gomas***
to make a mistake	*cometer un error / una falta*
to rub out	*borrar*
an ink rubber	*un borrador de tinta*

Rulers	***Reglas***
metric / imperial	*(regla) métrica / británica*
to measure	*medir*
to draw a straight line	*dibujar / trazar una línea*
to underline / double underline	*subrayar / volver a subrayar*

GEOMETRY EQUIPMENT	***EQUIPO DE GEOMETRIA (f)***
a compass	*un compás*
a protractor	*un alargador / un brazo / un portador*
a set square	*una escuadra / un cartabón*
to draw an angle	*trazar / dibujar un ángulo*
to measure an angle	*medir un ángulo*

STATIONERY cont. — *ARTICULOS DE ESCRITORIO Y OFICINA cont.*

OTHER EQUIPMENT — *OTROS MATERIALES*

Scissors	***Las Tijeras***
to cut	*cortar*
sharp / blunt	*afiladas / desafiladas*
to cut along a line	*cortar siguiendo una línea*
to cut out	*cortar*

Fastening things together	***Juntando Cosas***
glue	*pegamento*
sellotape	*cinta adhesiva / scotch*
double sided sticky tape	*cinta doble-adhesiva*
a stapler / to staple / a staple	*una grapadora / grapar/ una grapa*
to run out of staples	*quedarse sín grapas*
Have you any more staples?	*¿Tienes más grapas?*
How do you load the staples.	*¿Cómo se recarga la grapadora?*

Hole punchers	***Una máquina de hacer agujeros / taladradora***
to punch holes	*taladrar*
to use ring reinforcers	*usar anillas*

Stencils	***Plantillas***
to stencil / a stencil	*imprimir con plantilla / una plantilla*
an alphabet stencil	*plantilla de letras*
capital letters / lower case letters	*mayúsculas minúsculas*

CURRENT EVENTS
SUCESOS COTIDIANOS
SUCESOS CORRIENTES

POLITICS — *POLÍTICA*

ELECTIONS	***LAS ELECCIONES***
to call / hold an election	*convocar / tener elecciones*
to hold a referendum	*tener un referéndum*
a general election	*una elecciones generales*
to nominate / a nomination	*nombrar / una nominación*
to choose a candidate	*elegir un candidato*
to stand at an election	*presentarse a una elección*
to canvass opinion	*hacer una colecta de opinión*
to campaign	*hacer una campaña*
to give a speech	*dar un discurso*
the election day	*el día de la elección*
a polling station	*el punto electoral local / el colegio electoral*
a ballot paper / to put a cross	*un voto / señalar con una cruz*
to vote for / against	*votar (en favor / en contra) de*
to vote by secret ballot	*hacer uso del voto secreto*
a postal vote	*un voto postal*
the results of an election	*los resultados de la elección*
to announce the result	*anunciar los resultados*
to win / lose an election	*ganar / perder unas elecciones*
by a narrow margin	*por un margen muy ligero*
by a large majority	*por una mayoría cómoda*
to be elected // defeated	*ser elegido // ser vencido/derrotado*
to demand a re-count	*pedir un segundo cuento de votos*
How would you vote?	*¿Cómo vas a votar?*
I don't bother to vote / I voted for..	*No me molesto en votar / Voté por*
private versus public life	*vida privada frente a la vida pública*
media attention	*la atención de los medios de comunicación*

CURRENT EVENTS cont. / *SUCESOS COTIDIANOS cont.*

THE ECONOMY	***LA ECONOMIA***
to pay taxes	*pagar tasas*
high / low taxation	*india de tasas alto / bajo*
V.A.T.	*IVA*
income tax	*impuesto sobre la renta*
exempt from tax	*exento de tasas*
the Budget	*los impuestos*
the recession	*la crisis / recesión*
inflation	*la inflación*
the depression	*la depresión*
unemployment	*el paro*
the Welfare State	*El Bienestar Estatal*

THE WORKERS	***LOS TRABAJADORES***
a Trades Union	*un sindicato*
to call a strike	*llamar a la huelga*
to go on strike	*ir a la huelga*
to go out in sympathy	*ir en apoyo / simpatizar con una causa*
to demand	*demandar / exigir*
• a pay rise	• *una subida salarial*
• better hours	• *una jornada de trabajo mejor*
• better conditions	• *mejores condiciones*
• equality	• *igualdad*
• a minimum wage	• *un salario mínimo*
to wave a banner	*agitar una pancarta*
to picket	*hacer un piquete*
a peaceful / violent demonstration	*una manifestación pacífica / violenta*

CURRENT EVENTS cont. — *SUCESOS COTIDIANOS cont.*

EMERGENCIES — *EMERGENCIAS*

EMERGENCIES	*EMERGENCIAS*
to declare a state of emergency	*declarar un estado de emergencia*
a riot	*un levantamiento*
the riot police	*una redada policiaca*
shields / truncheons / tear gas	*escudos / trincheras / protectores*
a bomb scare / a car bomb	*una amenaza de bomba / un cochebomba*
terrorists	*terroristas*
to evacuate the area	*evacuar el área*
the bomb disposal squad	*el grupo / cuerpo de artificieros*

WAR	*GUERRA*
to declare war on	*declarar la guerra*
to be at war with	*estar en guerra con*
to fight / to wound	*luchar / herir*
casualties / the wounded	*heridos / heridos*
the number of dead	*el número de muertos*
guerrilla warfare	*el impuesto de guerra para los guerrillistas*
nuclear war / a nuclear explosion	*una guerra nuclear / una explosión nuclear*
radiation / fall out	*radiación / escape*
an anti-nuclear protest	*una protesta antinuclear*
to be a pacifist	*ser un pacifista*
to campaign for	*hacer una campaña en favor de...*
a protest march	*una marcha*
a peaceful demonstration	*una manifestación pacífica*
unilateral / multilateral disarmament	*desarmamento unilateral / multilateral*
to declare a truce	*declarar una tregua*
to cease fighting	*una tregua de alto el fuego*

CURRENT EVENTS cont. / *SUCESOS COTIDIANOS cont.*

LAW AND ORDER	***LEY Y ORDEN***
the police	*la policía*
a policeman / a policewoman	*un policía / una policía*
a police car / a siren	*una patrulla / una sirena*
to break the law	*romper la ley*
to break the speed limit	*pasar el límite de velocidad*
speed cameras	*cámaras de velocidad*
to be over the breathalyser limit	*estar sobre el límite de alcoholemia*
to be disqualified from driving	*ser suspendida la licencia de conducir*
to take illegal drugs	*tomar drogas ilegales*
to be under age	*ser menor de edad*
to caution / to arrest / to imprison	*retener / arrestar / meter en la cárcel*
to witness / to give evidence	*ser testigo / dar evidencia*
to sign a statement	*firmar una declaración*
to telephone your home	*llamar a tu casa*
to ask for a solicitor	*pedir un abogado de oficio*
to remain silent	*permanecer en silencio*

LAW COURTS	***LOS JUZGADOS***
the judge / the jury	*el juez / los jurados*
to try	*intentar*
the case for the prosecution	*el caso de la acusación*
to prosecute	*acusar*
the case for the defence	*el caso de la defensa*
to defend	*defender*
a solicitor	*un abogado de oficio*
a barrister	*un abogado*

CURRENT EVENTS cont. — *SUCESOS COTIDIANOS cont.*

LAW AND ORDER cont. — *LEY Y ORDEN cont.*

a summons	*una citación judicial / un emplazamiento*
a criminal	*un criminal*
to acquit	*absolver exculpar*
to get let off	*conseguir ser absuelto*
to find guilty	*ser juzgado culpable*
a sentence / a fine / to fine	*una pena / una multa / multar*
to be put on probation	*ser dejado en libertad condicional*
a term of imprisonment	*una sentencia de encarcelamiento*
censorship / freedom of speech	*censura / libertad de expresión*

SEXUALITY	***SEXUALIDAD***
heterosexual	*heterosexual*
homosexual	*homosexual*
lesbian / gay	*lesbiana / gay*
sexually transmitted disease	*enfermedad de transmisión sexual*
HIV positive	*Enfermo de SIDA*
AIDS	*SIDA*
a blood test	*un test de sangre*
a clinic	*una clínica*
confidential	*confidencial*
pornography	*pornografía*
prostitution	*prostitución*
equal opportunities	*igualdad de oportunidades*
sexual discrimination	*discriminación sexual*

CURRENT EVENTS cont. — ***SUCESOS COTIDIANOS cont.***

THE MONARCHY	*LA MONARQUIA*
the King / the Queen	*El Rey / La Reina*
the Prince / the Princess	*El Príncipe / La Princesa*
the heir to the throne	*el heredero del trono*
the Queen Mother	*la Reina Madre*
to be a member of the royalty	*ser un miembro real*
What do you think of the future of the monarchy?	*¿Qué piensas sobre el futuro de la monarquía?*
Do you think we should become a republic?	*¿Crees que deberíamos convertirnos en una república?*
Are you glad you have a royal family?	*¿Te gusta la Familia Real?*
Do you wish you had a royal family?	*¿Eres partidario de la Familia Real?*
Have you ever met any of the royal family?	*¿Has conocido a algún miembro de la Familia Real?*
I saw the Queen once.	*Ví a la Reina una vez.*

CURRENT EVENTS cont. — *SUCESOS COTIDIANOS cont.*

THE NATIONAL LOTTERY	***LA LOTERIA NACIONAL***
to buy a lottery ticket	*comprar un boleto de lotería*
to buy an instant lottery ticket	*comprar una tarjeta de rascar*
to choose your numbers	*elegir tus números*
a bonus number	*un número reintegro*
to watch the lottery draw	*ver el sorteo de lotería*
The first ball / the final ball is…	*La primer bola / la última bola es...*
The results of the lottery were..	*Los resultados de la bonoloto son...*
The jackpot is..	*El bote es...*
a roll-over week	*un bote acumulado para la próxima semana*
No-one won the lottery.	*Ningún acertante de la máxima categoría.*
a ten pound prize	*un premio de diez libras*
a syndicate	*un sindicato / grupo de apostantes*
to share the winnings	*compartir las ganancias*
How much is the lottery jackpot this week?	*¿Cuál es el bote de este semana?*
Do you approve of the lottery?	*¿Qué opina sobre la lotería?*
The charities are suffering because of the lotteries.	*Las organizaciones caritativas están siendo perjudicadas por la lotería.*
It gives people an interest.	*Da alegría a la gente.*
It's just good fun.	*Es divertido.*
Some people get addicted to it.	*Algunos son adictos a la lotería.*
What would you do if you won the lottery?	*¿Qué haría si ganases la lotería?*
I only got two numbers right.	*Solo tengo dos aciertos.*

TRAVEL
VIAJAR

SIGNS — *SENALES*

TOILETS	*SERVICIOS*
Ladies / Gentlemen	*Señoras / Caballeros*
vacant / engaged	*ocupado / desocupado*
out of order	*averiado*
hot water / cold water	*agua caliente / fría*

ENTRANCES	*ENTRADAS*
push / pull / no entry	*empujar / tirar / cerrado*

EXITS	*SALIDAS*
Fire Exit	*Salida de emergencias*
Fire Escape	*salida de evacuación*

LIFTS	*ASCENSORES*
up / down	*arriba / abajo*
It's coming	*ya viene*
Push the button.	*presiona el botón*
Which floor do you want?	*¿A qué piso quieres ir?*
I want the third floor.	*Quiero ir al tercer piso.*
Which floor is it for..?	*¿A qué piso va...?*
the top floor / the ground floor	*al piso de arriba / al bajo /*
the basement	*al sótano*
Excuse me, I want to get out here.	*Perdone, quiero salir de aquí.*

TRAVEL - SIGNS cont. / *VIAJAR - SENALES cont.*

ESCALATORS	***LAS ESCALERAS ELECTRICAS***
the up escalator	*la escalera eléctrica para subir*
the down escalator	*la escalera eléctrica para bajar*
Hold on to the hand rail.	*sujétese a la barandilla*
Stand in the middle.	*Permanezca de pie en el centro*
Mind your feet.	*Cuidado con el suelo / cuidado al poner los pies.*

OPEN	***ABIERTO***
When do you open?	*¿A qué hora abren?*
We open at..	*Abrimos a las...*
Opening hours	*Horas de apertura*
Open from……until.	*Abierto de.......hasta*

CLOSED	***CERRADO***
When do you close?	*¿Cuándo cierran?*
We shut at..	*Cerramos a las...*
We are just about to close.	*Estamos a punto de cerrar.*

SALE	***REBAJAS***
Great reductions!	*¡Super Rebajas! ¡Descuentos increíbles!*
10% off everything. / One third off.	*10% de descuento en todos los artículos./ Un tercio de descuento.*
Half price / a bargain	*A mitad de precio / una ganga*
Closing down sale.	*Rebajas por cierre. Liquidación.*
Sale ends on…	*La rebajas acaban el día...*

PRIVATE	***PRIVADO***
No Admittance	*Admisión reservada*
Strictly Private	*Estrictamente privado*
Staff Only	*Solo Personal*
Trespassers Will Be Prosecuted.	*No traspasar*

TRAVEL - SIGNS cont. — *VIAJAR - SENALES cont.*

NO SMOKING	***PROHIBIDO FUMAR***
BEWARE OF THE DOG.	***CUIDADO CON EL PERRO***

TRAVELLING BY TRAIN — *VIAJANDO EN TREN*

AT THE STATION	***EN LA ESTACION***
the entrance	*la entrada*
the main concourse	*la estación / el edificio explanada principal*
Shall we meet by the..	*¿Nos encontramos en...?*
the book stall	*los tenderetes de revistas y libros*
the newspaper kiosk	*los kioscos periódicos*
the big clock	*el reloj grande*

THE BUFFET	***EL AUTOSERVICIO***
to buy	*comprar*
a sandwich	*un bocadillo*
a coffee / a cup of tea	*un café / una taza de té*
a bottle of water	*una botella de agua*

THE WAITING ROOM	***LA SALA DE ESPERA***
Toilets - see page 61 for using the loo and page 371 for public toilets.	*Servicios*

TRAVELLING BY TRAIN cont. VIAJANDO EN TREN cont

THE LEFT LUGGAGE OFFICE	LA CONSIGNA
I have lost my..	*He perdido mi...*
Has my wallet been handed in?	*¿Han traido mi cartera aquí?*
Can I leave my suitcase here?	*¿Puedo dejar mí maleta aquí?*
Do you have lockers?	*¿Tienen taquillas?*
How much are they?	*¿Cuánto es? / Cuánto cuesta?*
What coins do they take?	*¿Qué monedas se necesitan?*
Do you have any change?	*¿Tiene cambio?*
How do they work?	*¿Cómo funcionan?*

THE TAXI RANK	*LA PARADA DE TAXIS*
Shall we take a taxi?	*¿Cogemos un taxi?*
There is a very long queue.	*Hay una fila larguísima.*
to give a tip	*dar una propina*
How much would it cost for a taxi to…?	*¿Cuánto cuesta ir a... en taxi?*

THE ENQUIRY OFFICE	*LA OFICINA DE INFORMACION*
Could I have a timetable for..?	*¿Me puede dar un horario?*
What time is the next train for..?	*¿A qué hora es el próximo tren?*
Is it a through train?	*¿Es un tren directo?*
Do I have to change?	*¿Tengo que cambiar?*
Where do I have to change?	*¿Dónde tengo que cambiar?*
Is there a good connection?	*¿Hay una buena conexión?*

TRAVELLING BY TRAIN cont. / *VIAJANDO EN TREN cont*

THE ENQUIRY OFFICE cont. / *LA OFICINA DE INFORMACION cont.*

What time is the connection?	*¿A qué hora es la conexión / el transbordo?*
What time does it arrive at..?	*¿A qué hora llega?*
What time is the one after that?	*¿A qué hora es el siguiente?*
How long does it take?	*¿Cuánto se tarda?*
What platform does it leave from?	*¿De qué andén sale?*

THE TICKET OFFICE	*LA VENTANILLA DE VENTA DE TIQUET*
May I have..?	*¿Quiero...?*
How much is..?	*¿Cuánto es...?*
• a return ticket	• *un billete de ida y vuelta*
• a day return ticket	• *un billete de ida y vuelta en el mismo día*
• returning tomorrow	• *para volver mañana*
• returning next week / next month	• *para volver la próxima semana / el próxima mes*
• a single ticket	• *un billete de día*
• first class	• *primera clase*
• second class	• *segunda clase / clase turismo*
• a child rate ticket	• *un billete para niño*
• a student rate ticket	• *un billete de estudiante*
• a season ticket	• *un billete de temporada*
• for a week / a month	• *para una semana / un mes*
• a book of tickets	• *un taco de billetes*
May I reserve a seat on..?	*¿Quisiera reservar un asiento en...?*
Is there a reduction for students?	*¿Hacen descuentos para estudiantes?*
Do you have a student card?	*¿Tienes carnet de estudiante?*
Do you have proof of your age?	*¿Puedes probar tu edad?*

TRAVELLING BY TRAIN cont. *VIAJANDO EN TREN cont*

THE ARRIVALS / DEPARTURES BOARD	*PANTALLA DE LLEGADA / SALIDAS*
due to arrive / depart at..	*se espera a / sale a*
delayed by ten minutes	*con retrase de diez minutos*
on time	*puntual*
early	*temprano*
just arrived	*acaba de llegar*
leaving from Platform Nine	*sale del andén número nueve*
now boarding	*embarcando ahora*

ANNOUNCEMENTS	*ANUNCIOS*
What was that announcement?	*¿Qué dijeron en los altavoces?*
I didn't hear what he / she said.	*No pude oír lo que dijo.*
The next train to depart from Platform One is the three forty five for Paddington, calling at all stations.	*El próximo tren que sale del andén uno es el tren de las tres y cuarenta y cinco que va a Paddington, parando en todas las estaciones.*
The train just arriving at Platform Four is the two thirty from Edinburgh.	*El tren que acaba de llegar en el andén cuatro es el de las dos y media de Edimburgo.*
We apologize for the delay.	*Disculpen por el retraso.*

THE TICKET PUNCHING MACHINE	*LA PICADORA*
to punch your ticket	*picar el billete*
You have to punch your ticket before boarding the train.	*Tienes que picar tu billete antes de subir al tren.*

TRAVELLING BY TRAIN cont. *VIAJANDO EN TREN cont*

THE PLATFORM	***EL ANDEN***
a barrier	*una barrera*
a ticket inspector	*un revisor / un revisor de billetes*
to catch / miss the train	*coger / perder el tren*
a seat	*un asiento*
to sit down	*sentarse*
a luggage trolley / a porter	*un carrito / un portero*

TYPES OF TRAIN	***TIPOS DE TRENES***
an intercity	*un interurbano*
an express train	*un talgo / un tren expreso*
a local train	*un tren de cercanías*
a sleeper	*un tren litera*
British Railway system (B.R.)	*El sistema de redes de trenes Británico.*
Spanish Railway system	*Red Nacional de Ferrocarriles Españoles (R.E.N.F.E.)*
Spanish high speed trains	*Alta Velocidad Española (A.V.E.)*

THE CHANNEL TUNNEL TRAIN	***EL TREN DEL CANAL (EUROSTAR)***
to drive on	*poner el coche (en el tren)*
to drive off	*descargar (el coche del tren)*
to sit in your car	*sentarte en tu coche*

BOARDING A TRAIN — *SUBIENDO AL TREN*

THE CARRIAGES	***LOS VAGONES***
the front / rear carriage	*el vagón de cabeza / del final*
a compartment	*un comportamiento*
No Smoking / Smoking	*Prohibido fumar / fumadores*
First Class / Second Class	*Preferente / de turismo*
the buffet	*el autoservicio*
the dining car	*el vagón restaurante*
the bar	*el bar*
a snacks trollet	*un carrito con comida*
the sleeping compartment	*la litera / el camarote*
the Guard's van	*el comportamiento del revisor*

The door	***La puerta***
to open / to close	*abrir / cerrar*
Press the button to open the door.	*Presionar el botón para abrir la puerta.*

The windows	***Las ventanillas***
Do you mind if I open / shut the window?	*¿Te importa sí abro / cierro la ventanilla?*

The corridor	***El pasillo***
to walk along / to look for a seat	*andar a lo largo / buscar un asiento*

The communication cord	***La cuerda de emergencia***
to pull	*pulsar*
an emergency	*una emergencia*
to stop the train	*parar el tren*

TRAVELLING BY TRAIN cont. / *VIAJANDO EN TREN cont*

The seats	***Los asientos***
Is this seat taken?	*¿Está ocupado?*
May I sit here?	*¿Puedo sentarme aquí?*
I'm sorry, someone is sitting here.	*Lo siento, está ocupado.*
That is a reserved seat.	*Ese sitio está reservado.*
Would you like to sit by the window?	*¿Quiere sentarse en la dirección en la que viajamos?*
Do you prefer to face the way we are going?	*¿Quiere sentarse en la dirección en la que viajamos?*
Shall we sit together?	*¿Nos sentamos juntos?*

The luggage rack	***El portamaletas***
Can I help you to put your case up?	*¿Puedo ayudarle a subir su maletín?*
Can you manage to get your coat down?	*¿Necesitas ayuda para bajar su abrigo?*

THE PASSENGERS AND RAILWAY STAFF	***LOS PASAJEROS Y EL PERSONAL DE LA ESTACION DE TRENES***
a commuter	*un viajero*
the driver	*el conductor*
the guard	*el guarda*
The ticket inspector	***El revisor de tiquets / billetes***
Tickets please.	*su tiquet por favor.*
Could I see your ticket, please?	*¿Puedo ver su tiquet?*
I didn't have time to buy one, I'm afraid.	*No me dió tiempo a comprar uno, me temo.*
Can I pay now, please?	*¿Puedo comprarlo ahora?*
The ticket office was shut.	*La ventanilla de ventas de tiquets / billetes estaba cerrada.*
I can't find my ticket.	*No puedo encontrar mi billete*
to be fined	*poner una multa / multar*
to be surcharged / to pay extra	*pagar más / pagar extra*

TRAVELLING BY UNDERGROUND — *VIAJANDO EN EL METRO*

COMMON EXPRESSIONS	*EXPRESIONES COMUNES*
Shall we go by tube?	*¿Vamos en el metro?*
Which lines is this station on?	*¿En qué línea está esta estación?*
Which line do we need to take?	*¿Qué línea necesitamos?*
What is this line called?	*¿Cómo se llama esta línea?*
What is this line number?	*¿Cuál es el número de esta línea?*
Let's look at a plan of the underground.	*¿Por qué no miramos un plano del metro?*
We are here.	*Estamos aquí.*
We need to go there.	*Tenemos que ir allí.*
Which line do I take for Buckingham Palace?	*¿Qué línea necesito para ir al Palacio de Buckingham?*
Take this line.	*Toma esta línea.*
Where do I get off for ..?	*¿Dónde tengo que bajarme para ir a...?*

CHANGING TRAINS	*CAMBIANDO DE TREN*
You need to change at Euston.	*Tienes que cambiar en Euston.*
We will have to change here.	*Tenemos que cambiar aquí.*
a connecting station	*una estación para hacer conexión / transbordo*

ZONES	*ZONAS*
the central zone	*la zona central*
an outer zone	*la zona periférica*
zone one / two / three	*zona uno / dos / tres*

TRAVELLING BY UNDERGROUND cont. / *VIAJANDO EN EL METRO cont.*

BUYING TICKETS AT THE TICKET OFFICE	***COMPRANDO EL BILLETE EN LA VENTANILLA***
Please could I have two tickets for..	*Por favor, dos billetes para ir a...*
to buy..	*comprar...*
• a single / a return	• *uno de ida / de ida y vuelta*
• a child's ticket	• *un billete para niños*
• an adult's ticket	• *un billete para adultos*
• a student's ticket	• *un billete para estudiante*
• a daily pass	• *un billete para el día / un pase de día*
• a weekly pass	• *un billete semanal / un pase semanal*
• a book of ten tickets	• *un taco de diez pases*
Can you use the passes on the buses too?	*¿Se puede utilizar el pase de autobús también?*
Is it more expensive at certain times of the day?	*¿Es más caro dependiendo de las horas del día?*
When does the cheap rate start?	*¿Cuándo es más barato?*
There is a flat rate fare.	*Hay una tarifa fija.*

AT THE TICKET BARRIER	***EN LOS CONTROLES DE BILLETES***
Put your ticket in here.	*Pon tu pase aquí.*
Take your ticket out there.	*Saca el pase por allí.*
You have to show your ticket.	*Tienes que enseñar el pase.*
The barrier isn't working.	*El control no funciona*

ESCALATORS	***LAS ESCALERAS ELECTRICAS***
a down / up escalator	*una escalera eléctrica de bajada / de subida*
to read the advertisements	*leer los carteles publicitarios*
to stand on the right	*permanecer a la derecha*

TRAVELLING BY BUS — *VIAJANDO EN EL AUTOBUS*

BUS STOPS	***LAS PARADAS DE AUTOBUS***
Which buses stop here?	*¿Qué autobuses paran aquí?*
Is this the right bus stop for..?	*¿Es ésta la parada de autobús para...?*
How often do the buses run?	*¿Con qué regularidad paran los autobuses?*
Have I just missed a bus?	*¿He perdido el autobús?*
How long have you been waiting?	*¿Cuánto tiempo llevas esperando?*
to look at the timetable	*mirar al horario*
a request stop	*una parada opcional / solicitada*
the next stop	*la siguiente parada*
You have to put your arm out to stop the bus.	*Tienes que levantar el brazo para parar al autobús.*
This is the bus you want.	*Esta es el autobús que quieres.*
to get on / off the bus	*subirse / bajarse (al / del) autobús*

TYPES OF BUS	***TIPOS DE AUTOBUS***
a single / double decker	*un autobús / un autobús de dos pisos*
a coach	*un autocar*

GETTING ON THE BUS	***SUBIÉNDOSE AL AUTOBUS***
Do you want to sit upstairs or downstairs?	*¿Quieres sentarte arriba o abajo?*
Shall we go upstairs?	*¿Por qué no vamos arriba?*
Press the button to stop the bus.	*Pulsa el botón para parar el autobús*
You pay the driver / conductor.	*Pagas tú al conductor / paga al conductor*

TRAVELLING BY BUS cont. — *VIAJANDO EN EL AUTOBUS cont.*

TICKETS	***BILLETES***
Could I have a single ticket to..?	*Deseo un billete de ida a....?*
a return ticket to..	*un billete de ida y vuelta a...*
I have a bus pass.	*Tengo un pase de autobús*

TRAVELLING BY AIR — *VIAJANDO POR AVION*

AIRPORTS — *AEROPUERTAS*

THE TERMINAL	***LA TERMINAL***
Which terminal does Iberian Aairways use?	*¿Qué terminal usa la línea Iberia?*
British Airways flights use Terminal…	*Los vuelos de la British Airways salen de la terminal....*
Which airline are you flying with?	*¿Con qué línea aérea vuelas?*

THE CAR PARK	***EL APARCAMIENTO***
a short stay car park	*un aparcamiento de plazo corto*
a long stay car park	*un aparcamiento de larga estancia*
to get a ticket	*coger / sacar un billete*
You pay before leaving.	*Paga / pagas antes de salir*
How much is the ticket?	*¿Cuanto cuesta el billete?*
Can we take a bus to the terminal?	*¿Podemos coger / tomar un autobús hasta la terminal?*

TRAVELLING BY AIR cont. / *VIAJANDO POR AVION cont.*

LUGGAGE TROLLEYS	*CARRETILLAS PARA MALETAS*
Can you find a luggage trolley?	*¿Puedes encontrar una carretilla*
to push / to pull	*empujar / tirar*
to steer // to brake	*guiar/ dirigir // parar / frenar*

AT THE TERMINAL	*EN LA TERMINAL*
automatic doors	*las puertas automáticas*
an escalator	*una escalera eléctrica*
a moving floor	*una cinta transportadora*
a lift	*un ascensor*
the shops	*las tiendas*
the toilets	*los servicios*
a restaurant / a bar	*un restaurante / un bar*

THE ARRIVALS / DEPARTURES BOARD	*LA PANTALLA DE LLEGADAS / DE SALIDAS*
destination	*destino*
due to arrive at	*hora de llegada*
just arrived	*aterrizo(a)*
delayed	*atrasado*
about to depart	*a punto de salir*
last call	*última llamada / aviso*
now boarding	*embarcando*

THE INFORMATION DESK	*EL PUNTO DE INFORMACION*
Can you tell me..?	*¿Me puede decir...?*
Has flight number .. arrived yet?	*¿Ha llegado ya el vuelo número...?*
Is the flight delayed?	*¿Trae retraso el vuelo?*
How late is it likely to be?	*¿Cuánto retraso se cree que trae?*
Why is it so late?	*¿Por que llega tan tarde?*
Is there a problem?	*¿Hay problemas?*

TRAVELLING BY AIR cont. — *VIAJANDO POR AVION cont.*

THE INFORMATION DESK cont.	*EL PUNTO DE INFORMACION cont.*
Where is the meeting point?	*¿Dónde esta el punto de encuentro?*
I am supposed to meet a passenger called….but I can't find him / her.	*Estoy buscando a un pasajero que se llama... pero no puedo encontrarle(la).*
Have there been any messages left for me?	*¿Ha dejado algún mensaje para mí?*
My name is…	*Mi nombre es...*
Can you put a message out on the tannoy for me, please?	*¿Puede poner un mensaje, por favor?*

THE CHECK-IN DESK	*EL MOSTRADOR DE FACTURACION*
to queue	*hacer cola*
Can you put your luggage on the scales, please?	*¿Puede poner su equipaje aquí para pesarlo?*
to lift a suitcase up	*levantar la maleta*
How many suitcases do you have?	*¿Cuántas maletas tiene?*
Is this one yours?	*¿Es ésta suya?*
the baggage allowance	*el límite de equipaje*
excess baggage	*equipaje de exceso*
to pay a surcharge	*pagar por exceso de peso*
hand luggage	*el equipaje de mano*
Did you pack your suitcase yourself?	*¿Has hecho las maletas tú?*
Are there any prohibited articles in your luggage?	*¿Hay algun artículo no autorizado en su equipaje?*
Your hand luggage is too large.	*Su equipaje de mano es demasiado grande.*
It will have to be put in the hold.	*Lo tenemos que poner en la bodega / en lista de espera.*
Could I see your ticket, please?	*¿Puedo ver su carta de embarque?*

TRAVELLING BY AIR cont.	*VIAJANDO POR AVION cont.*
THE CHECK-IN DESK cont.	***EL MOSTRADOR DE FACTURACION cont.***
Do you prefer smoking or non-smoking?	*¿Quiere asiento para fumador o no fumador?*
This child is travelling alone and needs looking after.	*Este niño viaja solo y necesita álguien que le ayude.*
Could I have a seat with extra leg room, please?	*¿Me puede dar un asiento con espacio extra para las piernas?*
Could I possibly have an aisle / a window seat?	*¿Me puede dar un asiento junto al pasillo / a la ventanilla?*
Here is your boarding card.	*Aquí tiene su billete de embarque.*
Go to passport control when you are ready.	*Vaya hacia el control de pasaportes cuando este preparado(a).*

PASSPORT CONTROL	*CONTROL DE PASAPORTES*
to show your passport	*mostrar el pasaporte*
to put your hand luggage on the conveyor belt	*poner el equipaje de mano en la banda transportadora*
to walk through the detector	*atravesar el detector*
to be stopped / to be searched	*ser parado / ser registrado*
to have your bag searched	*inspeccionar la bolsa / registrar la bolsa*

THE DEPARTURE LOUNGE	*LA SALA DE ESPERA PARA EMBARCAR*
the duty free shop	*la tienda de artículos libres de impuestos / el duty free*
your duty free allowance	*el límite permitido de artículos libres de impuestos*
to buy	*comprar*
• perfume	• *colonia (f) / perfume (m)*
• cigarettes / alcohol	• *cigarros (m) / alcohol (m)*

TRAVELLING BY AIR cont. — *VIAJANDO POR AVION cont.*

THE BOARDING GATE	***LA PUERTA DE EMBARQUE***
Our flight has been called.	*Nuestro vuelo ha sido anunciado.*
Now boarding.	*Embarcando.*
Last call.	*La última llamada / aviso.*
They are boarding at gate..	*Embarque en la puerta de salida número...*
to show your boarding pass	*mostrar el billete de embarque*
Seats numbered…. board first / next.	*Los números... embarcarán primero / a continuación*
Please board from the front / rear of the aircraft.	*Por favor, embarquen desde la parte delantera / trasera del aparato.*
Excuse me, could I get to my seat, please.	*Perdone, me da paso ir a mi asiento, por favor.*

THE SATELLITE	***LA PISTA SATELITE***
Our flight is leaving from the satellite.	*Nuestro vuelo sale desde la pista satélite*
We have to take the monorail / a bus.	*Tenemos que coger el monorail / autobús*

THE FLIGHT — *EL VUELO*

THE CREW	***LA TRIPULACIÓN***
the Captain	*el piloto*
the steward	*el azafato / el oficial de vuelo*
the stewardess	*la azafata*
an air hostess	*una azafata*

TRAVELLING BY AIR cont. — *VIAJANDO POR AVION cont.*

SAFETY	*SEGURIDAD*
to fasten your seatbelt	*abrocharse los cinturones*
to keep your seatbelt fastened	*dejar el cinturón abrochado*
to remain seated	*permanecer sentado(a)*
to call the stewardess	*llamar a la azafata*
to undo your seatbelt	*desabrocharse el cinturón*
to extinguish cigarettes	*apagar los cigarrillos*
to put on a life jacket	*ponerse el chaleco salvavidas*
to fasten the strap / to inflate	*apretar la correa / inflar*
a whistle / to blow	*un silbato / soplar o tocar*
oxygen masks	*las mascaras de oxígeno*
an emergency	*una emergencia*
emergency lighting	*las luces de emergencia*
escape routes	*las rutas de evacuación del aparato*

THE TAKE OFF	*EL DESPEGUE*
the runway / to taxi	*la pista de salida / esperar turno*
to accelerate	*acelerar*
to take off / to lift off / to climb	*despegar / elevarse / subir*
My ears hurt.	*Me duelen los oidos.*
Would you like to suck a sweet?	*¿Por qué no masticas algo?*
the altitude / the speed	*la altura / la velocidad*
to look out of the window	*mirar a través de la ventana*
to get a good view	*tener una vista buena*
the clouds / turbulence	*las nubes / turbulencias*

THE DESCENT	*EL DESCENSO*
the touch down	*el primer contacto con tierra*
to land / a good landing	*aterrizar / un buen aterrizaje*
to remain in your seats until the plane has stopped	*permanecer sentado(a) hasta que el avión este parado.*
to disembark	*desembarcar*

TRAVELLING BY AIR cont. — *VIAJANDO POR AVION cont.*

BAGGAGE RECLAIM	***LA RECOGIDA DEL EQUIPAJE***
to collect your luggage	*recoger el equipaje*
a carousel	*un carrusel*
Can you see your suitcase?	*¿Ves tu maleta?*
There's mine.	*Ahí va la mía.*
How many cases do you have?	*¿Cuántas maletas tienes?*
Is that everything?	*¿Es eso todo?*
a trolley	*un carrito*
to push / to steer / to brake	*empujar / dirigir / parar*

CUSTOMS	***PUERTAS DE CONTROL / ADUANA***
to go through customs	*atravesar las puertas de control de aduana*
the green / red channel	*la salida verde / roja*
to have nothing to declare	*no tener nada que declarar*
to have something to declare	*tener algo que declarar*
Have you anything to declare?	*¿Tiene algo que declarar?*
to have your baggage searched	*Registrar tu equipaje*

TRAVELLING BY FERRY	*VIAJANDO EN UN BARCO DE PASAJEROS (EN UN FERRY)*
to go by ferry	*ir en barco de pasajeros*
to take the Cross Channel ferry	*ir en el Barco del Canal*

THE PARTS OF THE FERRY	*PARTES DEL BARCO DE PASAJEROS*

THE RAMP	*LA RAMPA*
to queue / to wait	*hacer cola / esperar*
to drive up the ramp	*subir la rampa con el coche*
to drive down	*bajar la rampa con el coche*
to embark	*embarcar*
to disembark	*desembarcar*

THE VEHICLE DECK	*EL NIVEL PARA VEHICULOS*
to follow the car in front	*seguir al coche de enfrente*
to go right up to the bumper	*ir hasta el final de la rampa*
to park / to lock the car	*aparcar / echar la llave al coche*
to take important things with you	*coger las cosas de valor*
to leave the car	*dejar el coche*
to remember where the car is parked	*recordar donde se dejó el coche*

THE PASSENGER DECKS	*EL NIVEL DE PASAJEROS*
the restaurant / the bar	*el restaurante / el bar*
the toilets	*los servicios*
the lounge / the shops / the cinema	*el comedor / las tiendas / el cine*
the telephone	*el teléfono*
to stay inside	*estar dentro (quedarse dentro)*
to go outside for some air	*salir para tomar el aire fresco*

TRAVELLING BY FERRY cont. / *VIAJANDO EN UN BARCO DE PASAJEROS cont.*

THE SLEEPING AREA	***LOS CAMAROTES***
to sit up all night	*quedarse en los asientos toda la noche*
to have a cabin booked	*tener un camarote reservado*
a sleeping berth	*una litera*

A ROUGH CROSSING	***UNA TRAVESIA CON LA MAR REVUELTA***
Do you feel seasick?	*¿Sientes náuseas?*
I feel dreadful.	*Estoy fatal.*
I am going to be sick.	*Voy a ponerme malo(a)*
Would you like to take a tablet?	*¿Quieres una pastilla?*
I can't walk straight.	*No puedo mantener el equilibrio?*
Hold on to the handrail.	*Sujetarte a la barandilla.*
Would you like to go outside for some fresh air?	*¿Quieres salir para tomar el aire fresco?*
I feel cold. Can we go back inside now?	*Tengo frío. ¿Por qué no volvemos a dentro?*
I have got wet by the spray.	*Estoy empapado por culpa del oleaje.*

SAFETY EQUIPMENT	***EQUIPO DE RESCATE***
a life belt	*un flotador*
a life jacket	*un chaleco salvavidas*
the safety drill	*el ejercicio de evacuación / el simulacro*
a siren	*una sirena*

TRAVELLING BY CAR — *VIAJANDO EN COCHE*

TYPES OF CAR	*TIPOS DE COCHE*
a saloon	*un turismo*
an estate car	*un coche familiar*
a hatchback	*un tres o cinco puertas*
a sportscar	*un deportivo*
an open car	*un coche descapotable*
a four wheel drive	*un todo terreno*
a two door car	*un coche de dos puertas*
a four door car	*un coche de cuatro puertas*
a five door car	*un coche de cinco puertas*
an automatic	*un coche de cambio automático*
a hire car	*un coche de alquiler*
a racing car	*un coche de carretas*

THE PARTS OF THE CAR — *PARTES DEL COCHE*

THE ROOF	*EL TECHO*
a roof rack	*una vaca*
to load / unload	*cargar / descargar*
to lift up	*levantar*
to tie / to secure	*atar / asegurar*

THE DOORS	*LAS PUERTAS*
to lock / to unlock	*cerrar con llave / quitar la llave*
central locking	*cierre centralizado*
to open / to shut	*abrir / cerrar*
the driver's door	*la puerta del conductor*
the passengers' doors	*las puertas para pasajeros*
the front / rear doors	*las puertas delanteras / traseras*

TRAVELLING BY CAR cont. *VIAJANDO EN COCHE cont.*

THE BOOT	***EL MALETERO***
to open / to shut	*abrir / cerrar*
to put something in the boot	*poner algo en el maletero*
to get something out of the boot	*sacar algo del maletero*

THE SEATS	***LOS ASIENTOS***
to adjust the seat	*ajustar el asiento*
to alter the height	*cambiar la altura*
to move the seat backwards / forwards	*mover el asiento hacía atrás / delante*
to fold the seat forwards	*echar el asiento hacía delante*
to put the seat back	*poner el asiento en su posición*
the headrest	*el reposacabezas*
the ashtray	*el cenicero*

THE SEATBELTS	***LOS CINTURONES DE SEGURIDAD***
to fasten / to unfasten	*abrochar / desabrochar*
Fasten your seatbelt, please.	*Ponte el cinturón, por favor*
How do you fasten the seatbelt?	*¿Cómo te pones el cinturón?*
Can you help me to fasten the seatbelt?	*¿Puedes ayudarme a ponerme el cinturón?*
I think the seatbelt is stuck under the seat.	*Creo que el cinturón está atrapado debajo del asiento.*

TRAVELLING BY CAR cont. / *VIAJANDO EN COCHE cont.*

THE WINDOWS	***LAS VENTANILLAS***
to open	*abrir*
May I open the window a little?	*¿Puedo abrir la ventanilla un poco?*
to shut	*cerrar*
Could you shut the window now, please?	*¿Puedes cerrar la ventanilla ahora?*
automatic windows	*ventanillas automáticas*
Press this button to open / close the windows.	*Presionar este botón para abrir / cerrar las ventanillas.*
the sun roof	*la ventanilla del techo*

THE MAIN CONTROLS / *LOS CONTROLES PRINCIPALES*

The ignition	***El arranque***
to start the car	*arrancar el coche*

The gears	***Las marchas***
the gear lever / the reverse gear	*la palanca / la marcha atrás*
to reverse	*echar la marcha atrás*
the clutch	*el embrague*

The brakes	***Los frenos***
to brake / to put the handbrake on	*frenar / poner el freno de mano*
to take the handbrake off	*quitar el freno de mano*

The accelerator	***El acelerador***
to accelerate	*acelerar*

The steering wheel	***El volante***
to steer / to turn	*conducir / dar vuelta*

TRAVELLING BY CAR cont. — *VIAJANDO EN COCHE cont.*

The indicators	***Los indicadores/los intermitentes***
to indicate right / left	*el indicador de la derecha / de la izquierda*
to turn on the hazard lights	*poner las luces de emergencia*

The horn	***El pito / El claxon***
to blow the horn	*tocar el claxon*

The headlights	***Las luces / Los faros***
to turn on / off	*encender / apagar*
to flash your lights	*lanzar una ráfaga*
full beam / to dip	*las luces largas / cambiar luces*
dipped headlights	*luces cortas / luces de cruce*
sidelights	*luces de estacionamiento*
fog lights	*los antinieblas*

The windscreen	***La luna***
dirty / to clean the screen	*sucia / limpiar la luna*
windscreen wipers	*los limpiaparabrisas (abbr. los limpia)*
to turn on / off	*poner / quitar*
the rear windscreen heater	*la resistencia antibao de la luna de atrás*
to get fogged up / to wipe / a duster	*ponerse empañado / limpiar / un trapo*

BASIC CAR MAINTENANCE — *MANTENIMIENTO BASICO DEL COCHE*

To need some petrol	***Necesita gasolina***
to put in petrol / to fill it up	*echar gasolina / llenarlo*
to undo the filler cap	*quitar el tapón del tanque*
to serve yourself	*echar gasolina*
lead free / leaded / diesel	*sín plomo / con plomo / diesel*
two / three / four star	*normal / super / extra super*

TRAVELLING BY CAR cont. ***VIAJANDO EN COCHE cont.***

BASIC CAR MAINTENANCE cont. ***MANTENIMIENTO BASICO DEL COCHE cont.***

Oil and water	***El aceite y el agua***
to check the oil / the water	*comprobar el aceite / el agua*
Where is the dipstick?	*¿Dónde esta la barra para medir el nivel?*
It needs more oil / water.	*Necesita más aceite / agua*
to pour the oil / water in	*echar aceite / agua*

Tyres	***Neumáticos***
to check the tyre pressures	*comprobar la presión de los neumáticos*
The tyres look a bit flat.	*Los neumáticos están un poco flojos.*
to pump up	*inflar*
to have a puncture	*tener un pinchazo / pinchar*
to change the wheel	*cambiar la rueda*
to fit the spare wheel	*poner la rueda de recambio*

LEARNING TO DRIVE
APRENDIENDO A CONDUCIR

DRIVING LESSONS	*LECCIONES DE CONDUCIR*
I am having driving lessons.	*Estoy tomando lecciones de conducir*
My sister / brother is learning to drive.	*Mi hermana / hermano está aprendiendo a conducir.*
I have had six lessons.	*He tenido seis lecciones / clases.*
My parents are teaching me.	*Mis padres me están enseñando.*
I am having lessons with a driving school.	*Voy a clases en una autoescuela.*
a dual control car	*un coche de autoescuela con controles dobles*
a driving instructor	*un profesor de autoescuela*

THE DRIVING TEST	*EL TEST DE CONDUCIR*
I am about to take my driving test.	*Voy a examinarme de conducir*
I have passed my test.	*He pasado mi test / examen*
I passed my test..	*Pasé mi examen / test*
• at the first attempt	• *a la primera*
• at the second / third attempt	• *a la segunda / a la tercera*
I failed my test.	*Suspendí mi examen / test*

LEARNING HOW TO..	*APRENDIENDO A*
to do a hill start	*arrancar en rampa*
to reverse	*conducir marcha atrás*
to park	*aparcar*
to do a three point turn	*hacer la "U"*
to do an emergency stop	*hacer una frenada de emergencia*
to overtake	*adelantar*

LEARNING TO DRIVE cont. — *APRENDIENDO A CONDUCIR cont.*

REMEMBERING ..	*RECORDAR...*
to look over your shoulder	*mirar sobre el hombro*
to look in your rear view mirror	*mirar el retrovisor*
to look both ways	*mirar a ambos lados*
to indicate	*poner los intermitentes*

PROBLEMS ON THE ROAD	*PROBLEMAS EN LA CARRETERA*
to break down	*tener una avería*
to have an accident	*tener un accidente*
to have a puncture	*pinchar*
to be delayed	*retrasarse*
long queues	*filas largas*
roadworks	*obras*
a diversion	*una desviación*
to run out of petrol	*quedarse sín gasolina*

TYPES OF ROAD	*TIPOS DE CARRETERAS*
a motorway	*una autopista*
a dual carriageway	*una carretera de doble calzada*
a ring road	*una circunvalación*
a main road	*una carretera*
a minor road	*una calzada*

JUNCTIONS	*INTERSECCIONES / CRUCES*
a roundabout	*una glorieta*
Give way to the right	*Ceda el pase a los que vienen por la derecha*
a cross roads	*un cruce*
traffic lights	*semáforo*
a pedestrian crossing	*un paso cebra / un paso de peatones*
a level crossing	*un paso elevado*

TRAVELLING BY BIKE — *VIAJANDO EN BICICLETA*

TYPES OF BIKE	*TIPOS DE BICIS*
a motorbike	*una motocicleta*
a bicycle	*una bicicleta*
a mountain bike	*una bicicleta de montaña*
a BMX	*una BMX*
a tricycle	*un triciclo*
a tandem	*un tandem*

PARTS OF THE BIKE — *PARTES DE LA BICICLETA*

The handlebars	***El manillar***
drop handlebars	*manillar de carreras hacía abajo*
raised handlebars	*manillar de carreras hacía arriba*
straight handlebars	*manillar de paseo*

The brakes	***Los frenos***
front / back	*delanteros / traseros*
to apply	*pulsar / apretar / accionar*
to brake	*frenar*
to slow down	*reducir la velocidad*

The gears	***Las marchas / la velocidades***
a gear lever	*una palanca del cambio*
to change gear	*cambiar marchas*
to go up a gear / down a gear	*subir de plató / bajar plató*
low / middle / top gear	*el plato pequeño / mediano / grande*
three / six / twelve gears	*de tres / seis / doce platos*
fifteen / eighteen / twenty one speed	*quince / dieciocho / veintiuna velocidades*

The frame	***El cuadro***
a kickstand	*una patilla*

TRAVELLING BY BIKE cont. / *VIAJANDO EN BICICLETA cont.*

The chain	***La cadena***
the chainguard	*el guardabarros*
to adjust the tension	*ajustar la tensión*
too loose	*demasiado floja*

The pedals	***Los pedales***
to pedal	*pedalear*
to back pedal	*pedalear hacía atrás*
to free wheel	*dejar rodar*

The seat	***El asiento***
to raise / to lower	*levantar / bajar*
too high / too low	*demasiado alto / bajo*
the height adjustment	*el ajustador de altura*
a clamp nut	*una nuez*
to screw / to unscrew	*destornillar / atornillar*
a release lever	*un nivelador*
to pull / to push	*sacar / meter*

The wheels	***Las ruedas***
a mudguard	*un guardabarros*
the spokes	*los radios*

The tyres	***Los neumáticos / la cámara***
Your tyres are flat.	*Las ruedas están flojas.*
Have you got a pump?	*¿Tienes una bomba de inflar?*
to unscrew / replace the dust cap	*desenroscar / volver a poner el tapón de la válvula.*
to pump up / to inflate	*hinchar / inflar*
the tyre pressure	*la presión de las ruedas*
I think I have a puncture.	*Creo que he pinchado.*
a puncture repair kit	*una caja de herramientas para arreglar pinchazos*

TRAVELLING BY BIKE cont. / *VIAJANDO EN BICICLETA cont.*

The lights	***Las luces***
a dynamo	*una dínamo*
to turn on / off	*encender / apagar*
a headlamp	*un faro delantero*
a rear lamp	*un faro de atrás*
a bulb	*una bombilla*
to replace	*cambiar*
The bulb has gone.	*la bombilla se ha fundido.*
a battery	*una batería*
a reflector	*un reflector*

EQUIPMENT	***EQUIPO***
a bicycle lock / a key	*un candado de bicicleta / una llave*
to lock / to unlock	*cerrar / abrir*
to padlock / a padlock	*poner un candado / un candado*
a crash helmet	*un casco*
a fluorescent strip	*un par de bandas fluorescentes*
cycling shorts	*pantalones de ciclismo*
gloves	*guantes*
sunglasses	*gafas de sol*
a pump	*una bomba de inflar*
a basket	*una cesta*
a water bottle	*una botella de agua*
a child seat	*un asiento para niños*
a seat belt	*un cinturón de seguridad*

TRAVELLING BY BIKE cont. — *VIAJANDO EN BICICLETA cont.*

USEFUL VERBS (abc)	*VERBOS UTILES*
to accelerate	*acelerar*
to borrow	*pedir prestado(a)*
to brake	*frenar*
to fall off	*caerse*
to get off	*bajarse*
to hire	*alquilar*
to lend	*dejar prestado(a)*
to lock	*cerrar con llave*
to lose your balance	*perder el equilibrio*
to mount	*montar*
to pedal	*pedalear*
to push	*empujar*
to ride	*montar*
to signal	*señalar / indicar*
to steer	*dirigir / conducir*
to wobble	*tambalearse*

EMERGENCIES
EMERGENCIAS

ACCIDENTS — *ACCIDENTES*

TELEPHONING EMERGENCY SERVICES — *LLAMANDO A LOS SERVICIOS DE EMERGENCIAS*

IN ENGLAND	*EN INGLATERRA*
Police - 999	***La Policía – 999***
Ambulance - 999	***Ambulancia – 999***
Fire Brigade - 999	***Los Bomberos – 999***

IN SPAIN	*EN ESPAÑA*
Police - 091 (National)	***La Policía - 091 (Nacional)***
- 092 (Local)	***- 092 (local)***
Ambulance - 006	***Ambulancias - 006 (Nacional & local)***
Fire Brigade - 006	***Los Bomberos - 006 (Nacional & local)***

CALLING OUT FOR HELP	*PIDIENDO AYUDA*
Help!	*¡Socorro!*
Come quickly!	*¡Venga pronto / deprisa!*
Fire!	*¡Fuego!*
Bomb scare!	*¡Hay una bomba! ¡Amenaza de bomba!*
Everybody out!	*¡Todo el mundo fuera de aquí!*
Call the …	*Llame a...*
• fire brigade	• *los bomberos*
• an ambulance	• *a una ambulancia*
• the police	• *a la policía*
• a doctor	• *al doctor*

EMERGENCIES cont. / *EMERGENCIAS cont.*

THERE HAS BEEN AN ACCIDENT	***HA HABIDO UN ACCIDENTE***
a traffic accident	*un accidente de tráfico*
a pile-up	*un accidente múltiple*
Warn other traffic.	*Avisa al resto de conductores.*
a warning triangle / hazard lights	*una señal de emergencia / un triángulo / luces de peligro*

SOMEONE HAS BEEN RUN OVER	***ALGUIEN HA SIDO ATROPEYADO***
They are injured.	*Hay heridos*
They are conscious / unconscious.	*Están conscientes / inconscientes*
a broken bone	*un hueso roto*
He / she is bleeding.	*El / Ella está sangrando*
to give mouth to mouth resuscitation	*hacer la respiración boca a boca*
to administer first aid	*dar primeros auxilios*

FIRE	***FUEGO***
Press the fire alarm button!	*¡Presiona la alarma contra incendios!*
That's the fire bell.	*Esa es la alarma de incendios.*
an alarm / to go off	*una alarma / dispararse*
a smoke detector	*un detector de humo*
a fire door	*una salida de incendios*
a fire exit	*una salida de incendios*
a fire blanket	*una manta para protegerse del fuego*
a fire extinguisher	*un extintor de incendios*
smoke	*humo*
flames	*llamas*
to be on fire	*estar ardiendo*
to burn	*quemarse*
to put out	*apagar*
water / sand	*agua / arena*

EMERGENCIES cont. / *EMERGENCIAS cont.*

A BOMB SCARE	*UNA AMENAZA DE BOMBA*
to clear the area	*evacuar el área*
to evacuate the building	*evacuar el edificio*
to call the bomb squad	*llamar a los bomberos*
a sniffer dog	*un perro entrenado*
to cordon off the area	*acordonar el área*
to detonate	*detonar*
to explode / to go off	*explotar / volar por los aires*
a false alarm	*una falsa alarma*
a suspicious package	*un paquete sospechoso*
an abandoned package	*un paquete abandonado*
to report a package to the police	*denunciar / avisar de la presencia de un paquete a la policía*

ILLNESS — *ENFERMEDAD*

INITIAL SYMPTOMS	*SINTOMAS INICIALES*
to feel off colour	*perder el color*
to feel ill	*sentirse malo*
to look ill	*tener mal aspecto*
to be taken ill	*ponerse malo*

GENERAL SYMPTOMS	*SINTOMAS GENERALES*
I am hot / cold	*Siento calor / frío*
I feel hot and cold.	*Siento escalofríos*
I feel shivery.	*Estoy temblando.*
I feel faint.	*Me siento flojo(a)*
I am thirsty.	*Tengo sed.*
I am not hungry	*No tengo hambre*
I have no appetite.	*He perdido el apetito.*
I couldn't eat a thing.	*No pude comer nada.*
I have a slight / a high temperature	*Tengo una poca / mucha fiebre*

I HAVE A HEADACHE	*TENGO DOLOR DE CABEZA*
I have a migraine.	*Tengo una jaqueca / migraña*
The light hurts my head.	*La luz me hace daño.*
Do you have any pain killers?	*¿Tienes tranquilizantes / aspirinas / paracetamol?*

FAINTING	*DESMAYANDOSE*
I feel dizzy.	*Estoy mareado(a).*
I think I am going to faint.	*Creo que me voy a desmayar.*
Put your head between your knees.	*Pon tu cabeza entre las piernas.*
Can I lie down, please?	*¿Quiero tumbarme, por favor?*
to pass out	*desmayarse*

ILLNESS cont. / *ENFERMEDAD cont.*

STOMACH UPSETS	***DOLOR DE ESTOMAGO***
I have indigestion.	*Tengo una indigestion.*
I have heartburn.	*Tengo acidez de estómago.*
I feel sick.	*Me siento mal.*
I am going to be sick.	*Voy a vomitar.*
I have been sick.	*He vomitado.*
My stomach hurts.	*Me duele el estómago.*
I have diarrhoea.	*Tengo diarrea.*
I think it's food poisoning.	*Algo me ha sentado mal.*
Could I have a drink of water, please?	*¿Puedo beber algo de agua, por favor?*
Could I have a bowl by my bed, please?	*¿Puedes dejar un cuenco junto a mi cama, por favor?*

MY THROAT IS VERY SORE.	***ME DUELE MUCHO LA GARGANTA***
I have tonsillitis.	*Tengo anginas.*
My throat is dry.	*Tengo la garganta seca.*
It hurts to swallow.	*Me duele cuando trago algo.*
My glands are swollen.	*Me duelen las anginas.*
to gargle	*Hacer gárgaras.*
to have a hot drink	*Beber algo templado.*
Have you any throat sweets?	*¿Tienes pastillas para la garganta?*
I like lemon ones/ honey /menthol /eucalyptus / blackcurrant.	*Me gustan las de limón / miel / menthol / eucalipto / moras.*

ILLNESS cont. / *ENFERMEDAD cont.*

I HAVE CAUGHT A COLD	***HE COGIDO UN RESFRIADO***
to sneeze / Bless you!	*Estornudar / ¡Jesús!*
to blow your nose	*sonarse la nariz*
a handkerchief	*un pañuelo*
paper handkerchiefs	*un pañuelo de papel*
to find it difficult to breathe	*no poder respirar bien*
a decongestant	*un remedio para la congestión*
a cold remedy	*un remedio para el resfriado*

I HAVE A BAD COUGH	***TENGO UN BUEN CONSTIPADO***
a tickly cough	*una tos molesta / una tos cosquillosa*
a dry cough / a productive cough	*una tos fuerte / una tos violenta*
a spasm of coughing	*un espasmo al toser*
to take cough medicine	*tomar jarabe para la tos*
to need antibiotics	*necesitar antibióticos*

ASTHMA	***ASMA***
to suffer from asthma	*sufrir asma*
to be asthmatic	*ser asmático*
to wheeze / to cough a lot	*resollar / toser mucho*
to control one's asthma	*controlar el asma*
to be allergic to..	*ser alérgico a...*
• dust	• *el polvo*
• animals	• *los animales*
• chest infections	• *las infecciones de pecho*
to use an inhaler	*usar un inhalador*
• to inhale	• *inhalar*
• Ventolin ® / Becotide ®	• *Ventolín ® / Becotide ®*
• steroids / a nebuliser	• *esteroides / un nebulizador*

ILLNESS cont. — *ENFERMEDAD cont.*

SKIN PROBLEMS — *PROBLEMAS DE PIEL*

SUNBURN	***QUEMADURA***
to be burnt	*quemarse*
to be sore	*ser doloroso*
to peel	*pelarse*
to apply after-sun lotion	*poner loción para después del sol*
calamine	*calamina*
to rub on	*restregar / poner*

A RASH	***UN SARPULLIDO***
an allergy	*una alergia*
to be allergic to	*tener alergia a*
nettle rash	*un sarpullido de ortiga*
prickly heat	*calor agobiante*
to itch / to scratch	*picar / rascarse*
to feel sore	*sentir dolor*
antihistamine cream	*crema antihistamínica*

SPLINTERS	***ASTILLAS***
I have a splinter in my foot / hand.	*Tengo una astilla en el pie / la mano*
to get it out	*sacarla*
a needle / tweezers	*una aguja / un par de pinzas*
surgical spirit / disinfectant	*desinfectante*

MINOR INJURIES	***HERIDAS SUPERFICIALES***
a spot	*un grano*
acne	*acne*
a scratch	*un arañazo*
a graze	*un rasguño*
a cut	*un corte*

ILLNESS cont. / *ENFERMEDAD cont.*

SERIOUS CUTS	***CORTES GRAVES***
to need stitches	*necesita puntos (m)*
butterfly stitches	*puntos cruzados*
local anaesthetic	*anestesia local (f)*
a bandage	*una venda*
an elastoplast	*una venda elástica*
a sticking plaster	*una tirita*
a blister	*una ampolla*

STINGS	***PICADURAS***
a wasp / bee sting	*una picadura de avispa / abeja*
a mosquito bite	*una picadura de mosquito*
I have been stung by something.	*Me ha picado algo.*
a jelly fish sting	*una erupción debido a una medusa*
insect repellent	*un repelente de insectos*
antihistamine cream / tablets	*crema antihistamínica / píldoras*

TOILET PROBLEMS	***PROBLEMAS DE DESARREGLOS DIGESTIVOS***
to have cystitis	*tener cistitis*
to have diarrhoea	*tener diarrea*
to take kaolin and morphine	*tomar kaolin y morfina*
to be constipated	*estar estreñido*
a laxative	*un laxativo*
to eat more roughage	*comer sólido*
to drink more water	*beber más agua*

ILLNESS cont. — *ENFERMEDAD cont.*

PERIOD PROBLEMS	*PROBLEMAS CON LA REGLA*
to have period pains	*tener dolores de la regla*
to take pain killers	*tomar tranquilizantes*
My period is..	*La regla se me está...*
• late	• *retrasando*
• heavy	• *manchando mucho*
• painful	• *Me duele el vientre mucho por la regla*
• prolongued	• *Se está alargando mucho la regla*

INJURIES	*HERIDAS*
I hurt here.	*Me duele aquí.*
I have bruised my..	*Me he hecho un cardenal en...*
I have cut my..	*Me he cortado...*
I have sprained my..	*Me he torcido...*
I have broken my..	*Me he roto...*
I have dislocated my..	*Me he dislocado...*
I have burnt my..	*Me he quemado...*
I can't move my..	*No puedo mover...*

PARTS OF THE BODY — *PARTES DEL CUERPO*

THE SKIN		*LA PIEL*	
dry	*seca*	cracked	*agrietada*
sore	*dolorida*	wrinkled	*arrugada*
burnt	*quemada*	soft / hard	*suave / áspera*

ILLNESS cont. ***ENFERMEDAD cont.***

PARTS OF THE BODY cont. ***PARTES DEL CUERPO cont.***

THE HAIR	***EL PELO***
straight / wavy / curly	*liso / ondulado / rizado*
blonde / auburn / brown	*rubio / castaño rojizo / moreno*
red / black	*pelirrojo / negro*
grey / white	*canoso / cano*
short / long	*corto / largo*
to wear it up	*recogérselo*
to wear it loose	*llevarlo suelto*
shoulder length	*por los hombros*
balding / to be bald	*clareando / quedarse calvo(a)*
dandruff	*con caspa*
oily / dry	*graso / seco*
dyed / streaked	*decolorado / colorado*
permed	*con permanente*

THE HEAD	***LA CABEZA***
the brain	*el cerebro*
the skull	*el cráneo*
the scalp	*el cuero cabelludo*

THE FACE	***LA CARA***
the cheeks	*las mejillas*
the cheekbones	*los pómulos*
to blush	*ponerse rojo*

THE EYES		***LOS OJOS***	
an eye	*un ojo*	an eyelash	*una pestaña*
the eyebrows	*las cejas*	the pupil	*la pupila*
the eyelid	*los párpados*	the iris	*el iris*

ILLNESS cont. / *ENFERMEDAD cont.*

PARTS OF THE BODY cont. / *PARTES DEL CUERPO cont.*

THE EYESIGHT	*LA VISTA*
to wear glasses	*llevar gafas*
to wear contact lenses	*llevar lentillas de contacto*
to be short / long sighted	*ser corto de vista / no ver de lejos*
to have good eyesight	*tener buena vista*
to have an eye test	*hacerse un chequeo de ojos*
to wear sunglasses	*llevar gafas de sol*
to be partially sighted	*tener visión parcial*
to be blind	*ser ciego*
a white stick / a guide dog	*un bastón guía / un perro guía*

THE NOSE	*LA NARIZ*
a nostril	*un agujero de la nariz*
to blow the nose	*sonarse las narices*

THE MOUTH	*LA BOCA*
the lips	*los labios*
the tongue	*la lengua*
the jaw	*la mandíbula*
the throat / the tonsils	*la garganta / la nuez*

THE TEETH	*LOS DIENTES*
a molar / a canine	*un molar / un canino*
an incisor / a wisdom tooth	*un incisor / una muela del juicio*
the gums	*la encías*
to clean one's teeth	*limpiarse / cepillarse los dientes*
a toothbrush / to brush	*un cepillos de dientes / cepillarse*
toothpaste / to squeeze the tube	*pasta dentífrica / apretar el tubo*
to floss	*pasar el hilo de seda*
to use mouthwash / to gargle	*usar licor dentífrico/hacer gárgaras*

ILLNESS cont. — *ENFERMEDAD cont.*

PARTS OF THE BODY cont. — *PARTES DEL CUERPO cont.*

THE EARS	*LAS OREJAS*
the ear lobe	*el lóbulo del oido*
the outer ear / the middle ear	*la oreja / el oido medio*
the ear drum	*el tambor*
earwax	*la cerilla*
an ear infection	*una infección de oido*
to be unable to hear properly	*no poder oir bien*
to be deaf	*estar sordo*
a hearing aid	*un sonotone*

THE BEARD	*LA BARBA*
clean shaven	*recortada*
to grow a beard	*dejarse la barba*
to shave (See page 60)	*afeitarse*
a moustache	*un bigote*
sideburns	*patillas*
a chin	*una barbilla*

THE BODY		*EL CUERPO*	
the neck	*el cuello*	a rib	*una costilla*
the shoulder	*el hombro*	the rib cage	*la caja torácica*
the back	*la espalda*	the waist	*la cintura*
the spine	*la espina dorsal*	the hip	*las caderas*
the bottom	*el culo*	the stomach	*el estómago*
the chest	*el pecho*	the abdomen	*el abdomen*

ILLNESS cont. — *ENFERMEDAD cont.*

PARTS OF THE BODY cont. — *PARTES DEL CUERPO cont.*

THE ARMS	*LOS BRAZOS*
the upper arm	*el brazo*
the forearm	*el antebrazo*
the elbow	*el codo*
the funny bone	*el hueso de la risa*
the wrist	*la muñeca*

THE HANDS	*LAS MANOS*
the palm / the back of the hand	*la palma / la mano*
the knuckles	*los nudillos*
the fingers / the thumbs	*los dedos / los dedos gordos (o) pulgares*
left / right	*izquierdo(a) / derecho(a)*
a fingernail	*una uña*
a cuticle	*una cutícula*
a manicure / to manicure	*una manicura / hacer la manicura*
an emery board / a nail file	*una tabla de manicura / una lima*
nail varnish / nail varnish remover	*un esmalte / un quita esmaltes*

THE LEGS	*LAS PIERNAS*
the thigh	*el muslo*
the knee	*la rodilla*
the calf	*la pantorrilla*
the shin	*la espinilla*
the ankle	*el tobillo*

ILLNESS cont. — *ENFERMEDAD cont.*

PARTS OF THE BODY cont. — *PARTES DEL CUERPO cont.*

THE FEET	*EL PIE*
a foot	*un pie*
the heel / the sole	*el talón / la planta del pie*
the toes / the big toe / the little toe	*los dedos del pie / de pulgar / el meñique*
a toenail	*una uña*
to cut the toenails	*cortarse las uñas*
nail scissors / nail clippers	*unos alicates / un cortauñas*
hard skin / bunions	*cayos / durezas*
a pumice stone	*una piedra pómez*

THE MAIN INTERNAL ORGANS		*LOS PRINCIPALES ÓRGANOS INTERNOS*	
the lungs	*los pulmones*	the intestines	*los intestinos*
the heart	*el corazón*	the bowel	*el vientre*
the liver	*el hígado*	the bladder	*la vejiga*
the kidney	*el riñón*	the digestive system	*el sistema digestivo*

THE CIRCULATION	*LA CIRCULACION*
the blood	*la sangre*
to be anaemic	*estar anémico*
an artery / a vein	*una arteria / una vena*
to bleed	*sangrar*
to haemorrhage	*tener una hemorragia*
to bruise	*hacerse un moratón*
to clot / to form a scab	*coagularse / formarse una cicatriz (cicatrizar)*

ILLNESS cont. | ***ENFERMEDAD cont.***

PARTS OF THE BODY cont. | ***PARTES DEL CUERPO cont.***

THE MAIN MUSCLES	LOS MUSCULOS PRINCIPALES
the biceps / the triceps	*el biceps / el triceps*
the pectorals	*los pectorales*
the ham string	*el tendón de la corva*
the Achilles tendon	*el tendón de Aguiles*

THE MAIN BONES		LOS HUESOS PRINCIPALES	
the skeleton	*el esqueleto*	the shoulder blade	*el omoplato*
the skull	*el cráneo*	the ribs	*las costillas*
the collar bone	*la clavícula*	the hip bone	*el hueso de la cadera*
the spine	*la espina dorsal*	the thigh bone	*el fémur*
the vertebrae	*las vertebras*	the shin bone	*la tibia*
the coccyx	*el coxis*	the knee cap	*la rótula*

THE CENTRAL NERVOUS SYSTEM	EL SISTEMA CENTRAL NERVIOSO
the cerebellum	*el cerebelo*
the spinal chord	*la médula espinal*
the nerves	*los nervios*

MALE / FEMALE CHARACTERISTICS		RASGOS MASCULINOS Y FEMENINOS	
the penis	*el pene*	the breasts	*los pechos*
the testicles	*los testículos*	the nipples	*los pezones*
a broken voice	*una voz de gallito*	the womb	*el vientre*
		the vagina	*la vagina*

THE BODY cont. — *EL CUERPO cont.*

PREGNANCY	***EMBARAZO***
to do a pregnancy test	*hacerse una prueba de embarazo*
positive / negative	*positivo / negativo*
to be pregnant	*estar embarazada*
to be three months pregnant	*estar embarazada de tres meses*
to be at full term	*haber cumplido*
to go into labour	*ir de parto / romper aguas*
to have a baby	*tener un bebé*
the embryo / the foetus	*el embrión / el feto*

THE FIVE SENSES — *LOS CINCO SENTIDOS*

TOUCH		***EL TACTO***	
to touch	*palpar / sentir*	rough	*áspero(a)*
hot	*calor / caliente*	smooth	*suave*
cold	*frío(a)*	painful	*doloroso(a)*

TASTE		***GUSTO***	
to taste	*de gusta / probar*	sour	*agrio(a)*
bitter	*amargo(a)*	savoury	*salado(a)*
sweet	*dulce*		

SMELL		***EL OLFATO***	
to smell	*oler*	unpleasant	*desagradable*
pleasant	*agradable*	to stink	*apestar*

HEARING		***EL OIDO***	
to hear	oir / *escuchar*	noisy	*ruidoso(a)*
loud	*alto(a)*	quiet	*tranquilo(a)*

SIGHT		***LA VISTA***	
to see	*ver / mirar*	blurred	*turbio(a)*
to focus	*enfocar*	clear	*claro(a)*

THE DOCTOR — *EL DOCTOR*

GETTING TREATMENT	***SIENDO TRATADO***
Shall I call..?	***¿Llamo a...?***
Can I make an appointment to see ..?	***¿Podría darme cita para ver a...?***
• the doctor / the nurse	• *el doctor / la enfermera*
• the dentist	• *el dentista*
• the hospital	• *el hospital*

THE DOCTOR'S SURGERY	***LA CONSULTA DEL DOCTOR***
the waiting room	*la sala de espera*
to sit down / to wait	*sentarse/ esperar*
to read a magazine	*leer una revista*
I have an appointment to see..	*Tengo una cita para ver a...*

THE CONSULTATION	***LA CONSULTA***
I am going to ..	***Voy a...***
• to take your blood pressure.	• *Tomarte la presión sanguínea.*
• to take your pulse.	• *Tomarte el pulso.*
• to take a blood sample.	• *Tomar una muestra de sangre.*
• to do a urine test.	• *hacerte un test de orina.*
• to listen to your heart / chest.	• *ocultarte el corazón / el pecho*
• to look down your throat.	• *mirarte la garganta*
• to look in your ear.	• *mirarte en el oído.*
• to test your reflexes.	• *comprobar los reflejos.*

THE DOCTOR cont. — *EL DOCTOR cont.*

COULD YOU..	*PODRIA...*
• roll up your sleeve.	• *Subirse las mangas.*
• undo your jacket.	• *Quitarse la chaqueta.*
• lift up your shirt.	• *Levantarse la camisa.*
• take off your clothes.	• *Quitarse la ropa.*
• take everything off except your pants.	• *Quitarse todo salvo la ropa interior.*
• put this gown on.	• *Ponerse esta bata.*
• climb on the bed / lie down.	• *subirse a la cama / tumbarse*
• put this blanket over you	• *ponerse esta manta encima*
• open your mouth wide	• *abrir la boca.*
• do a urine / stool sample	• *hacer una muestra de orina / de caca (heces).*

SAYING WHERE YOU HURT	*DICIENDO DONDE TE DUELE*
Where does it hurt?	*¿Dónde te duele?*
Show me where it hurts.	*Muéstrame donde te duele.*
Does it hurt…	*¿Te duele aquí...*
• badly?	• *muchísimo?*
• much?	• *mucho?*
• when I touch it?	• *cuando presiono?*
• when you move it?	• *cuando te mueves?*
Can you move your… (See parts of the body - pages 411-417)	*¿Puedes mover...*

ILLNESS cont. — *ENFERMEDAD cont.*

THE DOCTOR'S INSTRUCTIONS	*LAS INDICACIONES DEL DOCTOR*
You should stay in bed.	*Debes guardar cama.*
You should not go to work / school / travel.	*Debes darte de baja / no debes ir "al colegio" / "de viaje".*
I would like to do further tests.	*Me gustaría hacer más pruebas.*
You need an X-ray.	*Necesito hacer rayos X.*
You need a scan.	*Necesito un scan.*
I will make an appointment at the hospital for you.	*Te voy a arreglar una cita para que vayas al hospital.*
I would like a second opinion.	*Me gustaría tener una segunda opinión.*
It is nothing serious.	*No es nada grave.*
You will be better soon.	*Te pondrás bien pronto.*
Are you allergic to anything?	*¿Tienes alguna alergia a algo?*

THE TREATMENT	*EL TRATAMIENTO*
a prescription	*una receta*
Take it to the chemists.	*Llévala a la farmacia.*
to get the prescription made up	*hacer una prescripción.*
antibiotics / penicillin	*antibióticas / penicilina*
a tablet / a capsule	*una pastilla / una cápsula*
medicine / linctus	*medicina / jarabe para la tos*
a five millilitre spoon	*una cucharadita de cinco mililitros*
the dosage	*una dosis*
to swallow / to take	*tragar / tomar*
Shake the bottle before use.	*Agitar la botella antes de usar.*

ILLNESS cont. — *ENFERMEDAD cont.*

MEDICINE cont. — *MEDICINA cont.*

three times a day	*tres veces al día*
before / after meals	*antes / después de la comidas*
Take with food.	*Tómese con las comidas.*
Take on an empty stomach.	*Tómese en ayunas.*
Do not drink alcohol.	*No beba alcohol.*
Do not mix with other tablets.	*No tome otros medicamentos.*
Do not take if pregnant.	*No tome esto en case de embarazo.*
a suppository	*un supositorio*
an inhaler	*un inhalador*
antihistamine cream	*una crema antiestamínica*
antiseptic cream	*una crema antiséptica*
ointment / to rub on	*ungüento / restregar*
aspirin / paracetamol	*aspirina / paracetamol*

GOING TO HOSPITAL	*YENDO AL HOSPITAL*
an ambulance	*una ambulancia*
a stretcher	*una camilla*
the outpatients' department	*la sección de pacientes externos / no hospitalizados*
casualty	*la sección de emergencias*
the enquiry desk	*el mostrador de información*

ILLNESS - GOING TO HOSPITAL cont. / *ENFERMEDAD - YENDO AL HOSPITAL cont.*

BEING ADMITTED	***SER INGRESADO***
Can you fill in this form, please?	*Por favor ¿Podría rellenar esta ficha?*
Can I take your details, please?	*¿Puede darme sus datos?*
• Surname	• *Apellido*
• Christian Name	• *Nombre*
• Age	• *Edad*
• Date of Birth	• *Fecha de nacimiento*
• Place of Birth	• *Lugar de nacimiento*
• Nationality	• *Nacionalidad*
• Address / Telephone Number	• *Dirección / Número de teléfono*
• Next of Kin	• *Tutor / pareja / familiar cercano*
• Medical History	• *Historial médico*
• Details of previous operations	• *Detalles sobre previas operaciones*
• Serious illnesses.	• *Enfermedades*
• Allergies	• *Alergias*
• Have you ever had any of the following illnesses?	• *¿Ha tenido alguna de estas enfermedades?*

THE FRACTURE CLINIC	***LA CLINICA DE FRACTURAS***
to be assessed / examined	*ser examinado*
to have an X-ray	*hacer una prueba de rayos X*
to have one's arm in a sling	*poner un brazo en cabestrillo*
to be bandaged up	*vendar*
to be given a plaster cast	*poner una escayola*
to have a splint	*poner tablillas*
to walk with crutches / to hop	*andar con muletas / saltar*
to lean on someone	*apoyarse en alguien*
to use a wheelchair	*usar una silla de ruedas*
to push / to steer	*empujar / dirigir*

ILLNESS - GOING TO HOSPITAL cont. / *ENFERMEDAD - YENDO AL HOSPITAL cont.*

PHYSIOTHERAPY	***FISIOTERAPIA***
a physiotherapist	*un fisioterapeuta*
to do exercises	*hacer ejercicios*
to increase mobility	*aumentar la movilidad*
to use an ice pack	*usar una bolsa de hielo*
to use a bag of frozen peas	*usar una bolsa de guisantes congelados*
to wrap in a towel	*envolver en una toalla*
to reduce the swelling	*reducir la hinchazón*
to reduce the inflammation	*reducir la inflamación*
to use a heat compress	*usar una compresa caliente*
to have ultrasound treatment	*tratar con ultrasonidos*
to do exercises every hour	*hacer ejercicios cada hora*
three times a day	*tres veces al día*
to push / to pull	*empujar / tirar*
to squeeze	*apretar*
to lift / a weight	*levantar / una pesca*
to raise / to lower	*elevar / bajar*
to massage	*masajear / dar un masaje*

OPERATIONS	***OPERACIONES***
to have nothing to eat or drink	*ayunar*
to sign a consent form	*firmar una declaración de consentimiento*
to put on an operating gown	*ponerse una bata de operación*
to be given a pre-med	*dar premedicación*
to feel drowsy	*sentirse adormilado*
to have a local anaesthetic	*administrar anestesia local*

ILLNESS - GOING TO HOSPITAL cont. / *ENFERMEDAD - YENDO AL HOSPITAL cont.*

OPERATIONS cont. / *OPERACIONES cont.*

to be numb	*estar entumecido*
an injection	*una inyección*
to be given gas and air	*poner oxígeno*
a mask	*una máscara*
to dull the pain	*eliminar el dolor*
to cover your nose and mouth	*cubrir la nariz y la boca*
to breathe in	*respirar*
to have a general anaesthetic	*administrar una anestésica global*
to come round	*recuperar la consciencia*
to have a sip of water	*tomar un trago de agua*
to have your pulse checked	*hacer un chequeo del pulso*
to have your temperature taken	*tomar la temperatura*
to listen to your heart	*oscultar el ritmo cardiaco*
to call the nurse	*llamar a la enfermera*
Can I get you anything?	*¿Quiere algo?*
Is anything wrong?	*¿Está todo bien?*
to ask for a bed pan	*pedir una cuña*
to ask for a drink	*pedir una bebida*
visiting hours	*las horas de visita*
to have a visitor	*tener una visita*
to be given flowers	*recibir flores*
to receive Get Well cards	*recibir cartas de ánimo*

DENTAL TREATMENT — *TRATAMIENTO DENTAL*

THE DENTIST — *EL DENTISTA*

to make an appointment	*concertar una cita*
to sit in the waiting room	*esperar sentado(a) en la sala de esperar*
to go into the surgery	*ir dentro de la sala de consulta*
the dentist's chair	*la silla del dentista*
My tooth hurts.	*Me duele un diente.*
My filling has come out.	*El empaste se ha salido.*
My tooth was knocked out.	*Me he roto un diente.*

DENTAL TREATMENT	***TRATAMIENTO DENTAL***
to have a look	*echar un vistazo*
to put a bib on	*poner un peto*
Open your mouth wide.	*Abrir la boca completamente.*
Does that hurt?	*¿Duele?*
Which tooth hurts?	*¿Qué diente le duele?*
to be given a local anaesthetic	*dar anestesia local*
an injection	*una inyección*
Is it numb now?	*¿Está dormido ahora?*
to drill a tooth	*limar un diente*
to extract a tooth	*sacar un diente*
a laser beam	*un rayo láser*
to put a filling in	*poner un empaste*
to bite one's teeth together gently	*morder despacio*
to polish the teeth	*limpiar los dientes*
to wash / rinse the mouth out	*limpiar / enjuagar la boca*
to spit / to dribble	*escupir / babear*
a tissue / to dry one's mouth	*un pañuelo / secarse la boca*
to find it difficult to talk / to drink	*encontrar difícil hablar / beber*
Don't eat anything for a couple of hours.	*No comas nada en las siguientes dos horas.*

THE OPTICIANS — *EL OPTICO / EL MEDICO DEL OJO*

My glasses have broken.	*Se me han roto las gafas*
Could you mend them for me?	*¿Tienen arreglo?*
I have lost a contact lens.	*He perdido una lentilla.*
Could I try to get a replacement?	*¿Me puede proporcionar otra?*
I can't see very clearly.	*No veo muy bien.*
I have double vision.	*Veo doble.*
I keep getting headaches.	*Tengo dolores de cabeza muy menudo.*
Could I get my eyes tested, please?	*¿Podría hacerme un test de visión?*
A screw has come out of my glasses.	*He perdido uno de los tornillos de mis gafas.*
Can you mend my glasses for me?	*¿Puede arreglarme las gafas?*
Will you have to send them away somewhere?	*¿Tiene que enviarlas a alguna parte?*
How long will it take to repair them?	*¿Cuánto va a tardar el arreglo?*
I am going back to England in five days.	*Vuelvo a Inglaterra dentro de cinco días.*
Will they be ready by then?	*¿Van a estar listas para entonces?*

EYE SIGHT TESTS	***UN TEST DE VISTA***
Do sit down.	*Siéntase por favor.*
Look over there.	*Mire hacia aquí.*
Look at the writing.	*Mire a las letras.*
Read as much as you can.	*Lea hasta que no pueda ver con claridad.*
Can you read the next row down?	*¿Puede ver la siguiente fila de abajo?*

EYE SIGHT TESTS cont. — *UN TEST DE VISTA cont.*

Take your glasses off.	*Quitése las gafas.*
I am going to try different lenses.	*Voy a probar con lentillas distintas.*
Does it look clearer like this or like this?	*¿Cómo ve mejor con éste o este otro?*
Clearer with this lens or without it?	*¿Cómo ve mejor con o sín las lentillas?*
I am going to look in your eye with a torch.	*Voy a mirarle los ojos con una literna.*
Look up / down / left / right / straight ahead.	*Mire arriba / abajo / a la izquierda / a la derecha / recto / al frente.*
You can put your glasses on again now.	*Ya te puedes poner las gafas.*

PREVENTIVE MEDICINE — *MEDICINA PREVENTIVA*

RELAXATION	*RELAJACION*
to avoid stress	*evitar el estrés*
to practise relaxation	*practicar la relajación*
to relieve tension	*eliminar la tensión*
to do breathing exercises	*hacer ejercicios respiratorios*
to meditate	*meditar*
to practise meditation	*practicar la meditación*

EXERCISE	*EJERCICIO*
to take enough exercise	*hacer ejercicio suficientemente*
to walk more	*andar más*
to keep fit	*estar en forma*
to go to keep fit classes	*ir a clases de mantenimiento*
to go jogging / swimming	*hacer jogging / ir a nadar*
aerobic / anaerobic	*aeróbicos / anaerobio (-a)*
to warm up / to stretch	*hacer calentamientos / estirar los múscolos*
suppleness exercises	*ejercicios preparatorios*

PREVENTIVE MEDICINE - EXERCISE cont.	***MEDICINA PREVENTIVA - EJERCICIO cont.***
weight lifting	*levantar pesas*
to get breathless	*quedarse sín aliento.*
to work up a sweat	*hacer un buen mantenimiento*
to exercise three times a week	*hacer ejercicio tres veces en semana*
to exercise for at least twenty minutes	*hacer ejercicio por al menos veinte minutos*

SLEEP	***DORMIR***
to get a good night's sleep	*dormir bien*
to need eight hours' sleep	*necesitar ocho horas de sueño*
to lie in	*quedarse dormido*
to get up early	*levantarse tarde*
to go to bed late	*ir a la cama tarde*
to dream	*soñar*
to have nightmares	*tener pesadillas*
to suffer from insomnia	*sufrir de insomnio*
to take sleeping tablets	*tomar pastillas para dormir*

DIET	***DIETA***
to eat a balanced diet	*tener una dieta equilibrada*
to eat sensibly	*comer bien*
vitamins / minerals	*vitaminas (f)/ minerales (m)*
carbohydrates	*carbohidratos (m)*
protein	*proteínas (f)*
fibrous foods	*alimentos ricos en fibra*
vegetarian / vegan	*vegetariano / vegetariano estricto (Vegan)*
to drink too much caffeine	*beber demasiada cafeína*
to count calories	*contar las calorías*
to cut down	*reducir*
to have small portions	*tomar pedazos pequeños*
to have a little of everything	*comer un poco de todo*
a calorie controlled diet	*una dieta de consumo de calorías limitadas*

PREVENTIVE MEDICINE — *MEDICINA PREVENTIVA*

DIET cont. — *DIETA cont.*

a strict diet	*una dieta estricta*
a diabetic diet	*una dieta para diabéticos*
to binge	*sobrepasarse*
anorexia nervosa	*anorexia nerviosa*
bulimia	*bulimia*
to lose / gain weight	*perder / poner peso*
to lower one's cholesterol level	*bajar el nivel de colesterol*
to be a desirable weight	*estar en tu peso ideal*
to be a little overweight	*estar un poco gordo*
to be underweight	*estar demasiado delgado*
to be obese	*estar obeso*

ALCOHOL CONSUMPTION	*CONSUMO DE ALCOHOL*
to drink sensibly	*beber normal*
a unit of alcohol	*una unidad de alcohol*
to be a social drinker	*beber con los amigos*
to drink too much	*beber demasiado*
to get drunk	*emborracharse*
to have a hangover	*tener resaca*
to be dehydrated	*estar deshidratado(a)*
to be an alcoholic	*ser un alcohólico*

SMOKING	*FUMAR*
cigarettes / cigars / a pipe	*cigarros / puros / una pipa*
tobacco / nicotine / tar content	*tabaco / nicotina / alquitrán*
How many do you smoke a day?	*¿Cuánto fumas al día?*
to try to cut down / to be addicted	*intentar reducir / ser adicto*
to inhale / lung cancer	*inhalar / cáncer de pulmón*

DRUGS	*DROGAS*
soft / hard drugs	*drogas blandas / duras*
stimulants	*estimulantes*
cannabis	*porros*
to smoke	*fumar*
ecstasy / an E	*éxtasis*
a tablet	*una pastilla*
to inject	*una inyección*
a pusher	*un camello*
illegal	*ilegal*
I think he / she has taken some drugs.	*Creo que ha tomado drogas.*
Do you know what he took?	*¿Qué ha tomado éste?*
to be unconscious	*estar inconsciente*
I think we should get help.	*Creo que lo mejor es buscar ayuda.*
He / she is drinking a lot of water.	*Esta bebiendo mucha agua.*

ALTERNATIVE THERAPIES — *TERAPIAS ALTERNATIVAS*

AROMATHERAPY	*TERAPIA DE AROMAS*
essential oils	*los aceites de esencias*
a drop	*una gota*
to blend	*mezclar*
a carrier oil	*un aceite base*
to massage / a massage	*dar un masaje / un masaje*
to inhale	*inhalar*
an essential oil burner	*un quemador de aceite perfumado*
to put in the bath	*poner en el baño*
a compress	*una compresa*

HERBALISM	*EL HERBOLARIO*
a herbalist	*un herborista*
a herb / to gather / to store	*una hierba / reunir / almacenar*
an infusion / a decoction	*una infusion / un ungüento hervido*
a tincture / a compress	*una tintura / una compresa*

ALTERNATIVE THERAPIES cont. | ***TERAPIAS ALTERNATIVAS cont.***

HOMOEOPATHY	***HOMEOPATIA***
a homoeopath	*un homeópata*
a remedy	*un remedio*
constitutional treatment	*un tratamiento de acuerdo de tu constitución*
the potency	*la fuerza*
the dose	*una dosis*

CHIROPRACTIC AND OSTEOPATHY	***QUIROPODO Y OSTEOPATA***
a chiropractor	*un quiropodo*
an osteopath	*un osteópata*
to manipulate	*manipular / tocar con la manos*
the joints	*las articulaciones*

CRIME — *CRIMEN*

THEFT	***ROBO***
I've been robbed.	*Me han robado.*
Someone has taken my..	*Alguien me ha quitado me...*
• bag	• *bolsa*
• wallet	• *cartera*
• purse	• *monedero*
• money	• *dinero*
• credit card	• *tarjeta de crédito*
• watch	• *reloj*
• jewellery	• *joyas*
a thief / a pickpocket	*un ladrón / un ladronzuelo (carterista)*
a car thief / a joyrider	*un ladrón de coches*
to break into	*forzar*
to steal / to snatch	*robar / tirar*
to mug	*asaltar*
to rob a bank	*robar un banco*
to steal from the till	*robar de la caja registradora*
to shoplift / a shoplifter	*robar en una tienda / un ladrón de tiendas*
a hijacking / to hijack	*un secuestro / secuestrar en un avión*
a kidnapping / to kidnap	*un secuestro / secuestrar*
to demand a ransom	*pedir / exigir un rescate*
to take a hostage / terrorism	*tomar un rehén / terrorismo*
to hold up / a hold-up	*retener / un encierro con rehenes*
a murder / to murder	*un asesino / asesinar*
to kick / to stab	*dar una patada / apuñalar*
to thump / to cosh	*dar golpes / aporrear*
to knock someone out	*derribar a álguien / asaltar a álguien*
to strangle / to suffocate	*estrangular / asfixiar*
rape / to rape / to be raped / a rapist	*violación / violar / ser violado(a) / violador(a)*

CRIME cont. / *CRIMEN cont.*

HELPING THE POLICE	*AYUDANDO A LA POLICIA*
a witness / to witness	*un testigo / ser testigo*
to say what happened	*decir lo que sucedió*
to recognize	*reconocer*
to identify	*identificar*
a suspect	*un sospechoso*
to be cautioned	*leer los derechos*
to be taken into custody	*ser puesto bajo custodia*
to be arrested	*ser arrestado*
to be let out on bail	*dejar salir tras pagar una fianza*
to be innocent	*ser inocente*
to be guilty	*ser culpable*

LOSING OR DAMAGING IMPORTANT POSSESSIONS — *PERDIENDO O ROMPIENDO COSAS IMPORTANTES*

I'VE LOST MY...(abc)	***HE PERDIDO MI...***
• bag	• *cartera / bolsa*
• briefcase	• *cartera*
• bus pass	• *pase para el autobús*
• camera	• *cámara de fotos*
• cheque book	• *chequera*
• cheque card	• *mi tarjeta*
• contact lens	• *mis lentes de contacto*
• credit cards	• *mi tarjeta de crédito*
• diary	• *mi agenda*
• foreign currency	• *mi dinero extranjero*
• glasses / spectacles	• *mis gafas*
• handbag	• *mi bolsa*
• Identity card	• *mi carnet de identidad*
• key / keyring	• *mi llave / mi llavero*
• money	• *mi dinero*
• passport	• *mi pasaporte*
• purse	• *mi billetera*
• rail pass	• *mi pase de tren*
• rucksack	• *mi mochila*
• shoulder bag	• *mi mochila*
• suitcase	• *mi maleta*
• ticket	• *mi entrada / tíquet*
• travellers cheques	• *mis cheques de viaje*
• wallet	• *mi billetera / mi cartera de bolsillo*
• watch	• *mi reloj*

LOSING OR DAMAGING IMPORTANT POSSESSIONS — *PERDIENDO O ROMPIENDO COSAS IMPORTANTES*

I'VE BROKEN MY..	***HE ROTO...***
• camera	• *mi cámara de fotos*
• contact lens	• *mis lentes de contacto*
• glasses / spectacles	• *mis gafas*
• watch	• *mi reloj*
I'm sorry but I have broken your…	*Lo siento pero he roto tu...*
I will pay for it.	*Pagaré lo que vale.*
My parents will get you another.	*Mis padres te darán otra.*

I'VE TORN MY..	***ME HE ROTO MI/S***
trousers / skirt / coat / dress / shirt	*pantalones / falda / abrigo / vestido / blusa*
Could you mend it for me, please?	*¿Puedes coserlo(a) por favor?*
I've lost a button.	*He perdido un botón.*
My button has come off.	*Se me ha caido un botón.*
Could I sew it back on, please?	*¿Puede darme aguja e hilo para coserlo?*
Have you a needle and thread I could use?	*¿Me puede dar aguja e hilo para coserlo?*
My zip has broken.	*La cremallera se ha roto.*
Do you have a safety pin?	*¿Me puedes dar un alfiler?*

FORM FILLING / PERSONAL INFORMATION — *RELLENANDO FICHAS INFORMACION PERSONAL*

Could you fill in this form, please?	***¿Rellene esta ficha, por favor?***
in block capitals	*en letras mayúsculas*
Please print clearly.	*Por favor, rellene la ficha con caridad.*
Please use pen or biro.	*Por favor, use bolígrafo.*
Have you a pen I could borrow, please?	*¿Puedes prestarme un bolígrafo?*
Please put one letter in each square.	*Por favor, rellene cada cuadrito con un letra.*
Please sign and date the form at the end.	*Por favor, firme y ponga la fecha al final.*

Personal details	***Detalles personales***
Title	*Título*
Surname / Christian names	*Apellido / Nombre*
Date of Birth	*Fecha de Nacimiento*
Place of Birth	*Lugar de Nacimiento*
Age	*Edad*
Gender / Sex	*Sexo*
Marital Status	*Estado civil*

ADDRESS	***DOMICILIO***
House name / number	*Nombre del domicilio / número*
Street	*calle*
Town	*localidad*
City	*ciudad*
County / Area	*autonomía / área*
Country	*País*
Postal Code	*Código postal*
Where are you staying at the moment?	*¿Dónde te alojas?*
Where do you live?	*¿Dónde vives?*

FORM FILLING / PERSONAL INFORMATION — *RELLENANDO FICHAS INFORMACION PERSONAL*

TELEPHONE NUMBER	***NUMERO DE TELEFONO***
Country code	*Código para el país*
Area code	*Prefijo*
Work telephone number	*Número del teléfono del trabajo*
Home telephone number	*Número del teléfono en el domicilio habitual*
Mobile telephone number	*Número del teléfono móvil*
FAX number	*Número del fax*

GETTING THINGS TO WORK	***HACIENDO QUE LAS COSAS FUNCIONEN***
How does this work?	*¿Cómo funciona esto?*
Can you show me how to use this?	*¿Cómo se usa esto?*
This isn't working properly.	*Esto no funciona bien.*
Is there something wrong with it?	*¿Le pasa algo a esto?*
Am I doing something wrong with this?	*¿Estoy haciendo algo mal con esto?*
Can I watch you use it?	*¿Puedo ver cómo lo haces?*
Can I try to use it now?	*¿Puedo intentarlo ahora?*
How did you do that?	*¿Cómo lo has hecho?*

YOUR SPANISH EXCHANGE INDEX

A
accidents
 broken bones 275, **411**
 general 403-405
 fire 403, 404
 sprains 411
 traffic 404
 bomb 403, 405
 skiing 273, 24
address 437-438
airports 383 - 389
alarm clock 16, **56**
alcohol **179**, 232, 422
allergy 169, **408**, 409
alone, wanting to be 23
ambulance 403, **422**
animals
 cats 71
 dogs71
 walking the dog 234
 horses 262-267
 pets 71-72
 zoo 213
 circus 211-212
ankle 237 415
antihistamine 409, 422
antiseptic cream 422
architecture
 stately homes 215-217
 churches 224
arm
 hurt 237
 broken 275
 parts of 415
arrivals
 trains 375, **376**
 planes 384
 post 334
arriving on exchange 13-16
art 227-231
 equipment 230
 galleries 227-231
 medium 229
 types of 228, 231
aspirin 422
asthma 408
athletics 292-296
aunt 320

B
babies 325-326
back (of body) 415
ballet 198-200
bandage 410
barbecues
 general 184-185
 on beach 313
bath, having a 57-59
bathroom 57-63
batteries
 run on 139
 weak 251
beach 309-317
 clothes & equipment 309
 sandcastles 310
 shells 311
 shrimping 311
 beach games 311-312
 eating on the beach 313
 jellyfish, broken glass 314
 warning/ safety signs 314
 sunbathing 316-317
bedroom 53-57
 sharing a bedroom 15
beds, making the 55
bedtime 17-19
bee 66, stung by 245, 410
Beetle (game) 123-124
bikes 399-402
birds
 types of 244
 feeding bread to 245
birth 325
biscuits 53
bite, Does it bite? 72
blankets 16
blister 237
blow drying hair 61
boarding gate 387
boats
 cruises 314-315, **390-391**
 types of 314
 hire of 218
 ferries 390-391
body, parts of 411-418
bomb scare 365, 402, **405**
bones 417
 broken bones 275, **411**
bonfire 67
 lighting fires 33
books 159-161, 162-164
bookshop 164
boots 234
 riding boots 262
 ski boots 268-269
 skating boot hire 282
 boots hurting 282
borrowing
 general items 16
 books 162-163
 wellingtons 234
bowls (the game) 69
boyfriend 322
brakes
 car 394
 bike 399
bread 45, **177**
bread bin 45
breakfast 17, 167
 full English breakfast 170
breakdown (car) 396, **398**
breaking things 436
bride, groom etc. 327
bridge (card game) 110-113
briefcase 348
broken bones 275, **411**
brother 319
brushing
 hair 56, 61
 teeth 59
 floor 50
budgerigar 71
burns 411
bus 382-383

butter 175
button, losing a 436
buying
  books 164
  gifts, postcards 219
  guidebooks 215
  presents 219
  programmes 191
  tickets - see 'tickets'

C
C.D.'s 153
cake 236
calamine lotion 317
camcorders 251-253
cameras 247-250
camping 129
candles 35
car
  car controls 394-395
  car maintenance 395-396
  driving lessons 396-398
card games 96-113
  Bridge 110-113
  Pontoon 106-109
  Rummy 103-106
  Snap 122-123
  Whist 102-103
cards 96-113
  dealing 98
  following suit 99
  shuffling 97
  suits, face cards etc.96-97
  trumps 99
cassettes 153
cat 71
catch (a train etc.) 373-379
C.D.'s 153
cereals 17
change, (money) 85, **209**
changing rooms 303
cheating (cards) 101
  breaking rules 76
check-in desk 385-386
cheese 176
Chemist's shop 238, **421**
Chess 113-115
churches 224-226
cigarettes 386, 388, **430**
cinema 189-190
circus 211-212
cleaning 49-52
climbing frame 130
cloakroom 345
clocks
  fast/slow 30
  What time is it? 30
  setting alarm 56
  cuckoo / grandfather 30
closing time 372
clothes
  for bad weather 234-235
  what to wear 20
  smart / old 20
  washing 47-48
  drying 48
  ironing 49
  mending 436
cloudy 150, 270, 317
clubs 201-203
Cluedo 89-95
coat 20
coffee 178
  coffee grinder 45
cold (I'm cold) 275, **406**
  weather 210, 270
  cold and cough 408
college 354-357
comb 16
commentary headphones215
communication cord 378
computer 131-138
computer games 139-144
  controls 140
  scoring 141-144
constipation 410
contact lenses 413
cooker 37-38
cookery books 173
cooking 173-185
  equipment 39-40
  ingredients 174-183
  terms 173-174
cosmetics 62-63
cough 408
cousin 320
cricket 297-300
crime 433-434
crockery 43
croquet 69
cruises 314-315, 390-391
cup of tea 167, **178**
current events 363-369
curtains open / shut 57
customs & excise 389
cutlery **34**, 41, **44**
cuts 411
  to cut 38

D
daily routine 15-19
darts 208
daughter 319
days out 19-20
  places to go 189-246
dealing cards 98
death 330
deckchair 67, 309, 316
degrees
  university 355-357
  centigrade 38, 270
delayed
  trains 376
  planes 384
dentist 426
deodorant 59
departures
  train 376
  plane 384
developing films 250
dialling tone 337
diarrhoea 407, 410
dice 77
dictionary **21**, 136, **160**
diet
  ideal diet 429-430
  vegetarian / diabetic 169
dining room 34-36
dinner 17, 167
dishwasher 42
disliking people 323
dislocations 411
diving 305, **307-308**
divorce 321-322
dizzy 211, **406**
doctor 418-422
dodgems 206
dog 71
  walking the dog 234
dominoes 117-119
donkey rides 312
draughts (the game) 115-116
dressing 59, **304**

drinks
- types of drinks 178-179
- hot/cold drinks 235
- drinks machine 303
- Like a drink?190, 203
- old enough to drink 327
- drink of water 407
- to drink too much 430
- at a bar 203

driving
- lessons 397-398
- test 397

drugs
- illegal 431
- medicine 408, **421-422**

drying
- clothes 48
- hair 61
- drying up dishes 41

dubbed (films) 190
ducks 244
duvet 16, 18

E

ears 404
- hurting in plane 378

early morning tea 167
eggs 176-177
Elastoplast 237, **400**
elections 363
electric blanket 18
electric razor 60
elevenses 167
emergencies
- telephoning for help 403
- accidents 404
- fire 404
- bomb scare 365, **405**

engaged tone 336-337
enjoyment
- of food 167
- of games 77
- of theatre etc. 196-197
- of music 155-156
- of exchange 25

envelopes 332
escalators 372
essay writing 350
exams 351-352
- degrees 356-357
- music 158

exercise 424, **428-429**
exhibitions 227-231
eye, parts of 412
eye test 427-428
eyesight 413

F

face 412
fainting 406
fairs 205-211
family 319-322
fancying someone 323
farms 239
father 319
feeding birds 245
feet, sore 237, 269
ferry 390-391
fiancé 322, **327**
files 359
filling (in tooth) 426
film
- at cinema 189-190
- camera film 250

fire alarm 404
fire brigade, calling 403
fire, lighting a 33, **67**
fireworks 68
flights 383-389
flour 182
flowers -garden / wild 65
- wreath 330

fog 271
fog lights 395
food 167-187
- barbecues 184-185
- barbecues on beach 313
- British 170-171
- chewing etc. 169
- cooking 173-183
- following recipes 173-174
- Spanish 172
- fruit picking 245-246
- hot dogs 210
- ideal diet 429-430
- ingredients 174-183
- likes and dislikes 167-168
- McDonald's 186-187
- trying new 168, 170-172
- vegetarian / diabetic 169

food processor 46
foot 416
football 276-281
footwear 234
forgetting to bring things 16
form filling 437-438
formal letters 335
freezer 41
French cricket 311-312
fridge 41
frightened of dark 18
- of ghost train 206

friends 322-324
fruit, types of 180
fruit picking 245-246
funeral 330

G

games 73-130
- beetle 123-124
- board games 73-78
- card games see "cards"
- chess 113-115
- Cluedo 89-95
- dominoes 117-119
- draughts 115-116
- I spy 125
- jigsaw puzzles 119-121
- Monopoly 79-88
- noughts & crosses 126
- outdoor games
  - hide & seek 127
  - hop scotch 127
  - kite flying 128
  - roller skating 128
  - skipping 127
  - tent 128
  - treasure hunt 127

gardening 69-70
gardens general 63-70
- at stately homes 217-218
- garden furniture 67
- play equipment
  - bowls 69
  - climbing frame 130
  - croquet 69
  - mini golf 68
  - seesaw & slide 130
  - swing 129
  - trampoline 69

gargle 407, **413**
gas fire 33
gas cooker 37

gatecrashers 201
gears
  on car 394
  on bikes 399
geometry equipment 361
getting letters 334
getting up 17
getting dressed 59, **304**
gift shop 219
girlfriend 322
glasses
  for drinking 35
  opera glasses 192
  spectacles 413, 427
  sunglasses 268
glue 362
going out with 322-323
goldfish 71
golf 287-289
grandparents 320
group, (pop) 156
guide book 215
guinea pig 72

H
hair
  types of 412
  brushing 57
  washing 60
  drying 61
  drying after swim 304
  plaiting etc. 200
hamster 72
hand 415
handkerchief 408
hangers 56
hangover 430
harbour 315
head 412
headache **406**, 427
heartburn 407
heating - central 33
  open fires 33
Help! (emergencies) 403
helping 53-54
  to lay table 34-35
  to clear table 35
  to wash up 40
  to dry dishes 41
  to load dishwasher 42
  to make beds 55
helping cont.
  to make toast 33, **45**
  to put kettle on **44**, 54
  to tidy up 54
  to dust **51**, 53
  to vacuum **50**, 54
  to walk dog 234
  to mow lawn 70
hi-fi 31, **153-155**
higher education 354-357
hiring
  videos 151
  skates 282
  skis 269-270
holidays 321, 334, **352**
home, contents of 27-72
homesickness 23
homoeopathy 432
hoover ® see vacuuming
hopscotch 127
horoscopes 165-166
horses 262-267
hospital 422-425
hot
  (I'm hot) 18, 275, **406**
  weather 150, **316**
hot dogs 210
hot water bottle 18
houses
  contents of 27-72
  types of 27
housework 53
hungry 235
  not hungry 168, **406**
hurry up 58
husband 321

I
ice cubes **41**, 179
ice skating 282-283
illness general 406-417
  asthma 408
  cold and cough 408
  constipation 410
  diarrhoea 407, 410
  feeling faint 406
  got a rash 409
  headache **406**, 427
  indigestion 407
  period pain 411
  seasickness 14, **315**, **391**
illness cont.
  sickness 207, 346, **407**
  sore throat 407
  stomach upset 407
I'm…
  I'm hot. 406
  I'm cold. 406
  I'm homesick. 23
  I'm hungry. 235
  I'm thirsty. 406
  I'm tired. 13, **17**, **23-24**
  ..tired of walking 237
  ..tired of skiing 275
indigestion 407
informal letters 335
information desk 384
inhaler 408, 422
injuries 409-411
  blisters 237
  fractures etc.275, **411**
  minor 409
  serious cuts 410
  splinters 409
  stings 410
insects 66
Internet 137-138
interval
  at cinema 189
  at theatre 191, **196**
introducing people 202
invitations to parties 201
ironing 49

J
jam 182
jam making 245
jellyfish 309, 314, **410**
jigsaws 119-121
journey, How was it? 13-14
joystick 131
junctions, types of 398

K
kettle 44
keyboard 133-135
kiss 324
kitchen 37-46
kitchen tools 39-40, 44-46
kite, flying a 128
kitten 71
knee 415

L
laundry 47-49
law and order 366
law courts 366
lawn 54, 64
lawn mowing 70
laying the table 34-35
learning
  school work 350-351
  to drive 397-398
leaving
  your exchange 25
  school 354
left luggage office 374
leg 415
lessons 349
  music lessons 157
  riding lessons 262
  ski school 272-274
  water skiing 313
letters
  formal 335
  informal 335
library 163
lie in 17
lifeguard 308, 314
lifts
  elevator **28**, 371
  back home 203
light not working 55, 401
lighting a fire **33**, 67
lights - electric 30
  candles 31, 35
  on or off at night? 18
liking people 322-324
lilo 301, 309
living room 29-33
loading computer games 139
lockers **304**, 345
locking doors 304
loo -cleaning the loo 52
  need more loo rolls 61
  using the loo 52
  Where is the loo? 15
losing possessions 435-436
lottery 369
luggage trolley 377, **384**
lunch 167

M
mack 20
magazines 162
mains, runs on 139, 251
make-up 62-63
making beds 55
manicure 415
maps 236
margarine 175
marital status 327
matches (box of) 31, 33, 35
maze 217
McDonald's 186-187
meals 167
meat 180
medical room 346
meeting people
  meeting the family 13
  meeting at airport 385
  introductions 202
mending things 427, 436
messages
  taking messages 337
  on answerphone 339
  Any messages for me? 385
middle age 329
milk 174
mini-golf **68**, 287
missing a train 377
missing home 23
modem 131
monarchy 222, **368**
money 20, 433
Monopoly 79-88
mosquito 410
mother 319
motor racing 290-291
mouse (computer) 131
mouse (rodent) 72
mouth 413
muscles 417
music
  listening to 153-156
  lessons / practice 157-158
  exams 158
  noisy 202, 252, 418
  adjusting volume 31, 154

N
national lottery 369
nationality 202
needing things 16
needle and thread 436
nephew & niece 320
newsagent's 238
newspapers 161-162, 373
news reports 149
nightmares **19**, 429
night-time 15, 17-19
  night lights on or off? 17
  problems at night 18-19
noisy music 202, 252
nose 413
No Smoking 373
notepaper 331
not working (objects) 438
number unobtainable 337
nuts (edible) 182

O
office equipment 359-362
oil for car 396
  suntan oil 316
old age 329
open fires 33
opening hours 372
opera 198-200
operations 424-425
opticians 427-428
outdoor games 127-130

P
pack of cards 96-97
paddling 240
painkillers 330, 422
paper 333, **359**
paper hankies 408
Paracetamol 422
parcels 332-333
parties 201-203
peace and quiet, wanting 24
pencils 92, 348, **361**
pens **360**, 437
pepper 35, 46, **183**
periods **62**, 324, **411**
personal details 437-438
petrol 395
pets 71-72
photo album 248
photography 247-250
physical relationships 324
physiotherapy 424
piano practice **158**, 343
picnics 235-236

pictures, taking 247
plans for the day 19-20
play - see 'games'
plots, following 164, **190**
police 365, 366, **403**, **434**
police station 238
pontoon 106-109
pop groups 156
posing for photos 247
post
  post box 334
  postal deliveries 334
  posting items 332-334
  post office 334
  postcards 219, **331**
pregnancy 324, **418**
presents
  buying 219
  giving 13
preventive medicine 428-430
printer 132
private 372
prizes 83, 127, **209**, 369
problems
  breakages 436
  broken glass 314
  broken zip 436
  crime 433-434
  forgetting things
    16,21,96,98,101
  frightened of the dark 18
  homesickness 23
  losing things 435
  losing a button 436
  missing trains 377
  needing things 16
  needing peace 24
  needing needle etc 436
  needing a safety pin 436
  on the road 398
  seasickness 14, 315, **391**
  sickness 207, 346, **407**
  sore feet 237, 269
  strange food 167-8, 172
  tearing things 436
  tired generally **17**, 23-24
  tired of walking 237
  tired of skiing 275
  not understanding 21
  want to phone home 23
  with speaking 21-22
programmes - T.V. 148-150
programme, buying a 191
pronunciation 22
puncture 291, **396**
pupils 347
puppy 71

R
radio 31, **154**
rain 150
rashes 409
razor blades 60
reading 159-166
recording on T.V.147-148
records (music) 153
reductions
  student 190, 215, 227
relatives 319-322
remote control for T.V. 145
repeat, Please repeat it. 21
rescue (ski slope) 274-275
reverse (a car) 394, 397
reverse ('phone charge) 338
riding 262-267
roads, types of 398
rollercoaster 207
roller skating 127
rooms 29-63
routes 236
royal family 368
rubbish disposal 52
rugby 281
ruler 361
rules for games 74, 76
Rummy 103-106

S
safety pin 436
salad 181
sales 372
salt 35, 46, **183**
  dishwasher salt 42
  bath salts 57
sandcastles 310
sanitary towels 62
school 341-353
  types of 341, 353
  buildings/ rooms 341-346
  staff and pupils 346-347
  clothes/equipm't 347-348
  school day 348-349
  school year 352
  describing teachers 354
  higher education 354-357
scissors 362
sea 309
  rough sea 14, **391**
  seasickness 14, **315**, **391**
seasoning 183
seatbelts
  in cars 393
  on planes 387
seating at table 36
seats, taken / free? 379
see-saw 130
self-service canteen 342
sellotape 362
senses, five 418
separation 321-322
setting alarm 56
sexuality 324, 367
shampoo 60
shaving 60
sheets (on bed) 55
shells 310, **311**
shoes general 20, 234
  hurting 237
  ballet shoes 200
  tennis shoes 256
  wellingtons 234
  size of shoes 282
shopping at gift shop 219
shops - see 'buying'
shoulder 414
shower, taking a 60
shuffling cards 97
sick, feel / am 207, 346, **407**
sightseeing 215-233
signs 371-373
sink 40
sister 319
skating 282-283
skiing 268-275
  clothes & equipment 268
  ski hire 269-270
  snow 270
  ski runs 271
  lifts 271-272
  ski school 272-274
  accidents 274-275
  après ski 274-275
  enjoying it or not 275

skiing cont.
stopping for a rest 275
skin 317, **409**
skipping 127
sleep general 429
where to sleep 15-16
bed / bedding 16, **18**, **55**
how long 17
sleep troubles 429
nightmares 19
slide 130
smoking 430
snack 53, **167**
Snap (card game) 122-123
snorkelling 310
snow 270
soap 58
soap operas 149
socks 234
software, computer 132-133
son 319
sore
sore feet 237, 269
sore throat 407
sunburnt skin 317, 409
speaking problems 21-22
spectacles 413, 427
spider 66
splinters 409
sport 255-300
athletics 292-296
cricket 297-300
croquet 69
football 276-280
French cricket 311-312
golf 287-289
ice skating 282-283
motor racing 290-291
riding 262-267
rugby 281
skiing 268-275
swimming 301-317
table tennis 284-286
tennis 255-261
water skiing 313
windsurfing 314
sprains 411
stamps 332
stately homes 215-223
stationery 359-362
steering wheel 394
sticking plaster 237, 410
stings 237, 410
stomach upset 207, 346, **407**
student reductions 190
& 215, 227
study (the room) 36-37
studying 350-351
sub-titles 190
sugar 178, 182
suits (of cards) 96
suitcase 14-15,
& 374, 385, 389
sun 241, 317
sunbathing 316-317
sunburn 317, 409
swimming 301-308, 309
clothes & equipment 301
tickets and sessions 302
spectating 302-303
getting changed 303-304
lockers 304
parts of pool 303, 305
wave machine 305
tubes & strokes 306
underwater & diving 307
racing 307

T
T.V. 145-151
controls 146-147
programmes 148-150
table tennis 284-286
talcum powder **59**, 304
tampons 62
taxis 374
tea 167, 178
tea room 219
teachers
form teacher, head,
subject etc. 344
describing 354
tearing things 436
teeth 413
dentist 426
cleaning 59
telephone 335-339
using equipment 336-339
phoning home 14, 15, 23
emergency numbers 403
national code,
area code etc 438
temperature - weather
hot/cold/thunder 241-242
weather forecast 150
snow & ice 270
for sunbathing 316-317
temperature - personal
I'm hot / cold 275
raised in illness 406
tennis 255-261
clothes 256
equipment 255
courts 256
serving 257
scoring 258-259
shots 259
tournaments 259-260
tent 129
theatre 191-197
booking seats 191
parts of stage 193
types of play 194
ballet 197-198
opera 198-200
theft 211, **433-435**
thirsty 13, **235**, 275
throat 407, 413
throat sweets 407
thunder 242
tickets for
art galleries 227
boat hire 218
bus 383
car park 383
cinema 190
clubs & parties 201
fairground rides 205
football 277
ice skating 282
library 163
lottery 367
stately homes 215
swimming 302
theatre 191-192
trains 375
underground 381
video hire card 151
ticket inspector 379
time, on time 375
time, What time is it? 30
timetable, school 348-349
tiredness 23-24

toaster **45**, 54
a toast, to drink to 328
toilets
going to loo 15, 52, **61**
public 371
toiletries 59-63
tones, dialling etc. 336-**337**
toothbrush paste 16, **59**, 413
torch 129
towel 16, **58**, 309
traffic 404
trains 373-379
trampoline 69, 342
travel 371-402
trains 373-379
underground 380-381
buses 382-383
by air 383-389
by ferry 390-391
cars 392-398
bikes 399-402
treasure hunt 128
trees 242-243
trumps (cards) 99
tubes (swimming) 306
tumble drier 61
turn up/down (volume) 147
typing 133
tyres 396

U
uncle 320
underground 380-381
understanding words 21
not understanding 21
underwater swimming 307
university 354-357
unpacking 14, **15**
utility room 47-54

V
vacuum cleaner **50,** 54
vegetables 169, **181**
video player 145-151
controls 146-147
playing videos 147
recording 147-148
video hire shop 151
video recorders
(camcorders) 251-253
vineyard 231-233

W
walks 234-246
crossing water 239-**240**
dog walking 234
footwear 20, 234
high ground 240
landmarks 237-241
problems 236
route 236
sore feet 237, 269
walking clothes 234-235
weather 241-242
waltzers 206
wanting to be alone 23
wardrobe 15, **56**
washing self 15, **58-59**, 345
washing line 48
washing machine 47-48
washing up **40-41**, 53
wasp 66 **245, 410**
waste bin 42, 52
water
bottle of 373
drink of 15, 19, 179, 407
for car 396
fountains etc. 218
rivers etc. 239
water - hot/cold 371
water chute 306
water skiing 313
watering the garden 70
wave machine 305
wear
what to wear 20
clothes for walks 234-235
wear hair up/down 412
wear glasses etc. 413
wear school uniform 347
weather
hot / cold / wet 241-242
thunder 242
weather forecast 150
snow 270
for sunbathing 316-317
weddings 327-329
wellingtons 234
Whist 102-103
wife 321
wild plants 65
wind (weather) 128, 150
windows in car 394
open / shut 16, **57**, 378
sit by the 379, 386
look out of 388
stained glass 225
French windows 217
windsurfing 314
wine tasting 233
winning
at football 278, 279
an election 363
games **77-78**, 286
lottery 369
prizes 209
the toss
spinning coin 76
at tennis 257
at cricket 298
word processing 135-137
work
How does it work? 438
It's not working. 438
studying 350-351
wrist 415
writing equipment 359-362
writing letters 335

X
x-ray 421

Y
yoghurt 175

Z
zip, broken 436
to zip / unzip 359
zoo 213

Whilst every care has been taken to prevent errors in the text and to make this reference book easy to use, Yarker Publishing would be grateful to be notified of any mistakes you may have noticed for correction in future editions and would also welcome any suggestions for further improvements by way of topics which might be included or any ideas concerning ways in which you might find it quicker to locate the vocabulary and phrases you need. Please address any comments to:-

Yarker Publishing
Gordon House
276 Banbury Road
Summertown
Oxford
OX2 7ED